Oral Traditions in Contemporary China

Studies in Folklore and Ethnology: Traditions, Practices, and Identities

Series Editors: Simon J. Bronner, University of Wisconsin Milwaukee and Elo-Hanna Seljamaa, University of Tartu

Studies in Folklore and Ethnology: Traditions, Practices, and Identities features projects that examine cultural traditions around the world and the persons and communities who enact them. Including monographs and edited collections, the series emphasizes studies of living folk practices, artists, and groups toward a broad understanding of the dynamics of tradition and identity in the modern world.

Oral Traditions in Contemporary China

Healing a Nation

Juwen Zhang

LEXINGTON BOOKS

Lanham • Boulder • New York • London

Published by Lexington Books
An imprint of The Rowman & Littlefield Publishing Group, Inc.
4501 Forbes Boulevard, Suite 200, Lanham, Maryland 20706
www.rowman.com

86–90 Paul Street, London EC2A 4NE

Zhang, Juwen. "Folklore in China: Past, Present, and Challenges" (*Humanities* 2018, 7 (2), 35; https://doi.org/10.3390/h7020035).

Zhang, Juwen. "Chinese American Culture in the Making" (*Journal of American Folklore*, 128 (510): 449–475, 2015).

Zhang, Juwen. "Intangible Cultural Heritage and Self-Healing Mechanism in Chinese Culture" (*Western Folklore*, 76: 197–226, 2017).

Zhang, Juwen. "Rediscovering the Brothers Grimm of China: Lin Lan" (*Journal of American Folklore*, 71 (2): 119–147, 2020).

Zhang, Juwen. "'Moon Man' Figure in the Tale of the 'Predestined Wife' (ATU 930A)" (*Journal of American Folklore*, 127 (503): 27–49, 2014).

Zhang, Juwen. "'Older Ginger Is Spicier': Life-Views on Old Age and Aging in Chinese Proverbs" (*Proverbium*, 38: 401–446, 2021).

British Library Cataloguing in Publication Information Available

Library of Congress Cataloging-in-Publication Data

Names: Zhang, Juwen, author.
Title: Oral traditions in contemporary China : healing a nation / Juwen Zhang.
Description: Lanham, Maryland : Lexington Books, 2022. | Series: Studies in folklore and ethnology : traditions, practices, and identities | Includes bibliographical references and index.
Identifiers: LCCN 2021041646 (print) | LCCN 2021041647 (ebook) | ISBN 9781793645135 (cloth) | ISBN 9781793645142 (epub)
Subjects: LCSH: Oral tradition—China. | Folklore—China. | China—Social life and customs.
Classification: LCC GR335 .Z394 2022 (print) | LCC GR335 (ebook) | DDC 398.20951—dc23
LC record available at https://lccn.loc.gov/2021041646
LC ebook record available at https://lccn.loc.gov/2021041647

To my wife, Jing Liu,
and our sons, Andy and Teddy.

Contents

Preface

This book has two goals. The first one is to provide a survey of the active oral traditions (e.g., tales, proverbs, and ballads/folksongs) in China. Second is to offer an interpretive theoretical framework—one I call a *cultural self-healing mechanism*—through which to understand the continuity and discontinuity of traditions in China (and in other cultures) over time. The central questions running through the book are: How have the traditions in China been continued as one cultural entity for several thousand years? How are they being practiced in contemporary China? Why do people practice what they perceive as their traditions, with which they reconstruct their personal and national identities?

This work took shape as I gradually realized in the midst of news about Chinese culture in public life in the United States and in the academic world as a folklorist, that there was an urgent need for a coherent theoretical framework to understand Chinese folklore and tradition. Such a framework would engage a global discourse on the issue of the continuity and diversity of human cultures. Furthermore, it would facilitate research to address the lack of information on Chinese culture in English-language reference works on folk and fairy tales, proverbs, and ballads (Clements 2006; Haase 2008; Zipes, Greenhill, Magnus-Johnston 2016). On a personal note, my status as a "bicultural" (in Hsu's sense, 1973) immigrant, an insider and outsider to both Chinese and American cultures, gives me a distinctive perspective which also informs the writing of this book.

Oral Tradition in Contemporary China: Healing a Nation is a culmination of my folkloristic work over the past three decades. I consider that folklore practice or everyday life of the common people not only expresses the fundamental beliefs and values in a culture but also the operation of the dynamic mechanism inherent to the vitality and continuity of a culture. If Chinese culture were a sailing boat, Chinese folklore, most distinctively conveyed through oral tradition, would be the flowing water that keeps the boat fulfilling its meaning and use. Early on, I began studies of folk narratives using text-centered methods of analyzing their origin and diffusion. While the approach was useful to find patterns of transmission of certain traditions such as tales about the match-maker Moon Man and Chinese Cinderella or Yexian, I later used context and practice-centered perspectives to address issues of cultural process. I introduced terms that represent concepts that came through in Chinese culture such as "folkloric identity," "vitality and validity of traditions," "core and arbitrary identity markers," "third culture," and "life-view." Subsequently, when I recently looked over my corpus of work, a larger theoretical framework emerged: *the cultural self-healing mechanism*.

In light of my work on oral tradition, I have substantially revised, expanded, and updated previously published essays. I reorganized those materials into new chapters that have become integral parts of the whole book. For example, the two chapters in part II on folk and fairy tales contain materials published in several articles in Chinese and English, and new writing about contemporary storytelling, folk tellers, the Intangible Cultural Heritage (ICH) movement, and collecting folk literature in China today. Similarly, other chapters also present the latest development in folk practice and in academic studies in China. Chapter 7 on *geyao* (ballads/folksongs), as a new chapter, for example, touches upon the issue of the performance of folksongs in public spaces during the COVID-19 pandemic of 2020–2021 as a means of *self-healing* on individual and societal levels. Building upon my previous study of the ancient text about a musical instrument (i.e., the clay-vessel-flute *xun*), chapter 8 connects its history, ethics, and musicality to its current reconstruction as a national identity marker, and further reflects upon my personal practice in a cross-cultural context from an experience-centered perspective. While each chapter can be read separately, taken together they cohere under the larger theoretical framework of the self-healing mechanism. They address general issues stemming from the study of oral tradition in China such as the continuity over millennia of folklore practices. In particular, they provide a perspective on the ways that oral traditions are healing contemporary China, a nation in search of its cultural roots while reconstructing its identity in this globalizing age.

"Oral traditions" in the book's title is used to refer to spoken and sung folk expressions, or performances in other distinctive forms (e.g., through playing musical instruments as discussed in chapter 8), that the folk express their sense of identity or cultural roots in line with their fundamental beliefs and values (chapter 2), and "life-views" (i.e., "entering the world," "exiting the world," "next world," and "passaging the world," chapter 6). Within China, folklorists are familiar with such structural and performance theories (in Chinese translations) as those presented by Albert Lord in his *The Singer of Tales*, a central work in the development of oral-formulaic theory (1960), Vladimir Propp in his *Morphology of the Folktale* (1968), Richard Bauman in his *Verbal Art as Performance* (1977), and John M. Foley in his *The Theory of Oral Composition: History and Methodology* (1988) and *The Singer of Tales in Performance* (1995). These ideas, among others, have been used widely in studies of certain oral or written texts, as well as in studies of how oral performances transmit traditions.

In the twenty-first century, practice theory emerged within folklore studies not only as corrective to the performance-centered approach in relation to the transition and transformation of traditions but also as a reorientation of folklore studies to everyday life. It gives attention to the repeated embodied actions of practitioners as the focus of study, departing from previous approaches concentrating on the relict lore and fossilized text (see a set of recently translated articles on practice theory by Simon Bronner, 2019b, 2021a, 2021b, 2021c; Buccitelli 2021; Buccitelli and Buccitelli 2021). This book builds on the effort to redefine folklore as *"traditional knowledge put into, and drawing from, practice"* (Bronner 2019a, 76, emphasis in original) to move beyond the text- and context-centered paradigm to a new norm of seeking "holistic understanding of culture" and "holistic study of community life" by connecting body and mind in multiple perspectives (Bronner 2019a:3, 290; 2021d).

Furthermore, "oral traditions" includes those items that have been preserved in writing throughout history (e.g., tales, proverbs, and ballads/folksongs from historical documents), and the material that has been recently recorded from live performances/tellings, which may still occur *in situ*. In China, "oral traditions" also means a body of works of oral provenance that is distinguished from the literati-authored works in print called, in early China, "anthologies" (*ji* 集), even though the "oral tradition" is often preserved in the anthologies by the elites. Certainly, "oral" is inseparable from non-oral actions of performing traditions, just as the intangible is inseparable from the tangible traditions. In this sense, "oral tradition" (*koutou chuantong* 口头传统) has been used in Chinese to refer to "folk literature" (*minjian wenxue* 民间文学), a concept developed in the early twentieth century to highlight the "oral literature" (*koutou wenxue* 口头文学) of the "folk" (common people; *pingmin* 平民) and all forms of "storytelling performances" (usually with musical instruments) (*quyi* 曲艺), even though *quyi* is often excluded in studies of "folk literature."

An example of different interpretations of these concepts can be seen in the English title of the American journal, *CHINOPERL: Journal of Chinese Oral and Performing Literature*, while its Chinese title shows *yanchang wenyi* (演唱文艺, literally *performing and singing literature and art*). As a result, Chinese folklorists and literature scholars have emphasized these three major categories of folk literature in the past century or so: *minjian gushi* (民间故事 folktales), *geyao* (歌谣 ballads/folksongs), and *yanyu* (谚语 proverbs). Therefore, these are the three categories included in this book. However, it should be noted that these categories are adopted from Western concepts of those genres and they redefine traditional Chinese notions and terms. Furthermore, there is no consensus among Chinese folklorists regarding those definitions and categories. For example, *geyao* refers to both folksongs (*minge* 民歌) and ballads or rhymes (*yao* 谣), but some Chinese folklorists treat *geyao* as a part of the larger category of folksongs. Moreover, the relationship between proverbs and other proverbial expressions, such as *suyu* (俗语 folk expressions) and *xiehouyu* (歇后语 two-part proverbs), is treated differently in various Chinese collections and studies. It is the complexity of these definitions and categorizations, used by both scholars and common people, that has also enabled them to adopt different historical and cultural elements to justify continuing a tradition that, in turn, reinforces their own group identity.

"Contemporary" covers the last two decades of the twentieth century and the first two decades of the twenty-first century. "China" in this book is limited to the geographic territory of the People's Republic of China where the Han Chinese language is the primary source and media of oral traditions. I focus on the Han Chinese people who use the Chinese language and constitute about 91 percent of the total population, while recognizing the influence of minorities on the broader tradition of folk literature (Mair and Bender 2011; Bender, Wuwu, and Zopqu 2019).

"Healing a Nation," the subtitle of this book, encapsulates my interpretive framework. To analyze the continuity of either a particular traditional item/practice, or the overarching heritage of a folk/cultural group, or a nation as a whole, scholars should examine the "vitality" and "validity"—the driving forces—of a given tradition. In doing so, they will find that those traditions that are rooted in the *fundamental beliefs and values* of a given culture sustain their power throughout social upheavals and cultural changes and are at the root of what we call culture. They can be identified by a few abstract concepts which are, in turn, expressed in everyday practices. Historically, those cultures that have operated with such awareness of their roots can also self-heal themselves when external destruction occurs; those that have not often are weakened or disappear. What I am proposing here is that the active oral traditions discussed in this book, representative of other traditions beside "oral traditions" in Chinese culture, constitute the evidence of the operation of this *cultural self-healing mechanism*. Moreover, in practice, traditionalization, heritagization, and localization are some of the expressions of the mechanism in operation, as discussed in part I. This mechanism applies not only to particular traditions such as the continuity of specific tales, proverbs, and folksongs examined in this book but also to Chinese culture and history in a broad sense. In fact, it can also be applied to understand the continuity and discontinuity of other cultures in human history.

The Chinese belief system is based on the polytheist, inclusive mixture of Confucianism, Daoism, Buddhism, ancestor beliefs, and local folk beliefs, while the Western system emanates from monotheistic, exclusive beliefs. This difference is the root of the conflicts exhibited in the current world affairs, particularly between China and the West. At least three major intertwined forces can be seen in the Chinese system: beliefs imposed and promoted by the ruling powers in different dynasties; the commonly accepted folk beliefs maintained as traditions; and various regional beliefs that continued as local customs through dialects/topolects.

In part I, the opening chapter provides a historiographical background for the study of oral traditions in China. Chapter 2 follows with a discussion of definitions and applications of work to safeguard ICH in China and elaborates the interpretive theoretical framework of this book. The two chapters in part II focus on the category of *gushi* (tales), an umbrella term for various forms of oral narratives. Chapter 3 further explores ways that terms such as "folklore" and "fairy tale" entered Chinese discourse. I discuss how Chinese scholars adopted the ideology of the Brothers Grimm in the early twentieth century. In this context, I analyze the popularization of the fairy tale in contemporary China. Chapter 4 scrutinizes the tale "Predestined Wife" with the historic-geographic method to demonstrate the development of this tale since the ninth century to its contemporary role in storytelling.

The two chapters in part III treat *yanyu* (proverbs) not only as a genre of oral literature but also as an expression of "life-view" reflecting the fundamental beliefs and values of Chinese culture. In chapter 5, I clarify several related categorical terms to put *yanyu* in a Chinese historical context, as well as to describe how *yanyu* have been treated by Chinese scholars in recent decades. I survey developmental history in stages, and present the scholarship on Chinese proverbs, including a review of European translations. Chapter 6 applies paremiological methods to study the origin, development, symbolism, and contemporary uses of a specific proverb, "Older ginger is spicier," through which Chinese "life-views" are articulated.

Part IV looks at the *geyao* (ballads/folksongs), a genre not only less known to the world outside China, but also less studied in Chinese scholarship, even though it is the richest source of oral traditions in China. However, the relationship between folksongs and ballads has been complicated in China and as a result some scholars restrict the term *geyao* to ballads, while others consider folksongs as an umbrella term that includes *geyao*. In this book, *geyao* includes both ballads and folksongs. In addition, I use it to refer to folk music that is often connected with folk narratives and rhythmic expressions.

Chapter 7 provides a survey of *geyao* in Chinese literary, social, and historical contexts, and connects *geyao* to various oral and musical performances because there have been scholarly tendencies to separate *geyao* as either "text" or "music" in different disciplines. Chapter 8 extends the discussion of oral traditions to storytelling without words—the role of musical instruments in promoting the continuity of oral traditions. Unlike European "classical music," for example, traditional Chinese music (e.g., the title of each piece) and musical instruments are explicitly associated with tales, legends and/or proverbs about certain historical figures, events, or locations. Such written records are also inseparable parts of all history books and literary anthologies. Today, each performance of an ancient instrument or a traditional musical composition is evidently a retelling of those tales as oral tradition. Focusing on the specific example of the clay-vessel *xun*-flute, in its transformation as a musical instrument and as an ethical symbol in its long history, this chapter also includes a personal narrative of my perspectives as a practitioner and researcher of this instrument. Reflecting on the processes of making, playing, and teaching the *xun*-flute in the China-US context, I elucidate the ways that nonverbal performative practices play an important role in maintaining the tradition (or, "flutelore" in Olsen's term, 2013) as a means of engaging in multicultural communication.

It is imperative to understand Chinese traditions to fight against the rampant racism which threatens world peace and prosperity. Ever since Chinese folklore and literature were introduced to the West about five centuries ago, China and its people have been portrayed as exotic, and often with racist motivations, particularly in the last two centuries. References in 2020 to COVID-19 as the "China Virus" and "Kung Flu" are but recent variants of earlier racist references to "Yellow Peril" and "Sick Man of Asia." Thus, the significance of studying Chinese oral traditions is to recognize how stereotypes can be created and how mutual understanding can be gained through tales, proverbs, and songs.

In this sense, exploring the inherent logic in the continuity of Chinese culture can provoke further investigations of the issues in Chinese and other cultural traditions. After all, cultural understanding of others is a way to know ourselves and make sense of what we do as traditions, and to coexist and thrive together in peace. The *cultural self-healing mechanism* discussed throughout this book is particularly relevant to analyzing the role of tradition in nation-building and finding the roots of cross-cultural conflicts in global communication, especially when a nation is in search of healing itself out of crises.

Acknowledgments

The book is a culmination of my folkloristic work over the past three decades. I developed some of the concepts and methodological issues in previous publications, but the material in this book is substantially revised, updated, expanded, and reorganized. Some sections and chapters (e.g., chapter 7) are new. It is definitely not a cliché for me to say that this book would not have been completed without the support and help from many individuals. Some provided specific constructive critiques on sections of this book, and others are owed more generally for friendship that has enriched my life each and every day.

For comments on the first two chapters in part I, I thank these scholars (in alphabetical order): Deming An, Tongju Diao; Bingzhong Gao, Tao Huang, Jifu Lin, Weihua Wang, Xiaobing Wang, Xiaochun Liu, Fang Xiao, Li Xing, Lihui Yang, and Shishan Zhang in China; Bin He and Xing Zhou in Japan; John Alley, Dan Ben-Amos, Marker Bender, Susan Blader, Anthony Bak Buccitelli, Simon J. Bronner, Michael Owen Jones, Paul Jordan-Smith, Fariha Khan, Margaret Magat, Wolfgang Mieder, Elliott Oring, Solimar Otero, Sharon Sherman, Sue Tuohy, and Daniel Wojcik in the United States.

For assistance with scholarship on folk and fairy tales in part II, I thank Professors Shouhua Liu and Fan Jiang, and storyteller Tan Zhenshan. I am grateful to James Leary, Thomas DuBois, Margaret Mills, and Dan Ben-Amos for their comments on my approach to Chinese folktales. I also want to acknowledge the help of Andrew Teverson, Cristina Bacchilega, Anne Duggan, Yongchao Chen, Xiaoming Xu, and the late Deqing Qin for their helpful comments. I am especially indebted to Jack Zipes for encouraging me to write on the Lin Lan fairy tale series and develop the topic into a book in the Oddly Modern Fairy Tales Series that he edited.

The two chapters on proverbs in part III are most recently written. I want to especially thank Wolfgang Mieder and Simon J. Bronner for their critical readings of the early drafts, and Deming An and Bill Long for their generous support and help on this topic. Their encouragement and support also extended to part IV. Chapter 7 is new, while chapter 8 is developed from several conference presentations and a section of a previous publication, with a new reflection of my own experience in connecting Chinese tradition to the practices in the United States. I benefited from illuminating conversations on ideas presented in chapter 8 with Susan Blader, Pamela Crossley, and Sarah Allan at Dartmouth College while I was teaching there in 2012–2013.

In my institutional home of Willamette University, I am fortunate to have colleagues Ron Loftus, Miho Fujiwara, Cecily McCaffrey, Patricia Varas, Michael Nord, John Doan, Hekun Wu, Elise Yun, Heidi Grew, and Jim Nafziger, as well as many students who learned with me about making and playing traditional Chinese musical instruments. I am grateful to have received several grants and awards that helped support my research: the Hewlett Grant (2011–2012), Center for Asian Studies (2013–2014), Atkinson Award (2015–2016), and Faculty Excellence in Teaching and Scholarship Award (2019–2020).

I am also grateful to those musician friends nearby, with whom I have had fun playing together: Jiyu Yang, Hai Bi, Jim Binkley, Jeremy Hickerson, Justin Luk, among others. I thank Ken Adams at radio station KMUZ in Salem for conducting several interviews and conversations with me, and Andy Cox for sharing his experiences in making the *xun*-flute in South Carolina. In particular, I want to recognize Bill Long of Salem for sharing his knowledge and insights with me on many topics. For their guidance and encouragement at Lexington Books, I am beholden to Simon J. Bronner and Elo-Hanna Seljamaa, editors of the Studies in Folklore and Ethnology series, and Judith Lakamper and Mikayla Mislak at the "home office." Last but not least, I thank my wife, Jing Liu, and our children, Andy and Teddy, to whom this book is dedicated, for their loving support.

Part I

INTRODUCTION

AN INTERPRETIVE FRAMEWORK FOR THE CONTINUITY OF TRADITIONS

The Chinese terms for *tradition* (*chuantong* 传统) and *folklore* (*minsu* 民俗) are often used to modify each other to emphasize either the traditionality of a folklore practice (*chuantong min-su*; traditional folklore) or the ongoing folk practice as a tradition (*minsu chuantong* folk/folklore tradition). At the turn of the twentieth century, this dual dimension of the concepts became more complicated when *literary tradition* (*wenxue chuantong* 文学传统) began to germinate a new branch, *folk literature* (*minjian wenxue* 民间文学 or *su wenxue* 俗文学) or *oral literature* (*koutou wenxue* 口头文学), by paying attention to the *oral tradition* (*koutou chuantong* 口头传统) among the common people. While the *written* literary tradition has a long history in China, this shift of attention signifies something greater than the re-categorization of literary forms itself. Today, in university curricular or academic degree programs, "folk literature" covers "oral literature" and is sometimes interchangeably used with "folklore/folkloristics" (*minsu xue* 民俗学), emphasizing *oral tradition.*

Semantically, *tradition/chuantong* in classic Chinese contains two actions: *chuan* means "to pass down or to; to hand over"; *tong* means "to unify many into one" (as in pulling one silk thread from one cocoon and then reeling and spinning many of them into one thicker thread for weaving). In this sense, *chuantong* embodies not only the meaning of *tradere* (to hand over or deliver) in Latin root, but also an additional layer of meaning of "unifying or synthesizing many into one." This extra layer of meaning is not expressed in *traditio* (the process) or *traditum* (for the thing transmitted) regardless of whether the "thing" is of what value. Thus, the Western *tradition* emphasizes the process of transmitting a thing or the value of the thing (Bronner 2019: 43), whereas the Chinese *chuantong* implies a certain *way* of transmitting things. It thus implies that *tradition* in Chinese practice may be much more complicated than what can be sorted in American folklore as "seven strands," namely, *lore, canon, process, mass, culture, langue,* and *performance* (Ben-Amos 1984). As for *minsu/folklore,* though a term directly borrowed from Japanese translation, the character *min/folk* refers to "common people" as a noun, in contrast to officials/*guan,* while *su/lore* means "custom" as a noun and "vulgar" as an adjective.

Ever since *folklore* was introduced to China in the early twentieth century, the meaning and translation of this term or concept in Chinese have been in debate, and the efforts to redefine and retranslate it have been continuing, as discussed in several chapters in this book. It is necessary to note here, though further discussed in the related chapters, that a number of key terms like "folklore" and "fairytale" were adopted from Japanese folklore scholarship, as folklore writings from the West were introduced into Japan during the Meiji period in the late nineteenth century, and then made their way to China, often via students studying in Japan. This is seemingly a semantic issue, but, as a matter of fact, it is at the core of disciplinary orientation and status, and national identity, and is certainly an ideological matter as well. It also relates to such questions as, how the imported terms and concepts should be understood and interpreted from Chinese perspectives within the Chinese context, whether they have limited the disciplinary growth, and why there has been, at the same time, a domestic discourse in contrast to an international discourse on the same concept or genre.

To keep in line with the present practice and scholarship in China, *oral tradition* in this book is used interchangeably with *folk literature,* and is discussed from these three major categories: folktales (*gushi*); proverbs (*yanyu*); and ballads (*geyao*). While *oral tradition* is emphasized, this book consciously tries to keep the oral within the context of a holistic view about oral and/or physical performances, and relate the intangible to the tangible, with the conviction that all traditional practices must be treated as organic parts of one cultural entirety. Indeed, the continuity of Chinese oral traditions must be understood within the broad context of how Chinese culture has continued as a whole for millennia. Limited by the length of this book, unfortunately, some other forms/genres of oral traditions like myths, epics, jokes, and riddles are not discussed in this book. Nevertheless, folk songs and musical instruments as oral performative traditions are discussed in the two chapters in part IV.

In this regard, the two chapters in this introductory part I are to "set the key" for the whole book. Chapter 1 surveys the developmental histories of oral traditions and folkloristic studies in China, laying out the background for the articulation of the theoretical framework in the chapter 2, which proposes the theoretical interpretive framework with a set of concepts that are essential to understanding Chinese culture as a whole. This framework, *cultural self-healing mechanism,* is intended to reason how Chinese culture has continued for several millennia, despite the fact that it is full of paradoxes in such aspects as dialects, languages, ethnicities, and religious beliefs. This interpretive framework is also meant to understand the continuity and discontinuity of human cultures or traditions in a broad sense, the rise and fall of a culture, and the change of a specific tradition.

Chapter 1

Folklore and Folkloristics in China

A survey of the history and reality of what is known as folklore (or oral/folk literature) and folkloristics (a discipline of folklore studies) in China from both insider and outsider perspectives will help understand the practice and transmission of oral traditions in Chinese cultural context. Even with a brief historical overview, one may gain an awareness of the mechanism that has enabled the continuity of the Chinese culture as one entirely for thousands of years, and thus can make sense of the theoretical framework discussed in the following chapter for interpreting the practices of those traditions in contemporary China.

This survey highlights these five aspects: (1) China's adaptation to Western influences since the sixteenth century; (2) the stages of collecting, categorizing, and practically applying folk literature throughout Chinese history; (3) the development of disciplinary studies of folk literature and folklore in the twentieth century; (4) current folkloristic efforts in the Intangible Culture Heritage (ICH) movement; and (5) Chinese folklore and folkloristics in perspective.

A GLIMPSE OF THE HISTORY OF CHINA-WEST INTERACTION

The interactions between China and the West can be traced back at least to the tenth century BCE when certain bronze technology was introduced from Central Asia, and to the massive exchange between China and the West around 2,000 years ago when the "Silk Road" (e.g., Buddhism to China; silk to the West) began to play its role in world history. Later on, through this Silk Road, as well as the maritime Silk Road, religious ideas and practices

5

of Christianity (e.g., Nestorian around the seventh century) and Islam (in the seventh century) entered China along with wars and traders. Stories of Marco Polo's travels to China in the thirteenth century certainly extended the European fantasies of the faraway land of China. But it was not until the sixteenth century, after the European exploration of the world with navigation technology, that a large-scale interactive relationship between China and the West began: the material influence from China to the West (e.g., silk, china, tea), and the ideological influences (along with science and technology) from the West to China. This pattern is essentially true as of today.

Two historical facts may well exemplify the Western influences to China. The first is related to ideological impact. Ever since the Jesuit missionary Matteo Ricci (1552–1610) arrived in China in 1582, Christianity began to take root in China and challenge traditional Chinese beliefs and values. This has continued until today through such ideologies as "colonialism," "imperialism," "racism," "modernization," and "universal values." Certainly, the missionaries' works on Chinese also stimulated some intellectual thinkers like the philosopher and mathematician G. W. Leibniz (1646–1716) and Max Webber (1864–1920), whose ideas have still been influential and quoted today. However, their comments on Chinese people and culture were to serve their own beliefs and ideologies.

The other fact is the combination of ideology, colonialism, militarism, and economic interests. In 1607, Dutch's East India Company shipped, for the first time, Chinese tea from Macau to Amsterdam, and thus began the tradition of tea drinking in Europe. The interest in tea further led to the introduction of some Chinese art forms, such as gardening, poetry, and music. Eventually, the combined desires out of those ideas and interests led to the Opium Wars in the 1840s–1860s and a subsequent century of wars between the European powers, including Japan, and China. This century is extremely crucial to understanding the Chinese minds and practices in everyday life and in world affairs today.

A few historical incidents provide a picture of what China was like in the late nineteenth and early twentieth centuries, and a brief review can help readers understand the use of folklore and fairy tales at that time. One factor was central: the transformation of the Manchu Qing Empire into the Republic of China had much to do with its relations with the West.

The First Opium War (or First Anglo-Chinese War, 1840–1842) and the Second Opium War (or Second Anglo-Chinese War; Anglo-French Expedition to China, 1856–1860) resulted in a series of unequal treaties (e.g., the Treaty of Nanjing with Great Britain in 1842 and the Treaty of Shimonoseki with Japan in 1895). This eventually led to the *guafen Zhongguo* (scramble for China 瓜分中国) movement through concessions by the Western powers and Japan in the early twentieth century (e.g., the Treaty of Versailles from the Paris Peace Conference in 1919 reinforced the previous unequal treaties that had divided and conquered China by the Western powers and Japan), resulting in dozens of "Concessions in China" and a "century of humiliation" (Ebrey, Walthall, and Palais 2009:315–316; Ebrey 2010:240). At the same time, these humiliations also stimulated the Chinese elites to seek their roots in their cultural traditions and to build their national identity through discourses in various domains, as a nation equal with the rest of the world (Ebrey, Walthall, and Palais 2009:407). These unprecedented humiliations created the colonial and imperial stereotypes that the Chinese were an inferior "race," which led to the public stereotypes of "Yellow Peril," "Sick Man of Asia," and even "China Virus" in 2020.

The epochal 1911 Revolution in China resulted in the termination of the Manchu Qing Dynasty (1644–1911) and the establishment of the Republic of China (1912). This social and political upheaval revealed various crises and hopes before and after the revolution, including, for example, the struggles between the Han-Chinese and the Manchu government, and between total Westernization and the restoration of *guocui* (national essence 国粹). However, there was a common goal among those different voices: to build a new China as a strong and modern nation in the world. It was this ideological drive within a particular historical context that led "nationalism" and "folklore," along with the wave of Westernization, to be introduced to China. In retrospect, two sets of discourses can be discerned from the New Culture Movement (1915–1923) launched by the Chinese intellectual elites at that time: one was domestic for the sake of restoring or building a new republic ruled by the Han-Chinese, and the other was for the sake of reconstructing this nation as strong and equal to other nations through international discourse (Zhang 2019a:335–336).

The May Fourth Movement in 1919 was the direct response to the aforementioned situation in China, but it was also the accumulated result of the previous decades (Ebrey, Walthall, and Palais 2009:411; Ebrey 2010:272). The Movement was a series of protests and marches initiated by university students in Beijing, supported by people of all walks of life, which eventually spread to many other cities in China. At the same time, the elites in China had begun to seek ways to rescue their country from total colonization.

The New Culture Movement was particularly meaningful to the rise of folklore in China. Specifically, the Folksong/Ballad (Folk Literature) Movement in 1918, launched from Beijing University, marked the birth of folklore studies in China. Central to this movement was Cai Yuanpei (1868–1940), who was then the university president (1916–1927), with experience of studying ethnology in Germany and other parts of Europe. It was during this period that a group of elites founded the fields of children's literature and folklore, among others, as part of these social and cultural movements.

Eventually, by the 1930s, the following people were responsible for the establishment of the academic discipline of folklore studies in China: Zhou Zuoren (1885–1967), Jiang Shaoyuan (1898–1983), Gu Jiegang (1893–1980), Zhong Jingwen (1903–2002), and Lou Zikuang (1907–2005) (Wang 2003:315–319). These pioneering folklorists—who were influenced by such Western ideas as evolutionism and social Darwinism and the establishment of academic disciplines such as ethnology, sociology, and anthropology, as well as folklore—had different opinions about how folklore should be used: (a) folklore as the weapon of an ideological revolution; (b) folklore as the tool of social reform; and (c) folklore as a force to expedite social changes with the involvement of the common people (e.g., promoting *baihuawen*, vernacular speech, to replace semi-classical usage of written Chinese that played a key role in Chinese culture).

Also during this period, the common goal for the elite began to educate or enlighten the public, influenced by the Brothers Grimm's idea of "enlightenment." In particular, they advocated for the education of women and children. While the term *minsu* (folklore) was not new in terms of the two characters (i.e., *min* meaning folk/people and *su* meaning customs), it introduced a totally new concept to the Chinese elite by borrowing the Japanese expression, which was a translation from English. Instead of focusing on *su* (customs), the elite found that one particular form, *tonghua* (fairy tale; *tong* meaning children, *hua* meaning story/tale), was the most explicit way to explain the concept of folktale to the public. Part of the reason was that the term *tonghua* was most directly related to the idea of "children's education" (through "children's literature" and "children's stories"); the term was also borrowed from Japanese characters through loan translation by the elites who studied in Japan—specifically, by Zhou Zuoren. (Chapter 3 will further discuss the transformation of European fairy tales to Chinese *tonghua*.)

From the First Opium War in 1840 to the New Culture Movement of the early twentieth century, Chinese social, political, and cultural life fell into deep predicaments. The European powers "scrambled" to divide China; everyday life of the common people in China was "abnormal" due to constant wars and famines. This was a rare period of cultural destruction not only in China but also in human history. During this period, Chinese culture faced constant crises which may be seen as a liminal stage, in which the Chinese lost their awareness of who they were and what China or Chinese culture meant. While there was a force to deny Chinese traditions that were represented by Confucian ethics and Chinese writing system, among others, the majority of Chinese people were relentlessly in search of new paths for development.

Through a long process—the establishment of the Republic of China (1912), the New Culture Movement, New China, and the Root-Seeking

(*Xungen*) Movement in the late twentieth century, Chinese culture finally seems to have returned to its roots, and most Chinese people have regained cultural self-awareness of and self-confidence in their own traditions, though the struggle has continued until today (Fei 1997; 2003; Fei and Zhang 2009). In this sense, the past two decades have witnessed the emphasis on "national tradition" (*minzu chuantong*) and "localizing" (*bentuhua*) various cultural elements with "Chinese characteristics" (*Zhongguo tese*), with a conscious reconstruction of Chinese national identity.

In addition to this China-West (including Japan) dichotomy in the recent centuries, there are also layers to the traumatic experiences of the Han-Chinese throughout the history of China. For example, the nomadic Xiongnu invasion from the north resulted in the building of the Great Wall over 2,000 years ago; the Mongols' invasion and ruling of China during the eleventh to fourteenth centuries; and the Manchu ruling from the seventeenth century to the early twentieth century, along with the periods of dis-unified China such as the Southern and Northern Dynasties (fourth to sixth century) and the Liao-Jin-Xia Dynasties (eleventh to thirteenth century) with a number of independent states of different languages, religions, and traditions. Yet, it was through these experiences in dealing with different peoples and cultures that the Han-Chinese have developed their cultural self-healing mechanism (to be further discussed in chapter 2), through which the Chinese culture has continued with vitality.

Within this dimension, how Chinese folklore has been known in the West (mostly in the English language world) also affects how Chinese intellectuals look at their own work. While the history of Sinology began about five centuries ago (Honey 2001), academic studies departing from the previous missionaries' works took the role mainly in the early twentieth century. However, previous descriptions and studies related to Chinese folklore have still played a fundamental role in the Western understanding of China, including stereotypes about Chinese people and culture as seen in the numerous publications on Chinese folk and fairy tales and proverbs (to be further discussed in the following chapters of this book).

FOLKLORE COLLECTION IN CHINESE HISTORY

The history of Chinese accounts and collections of folklore began when the writing system developed into its maturity as early as the seventeenth century BCE as seen in the Oracle Bone Inscriptions, which was used to divine and record the everyday events centered on the life of the Kings (Chang 1980; Song [1994] 2005). During the period of 500 BCE–300 BCE, all classics essential to Chinese culture (including folklore) were written down, including the most important three books on rites: *Book of Rites* (*Liji*), *Book of Zhou Rites* (*Zhouli*), and *Book of Etiquettes* (*Yili*), and other important classics such as the *Book of Songs* (*Shijing*, ca. 11th c. BCE–8th c. BCE) known as a grand collection that plays "an enormous part in the literary and cultural history of China" (Karlgren 1950:1), *Classic of Mountains and Seas* (*Shanhaijing*, ca. 3rd c. BCE–3rd c. CE) (Birrell 1999) known as a collection of myths, and *Biography of King Mu, Son of Heaven* (*Mu Tianzi Zhuan*, ca. 2nd c. BCE–3rd c. CE) known as a legendary narrative.

In the long history of collecting folk narrative (including fairy tales, myths, legends, and jokes in Western genres), a few collections are of special relevance to this discussion. For example, *Miscellaneous Morsels from Youyang* (*Youyang Zazu* 酉阳杂俎) is a collection by Duan Chengshi (803–863), containing thirty volumes (Duan 1981). The tales were categorized in "genres" such as *zhiguai* (strange/wonder/ghost tales) and anecdotes. The Chinese "Cinderella" tale, *Yexian* (叶限), was recorded under the genre of *nuogao*, a Daoist term for summoning ghosts and spirits. Duan recorded the tale and made a note at the end about the teller's background. (More discussion on the tale of *Yexian* in chapter 3.)

Also in the ninth century, similar collections were popularly known as *biji* (written notes 笔记), a prototype of the early forms of short stories. But by the twelfth century, *shuohua* (close to the later "storytelling" 说话) began to take shape, marking a big step forward in the history of folktales in China (Liu 2017:252). One example of this effort is the collection *Records of the Listener* (*Yi Jian Zhi*) by Hong Mai (1123–1202) (Hong 1981). Among the more than 2,700 stories in the collection, most were from oral sources, with relatively complete plots. Approximately 100 tales in the collection can be defined as complete folktales or legends in today's sense (Liu 2017:253). In the *History of Chinese Folktales* (2017), Liu Shouhua has examined 450 tale types from more than 40 collections compiled in the past 2,000 years in China. These tales demonstrate a clear continuity of development of form and content.

These classics, in addition to their political and social functions, also set up a model of collecting and categorizing folklore. This tradition continued until today as seen in the two national projects: *Grand Collections of Chinese Folk Literature* (1984–2009) and the ongoing *Compendium of Chinese Folk Literature* (2017–2025) (to be further discussed in the following parts on tales, proverbs, and ballads).

Through the long history of collecting, recording, categorizing, editing, and (re)printing folklore, two parallels traditions have developed: the "written" tradition and the "oral" tradition, which mutually benefit from each other in the making of the "practiced" history of traditions in China. This dynamic relationship has contributed to the interactive working system of orthodoxy (as the ruling and unifying ideology through texts) and orthopraxy (as the unifying norm of constructing common national and cultural identities in everyday practices, based on regional, linguistic, belief, and social differences). It has also illustrated the continuity of the unified Chinese culture, which is described as a model of "diversity within unity" (Watson and Rawski 1988) or the *duoyuan yiti geju* (a pattern of diversity in unity 多元一体格局) (Fei [1988] 1999:15, 38).

Therefore, folklore in China has functioned as a centripetal force not only for maintaining Chinese culture as a whole within geographic China, but also for the fluid "Cultural China" (Tu 1994; Li 1995), in which Chinese cultural influence reaches beyond geographic, linguistic, religious, and ancestral limits. However, in understanding "folklore in China" or "Chinese culture as a whole," one needs to bear in mind that Chinese people have never been a homogenous group in terms of lineage or kinship, language or dialect, and religion or belief. For this reason, the contemporary notions based on the Western racial/ethnic model of "racial/ethnic identity" must be abandoned; instead, it is the "folkloric identity" that has enabled the practice of traditions while absorbing various cultural elements from other cultures. Such a tradition is based on the inclusiveness of "Chinese culture" through its polytheist beliefs and values.

With the massive collections of folklore throughout history, the use of folklore in China is generally in accordance with what is seen in most other cultures. However, one crucial difference between the Chinese and the Western use of folklore began more than 2,000 years ago: folklore has been used to implement ethical guidelines in the polytheist practices in everyday life in China, whereas monotheist practices in the Judeo-Christian cultures have demonstrated strong exclusivity. Expressions of this fundamental difference are seen today in the political tensions in international affairs, as well as in academic discourses and interpersonal communication.

In folklore studies, generally speaking, the use or function of folklore has been understood from a functionalist perspective, representing "a paradigm absent in earlier diffusionist and literary approaches to folklore" (Oring 1996:656). For example, the functionalist folklorist William Bascom summarized four primary functions of folklore as: (a) "amusement" with "deeper meaning" and in the "concepts of compensation and the escape mechanism" [or, escaping from repressions imposed by society, and providing a release of personal anxiety, wonder or fantasy, often by means of entertainment]; (b) "in validating culture, [and] in justifying its rituals and institutions" [or, maintaining social norms]; (c) "in education, particularly, but not exclusively, in non-literate societies" [or, education of local and traditional knowledge];

and (d) "maintaining conformity to the accepted patterns of behavior" [or, applying social pressure and exercising social and political control in community-binding] (Bascom 1954:343–346). Although such a functional-istic "explanatory model was wholeheartedly accepted by folklorists in their attempts to explain their own peculiar subset of sociocultural phenomena" (Oring 1976:70), one may also need to step out the folklore "event" or "text" itself, and think about the use of folklore in constructing and maintaining identities at individual, group, and national levels in contemporary global-izing and digital communication (Bronner 2019).

In understanding Chinese practice of tradition, two other aspects stand out and deserve special attention: (a) the temporal dimension, that is, folklore in China as a synchronic force to maintain the continuity of a culture with-out changing its fundamental beliefs and values for so many centuries; and (b) the spatial dimension, that is, folklore in China as a diachronic force to integrate many different cultural groups into one umbrella-culture based on the Confucian ultimate principle of *heerbutong* (harmonizing with differ-ences 和而不同).

Given China's long history of collecting and using folklore, it is useful to consider this history in stages so as to understand the practice in context. In this regard, the first folkloristic effort to outline the long history of folklore collection in China was the six-volume *The History of Chinese Folklore* (2008), edited by Zhong Jingwen (1903–2002), who is regarded as the founder of contemporary Chinese folkloristics.

This series of six volumes covers the development of folklore collection from the pre-history (e.g., the Hemudu Culture about seven thousand years ago in China) to 1949, with commentaries on all important collections in each dynasty. It confirms that the terms "lore" (*su*), "social-lore" (*shisu*), "practical-lore" (*xisu*), and "current-lore" (*fengsu*), were used very much as today's "folklore" (*minsu*) as early as the fifth century BCE. This series also presents a general categorization of Chinese folklore, a categorization which has guided other major folkloristic textbooks in China since the 1980s, including: (1) material folklore; (2) social folklore; (3) spiritual folklore; and (4) linguistic folklore. Under these primary categories further subcategories are developed: material production (or modes of production); material life (foodways, dressing and housing); social organization (religious and other societies); annual festivals; life-cycle rituals; folk beliefs; folk technology and craftsmanship; folk literature; folk language; folk arts (music, dance, drama and handicraft); and folk games and entertainments.

Accordingly, folklore collection in China can be outlined in the following stages by highlighting the distinctive aspects and their continuity. This struc-tural arrangement is essential to showing the continuity of Chinese traditions, as argued in the *Introduction to Folkloristics* (Zhong [1998] 2009).

Stage One: The Pre-Qin Period (Prior to the Third Century BCE)

The character of "lore" (*su*) can be traced to the Bronze Inscriptions widely appearing from the eleventh to the third century BCE. By the fifth century BCE, the meaning of *su* was similar to today's usage. During this period, the fundamental beliefs and values in Chinese culture were established through everyday folklore practices, and were extensively discussed in all the major classics written at that time. This period is described as the "blossoming of a hundred schools of thought," but the most influential ideas were Confucian and Daoist (with Buddhist ideas integrated later on)—and are still essential to folklore practices today.

Confucius (551–479 BCE) interpreted myths of origin by relating them to human history, and, furthermore, differentiated the human from animals by making sense of the ethical relationship among human beings in the society—an ethical system deeply rooted in Chinese culture from individual life (friendship or brotherhood) to familial life (between husband and wife and father and son), and to social life (between different strata of society). Indeed, the Confucian ethical system has guided everyday folklore practices and united the different regional, linguistic, and ethnic practitioners through orthodoxy (text) and orthopraxy (practice) in China. His idea of promoting ethical behavior by ritualizing everyday behaviors as customs and by teaching through music (with songs/poetry) exemplified the use of folklore for individuals to become integrated into society and for the society to reinforce social norms.

Furthermore, his follower Xunzi (325–238 BCE), developed the idea of using folklore as a way of social ruling, that is, folklore as a unifier not only for small/familial groups but also for a state. He also pointed out that the primary difference between the Xia people (or the Han-Chinese) and the surrounding groups (or, today's *shaoshu minzu*, "ethnic minorities") was only in lifestyle choices (e.g., manner of dress), rather than the political system or blood ties. Such Confucian views revealed that the ancients recognized the differences of lifestyle among different groups, but considered that they were changeable with ethical education and adaptable to each other's customs.

Han Feizi (275–233 BCE), Xunzi's student, developed the idea that changing customs was the basis of changing social rules. This idea also proved the importance of folklore in unifying a state and improving social norms. The ancient ideas of "Great Unity" (*dayitong*) and "following local customs" (*ruxiang suisu*) are still discernible in today's folklore practice, and the following folk expressions are still common in contemporary language: "almost" (*chabuduo*), "giving face (to each other)" (*gei mianzi*), or the idea of "seeking common ground and letting differences exist" (*qiutong cunyi*).

The central Daoist insight regarding folklore is that it is essential to maintain the nature of human beings so that they can enjoy their existing customs developed through living a spontaneous life. This informed an ancient theory of "ideal life" which provided an outlet to "exit the world," escape or compensation for those who were frustrated by the stricter Confucian guide to "enter the world." Some of the ancient Daoist ideas were further developed into a religion by the third century, which, in turn, preserved many earlier myths and tales as the justification of a worldview and a metaphysical super-construction.

These two views, along with others in Chinese history (e.g., Buddhist ideas that became widespread by the third and fourth century), exemplified the idea of "diversity in unity" through different interpretations of diverse folklore practices. This inclusive model of adopting other ideas and folklore is also key to understanding the mechanisms of transmitting and transforming traditions, and of cultural self-healing processes in Chinese history.

Stage Two: Compiling and Annotating Folklore Collections during the Han and Wei Dynasties (3rd c. BCE–5th c. CE)

The integration of the "three-teaching-in-one" (Confucianism, Daoism, and Buddhism) during this period reshaped Chinese folklore and culture, both ideologically and practically. However, Buddhism added more ritual forms and everyday explanations (e.g., reincarnation and *karma*) to the previous Chinese fundamental beliefs of "the immortality of the soul" and "the unity of man and nature," rather than changing them. Besides the influence of the classics mentioned earlier, historiographies became essential not only to the history of the orthodox Great Tradition but also to collecting and maintaining folklore within the orthopraxy Little Tradition. The earliest and the greatest example is the *Records of the Grand Historian* (*Shiji*) by Sima Qian (145–90 BCE). In Sima Qian's view, history was related, but not equal, to folklore. Thus, he collected myths and legends to supplement his account of history. As a result, he established a model of historiography for the following twenty-four dynasties till the early twentieth century, a continued series of historiographies including aspects of folklore. In those orthodox history books, folklore became a category alongside categories such as "family history," "regional history," and "legendary history." This mutually supportive relationship between history and folklore is still characteristic of Chinese scholarship in the humanities.

Besides the historiography of the orthodox history in each dynasty, folkloregraphy (*minsuzhi*, a term used by Chinese folklorists) has been a distinctive feature of Chinese folklore collection, often appeared in the form and name of local history: *xianzhi* (County Annals) or *difangzhi* (Local/Regional

Annals). This tradition has continued since Sima Qian, and is still evident in the revision and writing of new *xianzhi* or *difangzhi* in contemporary China.

Two important examples of this tradition are the *Disquisitions* (*Lun Heng*) by Wang Chong (27–97) and the *Classics of Mountains and Seas* annotated by Guo Pu (276–324). The former is known as the representative work of atheist thought; the latter as the most important source of myths in China. In *Disquisitions*, Wang Chong discussed his views about folklore, in the context of the rise of Daoist and Buddhist ideas and the crisis of Confucian ideas during his time. He argued that folklore emerged out of actual experiences and was tested by history, and he criticized others for using folklore to serve their own political or ethical purposes. His view was welcomed because it considered that folklore should be treated as actual ways of living a life, but not necessarily determined by all kinds of gods and spirits. He denied his contemporary Daoist and Buddhist ideas about rebirth and *karma*.

As a Confucian and a Daoist scholar, as well as influenced by Buddhist ideas, Guo Pu helped justify the myths of origin for the believers. Through his annotations, the treasures of ancient myths were preserved and further developed in China and East Asia. The continuing influence of his book since his time shows how important his approach to folklore has been in Chinese culture and history.

Through such unorthodox folkloregraphies, there developed a rising category/genre of folklore around the fourth to fifth centuries: telling and recording (in writing) *zhiguai* (wonder and magic tales). The well-known Chinese versions of the tale types, "Swan Maiden" and "Cowherd and Weaving Girl," were recorded during this time. As a result, there began a history of using folkloregraphies to preserve the folklore excluded from orthodox historiographies, for example, *In Search of the Supernatural* (*Soushenji*) by Gan Bao (283–351) (1996) and the *Records of Strange Things* (*Shuyiji*) by Ren Fang (460–508).

Stage Three: The Tang and Song Dynasties (7th c.–13th c.)

This period saw the prevalence of folklore about agricultural-political changes and the beginnings of recording urban folklore. With the "three-teachings-in-one" as the ruling ideology and the ritualized everyday ethical norms in an agricultural society, folklore functioned not only as a unifier of the newly expanded empire in political and social sense, but also as the medium integrating new cultural elements from Central Asian and Europe through the Silk Road, and from Southeast Asia and Eastern African through the maritime Silk Road. This period experienced the most diverse cultural interaction and integration in Chinese history, and perhaps also in human history by that time. For example, the extreme dualistic conflicts in the monotheist societies between the Christian and the Islamic ideas (e.g., the Crusades) resulted in both Christian and Islamic ideas, along with the migration of the believers, being integrated into Chinese culture and folklore. Various records and objects have revealed the integration of peoples from Africa, Europe, and other parts of Asia into the "Chinese people" during the Tang dynasty. It is this inclusive mechanism inherent in Chinese culture that has further energized its vitality, a phenomenon not possible in an exclusive monotheist society.

The development of paper-making and printing during this period further enriched the history of the two dynamic and interactive social classes: the elite with written literature and the folk/commoners with oral literature. Three encyclopedic collections ordered by the Emperors from that era are the following: *Classified Collection of Arts and Literature* (*Yiwen Leiju*) edited by Ouyang Xun (557–641), the *Imperial Collection of the Taiping Era* (*Taiping Yulan*), and the *Extensive Records of the Taiping Era* (*Taiping Guangji*) edited by Li Fang (925–996). They became models for similar collections in later times, including the national projects of three grand folk literature collections (folktales, folksongs, and proverbs) initiated in the 1980s.

Widely circulated tales such as the "Predestined Wife" (*Dinghundian*, ATU 930A) and the "White Snake" (*Baishezhuan*), come from the *Taiping Guangji*. The well-known "Chinese Version of Cinderella" (*Yexian*, ATU 510A) was first collected in *The Miscellaneous Morsels from Youyang* by Duan Chengshi (803–863). Some other important folklore collections include: *Record of the Listener* by Hong Mai (1123–1202), the most comprehensive collection (in 420 volumes) of customs and strange tales in Chinese history; *Records of the Entertaining Performances* (*Jiaofangji*) by Cui Lingqin (fl. 740); and, *Notes of the Musical Performances* (*Bijimanzhi*) by Wang Zhuo (ca. 1081–1160) on folk drama, oral, and musical performances.

Although many tales collected during this period exhibit clear Buddhist marks of Indian origin, a close look can tell something more. For example, in Archer Taylor's (1959) seminal study of the "Predestined Wife" (930A), it was easy to tell that the matchmaker or the Moon Man (*yuexia laoren*) in the tale was a prophet reading Sanskrit, which indicates that the Buddhist idea of fate was adopted into Chinese tales. In contrast, tracing the image of the matchmaker, one can see that it was already widely used in Chinese literature and folklore as early as the fifth century BCE, long before Buddhism took root in China. What can be concluded from such examples is that, at least in the Chinese case, cultural integration was a long process based on its fundamental beliefs and values, and that foreign cultural elements were adopted often by changing names to reinforce those existing fundamental beliefs and values, or localizing—a syncretic mechanism characteristic of Chinese culture (Zhang 2014, 2017a; more discussion of the tale in chapter 4).

Recording urban folklore was also the result of developing metropolitan capital cities during this period, a new development of the traditional agriculture-centered folklore collection. Some of the important collections are: *New Records of the Two Capitals* (*Liangjing xinji*) by Wei Shu (?–757), *Records of the Dreamy Luxury in the Capital* (*Dongjing menghualu*) by Meng Yuanlao (ca. 1103–1147), *Fantastic Stories of the Capital City* (*Ducheng jisheng*) by Nai Deweng (fl. 1235), and *Records of Dreamy Life* (*Menglianglu*) by Wu Zimu (fl. 1274). They all vividly described the customs in the imperial courts and among the city residents, revealing the functions of education and justifying social norms through the imperial orders, as well as the lifestyle of the commoners who were still living on the agricultural calendar while transitioning to urban life. In addition, most traditional oral performances that still exist today in China were shaped and matured during this period.

Stage Four: The Yuan, Ming, and Qing Dynasties (1271–1911)

The two striking characteristics of this period are: (a) multicultural interactions: the Yuan (1271–1368) was ruled by the Mongols, the Qing (1644–1911) by the Manchu, and the Ming (1368–1644) by the Han-Chinese; and (b) the extensive interaction of high and low cultures. During the Yuan and Qing, both elites and commoners among the Han-Chinese used folk literature and folklore as a way to escape the social pressure (e.g., the Han-Chinese were classified as the lowest social class by the Mongols) and to compensate their nostalgic sentiment. As a result, folk performances were unusually developed during the Yuan and the Qing. In addition, folklore was developed as a means of enlightenment and education, particularly during the Ming, when, for example, the West was first known to the Chinese on a large scale (i.e., through the Jesuit missionaries in the sixteenth and seventeenth centuries).

Folkloregraphy played an important role in maintaining the unity of the empire during this period. Writing and rewriting "regional annals" at the county level all over the empire was the political task, while other records were also greatly encouraged. They were all compiled by the elites, who substantially used folklore and folklife materials. Thus, these records are considered very important to today's revitalization of local traditions. Furthermore, there were also "serendipitous" folklorists who, being scholar-officials at governmental or military posts, recorded folklore practices that turned out to be extremely valuable. For example, Xiao Daheng (1532–1612) was a general (and later the minister of defense) stationed at the border of the Ming Empire to defend against the Mongols. He wrote a booklet, *The Records of Mongolian Folklore* (*Yisuji*), which turned out to be the only written record of Mongolian folklore in both Chinese and Mongolian languages until the twentieth century (Zhang 2017b).

Another development is the change of the elite's attitude toward folk litera-ture and arts, which led to more and more folkloregraphies being produced. Many works by Feng Menglong (1574–1646) demonstrated not only his comprehensive collections and recollections of folklore but also his positive attitude toward folklore as a way of social education and entertainment. Pu Songling's (1640–1715) *The Strange Tales from Liaozhai* (*Liaozhai zhiyi*) (1989) is another classical collection of wonder or ghost stories (nearly 500 tales) in Chinese.

The multicultural interactions in everyday life during this period also high-lighted the value of languages in recording folklore practices. For example, the *Ancient Ballads and Proverbs* (*Guyaoyan*) by Du Wenlan (1851–1881) and *Records of Local Customs* (*Tufenglu*) by Gu Zhangsi (fl. 1791) recorded the popular expressions, folk sayings, and local slang, which greatly enriched the overall collection of verbal folklore.

By the late nineteenth century, folklore collection had become more sys-temic with distinctive categorization, paving the way for the later folkloristic studies. At the same time, Western concepts such as "nation," "nationalism," "ethnology," "ethnography," and "folklore" began to be introduced to China. Meanwhile, China was resisting the colonial and imperial powers "scram-bling for China" after the Opium Wars of the 1840s, which first led to a period of national survival without folklore collection or studies, and then, at the turn of the twentieth century, a wave of saving China with "folklore" in relation to "nationalism," or the birth of folkloristics in China.

FOLKLORE STUDIES IN THE TWENTIETH CENTURY

Even though the history of folkloristics in China is short (since the 1910s), it has been severely interrupted during the wars against Japan's invasion (1931–1945), the Civil War (1945–1949), and the Cultural Revolution (1966–1976). These extreme times of cultural crises also remind us how vulnerable the humanities can be when colonial invasions destroy a society.

There are different views about when the history of folkloristics in China actually began. However, these milestones are clear: the establishment of a (national) Folklore Society in 1927, its resumption in 1943, and the restora-tion/reestablishment of the China Folklore Society (CFS) in 1983.

One view is that it began with such folklorists as Huang Zunxian (1848–1905, a scholar-official and diplomat known as "the first person who opens himself up to and embraces the world" in modern China) and Zhang Liangcai (1870–1906, whose *Chinese Custom History* (Zhang [1912] 2013) is known as the first monograph on Chinese social/folklore history). In the 1910s–1920s, university-based elites such as Cai Yuanpei, Lu Xun, Liu

Bannong, and Shen Yimo further enabled the establishment of folklore studies in China. Eventually, in the 1930s, the following people were responsible for the establishment of the academic discipline of folklore studies: Zhou Zuoren, Jiang Shaoyuan, Gu Jiegang, Zhong Jingwen, and Lou Zikuang (Wang 2003:315–319).

Most Chinese folklorists, however, considered that the Folksong/Ballad (Folk Literature) Movement in 1918 connected folkloristics in China with the influence of European "nationalism." The Chinese wanted to use "folklore" to rescue the nation while facing their declining empire and the foreign invading powers, and as an effort to build a modern China (e.g., Hong 1985; Duara 1995). Many pioneering folklorists promoted these European ideas in China: evolutionism, social Darwinism, ethnology, sociology, and anthropology. Among them there were these schools of thoughts: (a) folklore as the weapon of an ideological revolution; (b) folklore as the tool of social reform; and (c) folklore as a force to expedite social changes with the involvement of the common people (e.g., promoting vernacular speech, *baihuawen*, to replace semi-classical usage that played a key role in Chinese culture). These thoughts were essential to the Folk Literature Movement and the May Fourth Movement or New Culture Movement in the 1910s–1920s, which were the turning points in modern China.

However, in reviewing the path of Chinese folkloristics from the 1910s, Bingzhong Gao (2008:5) holds a different view. He considers that the discipline was substantially constructed during the 1980s–2010s, because it was only since the 1980s that the discipline began to take shape in these three foundational areas: teams of folklorists and their training through curriculum in universities; folklore becoming public knowledge; and folklore and folkloristics becoming part of cultural production.

Despite these different views, this list of the pivotal events in the history of folkloristic studies since the 1910s may be helpful for the following discussion about the development, contributions, and challenges in current Chinese folkloristics:

- 1914: The term *minsuxue* (folkloristics 民俗学) was first introduced into Chinese by Zhou Zuoren (1885–1987) by borrowing the characters from Japanese. Previously, *folklore* was translated into different Chinese terms such as *minjian wenxue* (folk literature), *minxue* (study of people/folk), and *geyaoxue* (study of ballads and songs).
- 1915: The journal, *La Jeunesse (Xinqingnian)*, was launched and played a leading role in the New Culture Movement and the rise of folkloristics in China.
- 1918: *The Beijing University Daily* called for a national survey of ballads/folksongs, with the support of the university president, Cai Yuanpei

(1868–1940), an event which is often seen as the beginning of folkloristics in China.

- 1922: Beijing University launched *Ballads/Folksongs Weekly* (*Geyao Zhoukan*), which directly influenced the establishment of several associations or societies of folklore collection and studies.
- 1927: The Folklore Society was established in Sun Yat-sen (Zhongshan) University, and the journal *Folklore Weekly* was launched the following year.
- 1942: The multilingual journal, *Folklore Studies* (*minsuxue zhi*), was published in Beijing by Father Matthias Eder of Germany. (This journal was later moved to Japan as an English journal and renamed *Asian Folklore Studies*, and, currently, *Asian Ethnology,* hosted in Nanzan University, Japan.)
- 1950: China Folk Literature and Arts Association was established under the central government of the PRC. Folklore was included under the disciplinary field of Folk Literature and Arts. The journal, *Folk Literature* (*minjian wenxue*), was published.
- 1978: An open letter by a dozen leading folklorists was presented to the China Academy of Social Sciences proposing to restore folkloristics in China.
- 1983: The CFS was established in Beijing, and Zhong Jingwen was elected the president. CFS holds annual meetings, but does not have its own journal.
- 1984: The Ministry of Culture initiated the Three Grand Collections of Folk Literature Project: *Chinese Folktales Collections*; *Chinese Ballads and Songs Collections*; and *Chinese Proverb Collections*, with 90 volumes at provincial level, and more than 4,000 volumes at country level; all were published by 2009.
- 1985: The quarterly journal, *Folklore Studies* (*Minsu yanjiu*), was published in Shandong University, remaining a leading journal in the field.
- 1996: The International Asian Folklore Society was established in Beijing by scholars from China, Korea, Japan, Mongolia, and some other East and Southeast Asian countries. It is the only organization that connects East and Southeast Asian countries.

In writing the history of folkloristics in China, one view considers that it has undergone three stages: Shaping stage (1918–1937); Developing stage (1949–1966); and Reconstructing stage (1976–present) (Xing 2016:415–428). Another approach is to see it as having the following two stages (Wang 2003:342):

Stage One: The Beginning of Folkloristic Movement and Studies of Ancient Folklore (1910s–1940s). Characteristics of this period were the national survey and ballad collection (or oral folklore), the publication of those collections, and the establishment of folklore societies in several universities. Furthermore, there were the pioneering stage (1918–1927) and foundation-laying stage (1927–1949). The publications included these categories: studies of ancient folk literature (e.g., Yang 1933; Hu 1923); studies of different folklore practices (e.g., on Mongolian folklore by Luobusangquedan 1918; Jiang 1928); and, introduction of Western folklore studies (e.g., *Handbook of Folklore* by C. Burne, *English Folklore* by A. R. Wright, and *Le totémisme* by M. Besson).

Stage Two: The Establishment of Folkloristic Theories with Chinese Characteristics (1950s–2000). The first three decades of this period were mostly occupied with the collection of folk literature and the survey of the oral literature of the minority nationalities. Since the late 1970s, folkloristics in China was developed with the (re)establishment of CFS, along with increasing folkloristic publications and introduction of Western folklore theories. In this process, more than ten Chinese folklorists published their own works within a dozen years to define and categorize folklore. Their commonly accepted categorization of Chinese folklore includes: economic folklore, social folklore, folklore of belief, folk literature (or folklore of language), and folklore of entertainment (i.e., games and sports).

Wang points out these additional features as he describes this developmental history (from the collections in the fifth century BCE to the early twenty-first century): from making use of folk practices to enhance political power to collecting folklore in texts for the broad goal of enhancing social harmony; from collecting folklore as an individual practice to institutionalizing it as a collective enterprise; and from making use of folklore to enable social and cultural integration to establishing a discipline "with Chinese characteristics" (Wang 2003:344–345).

Folklorist Liu Tieliang considers that the development of Chinese folkloristics has undergone an "initiating stage" (1918–1926), a "maturing stage" (1927–1937), a "stagnating stage" (1937–1949) due to wars, a "shifting stage" (1949–1966) focusing on folk literature collecting, and a "revival stage" (after 1978) (Liu 1998). He also adds that since 2003, Chinese folkloristics has expanded its scope and diversified its topics, especially with the introduction of ICH, and has engaged in international discourse (Liu 2008).

Studies of Chinese folklore by Western scholars have also played a meaningful role in the development of Chinese folkloristics. Examples on specific areas will be further discussed in the following chapters (e.g., on fairy tales and proverbs), but here is a synopsis.

In terms of folkloristic studies, the turn of the 1930s from previous missionaries' works to academic studies marked a different approach. The folklorist R. D. Jameson (1895–1959) pioneered this path with his teaching in China, the well-quoted *Three Lectures on Chinese Folklore* (1932), and a survey of Chinese folklore in addition to at least two hundred entries in the *Fund and Wagnalls Standard Dictionary of Folklore, Mythology and Legend* (Jameson 1949). Wolfram Eberhard (1909–1988) published his *Typen Chinesischer Volksmärchen* (1937a). Chinese local folklorists also began their folklore investigation (Chao 1942). China's societal and political changes in the 1950s–1970s aroused a new look from the West on the use of folklore in "red China" (Moy 1952; Yen 1964; Hrdličková 1965; Eberhard 1970; Eminov 1975).

After the resuming of Chinese folkloristics in the 1980s, publications on Chinese folklore have tremendously increased. Local reflections upon the three decades of achievements, difficulties, and challenges have depicted a general picture of Chinese folkloristics (An and Yang 2015). Surveys from American perspectives on the use of folklore and ideology (Tuohy 1991) and changes in the new century with emphasis on ethnic minorities (Bender 2006a) provide another new look. The folklore of Chinese people abroad has also become a subject matter (Zhang 2006, 2015b). Furthermore, reflections upon the previous studies have pointed out how the early twentieth-century European depictions of Chinese folklore (e.g., in fairy tales, proverbs) aided the widespread stereotypes shaped by the early missionary works in translating, or making up, Chinese tales, proverbs, and ballads.

The reestablishment of the CFS in 1983 reflected a change in the social and academic climate in China. In 1984, the Ministry of Culture initiated the Three Grand Collections of Folk Literature Project (1984–2009), which was categorized into the *Grand Collection of Folktales*, *Grand Collection of Ballads and Songs*, and *Grand Collection of Proverbs*. The project was completed in 2009 and consisted of 298 volumes at the provincial level (Zhou 1984–2009) and more than 4,000 volumes at the national level, along with numerous unpublished archival materials. Besides this national project supported by the central government, two other encyclopedic series are worth mentioning: *Folklore and Folk Literature Series* (Lou 1971) (a reprint of the folklore collections by the Folklore Society in the 1920s, amounting to 200 volumes), marking the foundation of folkloristics in China; and the *Grand Series of Chinese Folklore* (Tao 2003–2004) in thirty-one volumes arranged by province, covering the studies and practices since the 1980s. Western studies of Chinese oral and folk literature and performance resulted in many publications, including *CHINOPERL: Journal of Chinese Oral and Performing Literature* and several important collections (e.g., Vibeke 1999; Mair and Bender 2011). There are also dictionaries and encyclopedias on regional or national folklore, based on previous literature or recent fieldwork.

FOLKLORE AND CULTURAL HERITAGE
IN THE TWENTY-FIRST CENTURY

The introduction of the concept of ICH through the UNESCO's ICH Convention (2003) to China marked a historical turn to folkloristics in China. However, to understand the present situation in China, one has to consider it as an organic development of the previous forty or so years. The current situation in China can be perceived from these aspects: disciplinary infrastructure; development and contributions; and challenges.

Disciplinary Infrastructure

Since the restoration of the CFS in 1983, the discipline of folkloristics in China has enjoyed a rising tide as its usefulness is increasingly recognized in the construction of a new national identity of China in the world, as well as a new cultural identity for the Chinese at home and abroad. Folkloristics in China is symbolized through the CFS—in gaining recognition among other disciplines and in unifying folklorists, as well as in obtaining governmental support for folklorists to engage in various cultural heritage projects. The CFS functions as an umbrella scholarly institution with nearly 3,000 members as of 2020, in addition to its annual meetings, and its online forum (http://www.chinesefolklore.org.cn) also plays an important role in attracting young scholars and public folklorists.

At present (2020), there are nearly fifty graduate degree programs in folklore/folk literature, seven of which are doctoral programs. On average, each folklore program has around ten to thirty graduate students. However, there is no undergraduate major in folklore. A growing number of Master's Programs in Cultural Industry (*wenhua chanye*) now exist in more than one hundred universities and are closely related to folklore programs. The first graduate programs in folkloristics (and Folk Literature) began in the 1980s, during the period of academic restoration, in Beijing Normal University which is regarded as the cradle of contemporary folkloristics in China.

Although "public folklore" is still a new concept in China for both academia and the government, there exists a national network of "public culture" posts: from the village level to the county, city, province (or autonomous regions), and the central government (i.e., Ministry of Culture) levels. This network has begun to function in the ICH movement in conjunction with folkloristic programs.

The leading journals in folkloristics are: *Folklore Studies (Minsu yanjiu)* published in Shandong University; *Folk Culture Forum (Minjian wenhua luntan)* by the Association of Folk Literature and Arts; *Cultural Heritage (Wenhua yichan)* by Sun Yat-sen University; and *National Arts (Minzu yishu)* by Guangxi Institute of Culture and Arts of the Nationalities. They are published in Chinese with the table of contents and abstracts in English.

Among the increasing folkloristic publications, two encyclopedic series are worth mentioning besides the above-mentioned *Three Grand Collections of Folk Literature* (China Folk Literature Collections Committee 1984–2009): *Folklore and Folk Literature Series* (ed. Lou [1970] 2004, a reprint of the folklore collections by the Folklore Society in the 1920s, amounting to 200 volumes), marking the foundation of folkloristics in China; and the *Grand Series of Chinese Folklore* (ed. Tao 2003–2004) in thirty-one volumes arranged by province, covering the studies and practices since the 1980s. There are also dictionaries and encyclopedias on regional or national folklore, based on previous literature or recent fieldwork.

Translations of international folkloristics have greatly contributed to the construction of folkloristics in China. Nearly all important theories and representative works in modern folkloristics have been introduced to China: from Vladimir Propp's work on morphology to contemporary European fairy tale studies, from *Kalevala* to Yanagita Kunio's works, from Edward Tylor's *Primitive Culture* (1871) to Franz Boas' *The Mind of Primitive Man* (1911), from European myth-ritual studies to American context and performance studies, from AT (ATU) Folktale Type Index to two indices on Chinese folktales (e.g., Eberhard 1937b; Ting 1978), and from linguistic and semiotic studies to phenomenological and hermeneutic studies.

Writing the history of the discipline is another essential component of folkloristics. Besides the above-mentioned six-volume *The History of Chinese Folklore* (Zhong and Xiao 2008), there are also three other books on the topic by Wang Wenbao (1987, 1995, 2003). They are supplementary to those major textbooks. Furthermore, the improvement in the textbooks demonstrates the development of the discipline (Zhang 1985). For example, two key textbooks edited by Zhong Jingwen are being updated with new ideas: in the *New Introduction to Folk Literature* (Wan 2011), "fairy tale" is no longer a genre as it was in the *Introduction to Folk Literature* (Zhong 1980); in the *New Introduction to Folkloristics* (Xing 2016), "folkloregraphy" and "image-narrative" (*tuxiang xushi*) are discussed without mentioning "ethnography" (*minzuzhi*) which was a key term in the *Introduction to Folkloristics* (Zhong [1998] 2009).

International exchanges among folklorists is another important aspect of the development of folkloristics in China. Beginning with interactions with Japanese folklorists in the 1980s, Chinese folklorists soon began to participate in seminars, summer schools, and conferences with European folklorists. Discrete and individual communications with American folklorists began in the 1980s, but institutional exchange between the CFS and the American Folklore Society did not begin until 2005 (Zhang and Song 2017). In the past decades, dozens of young folklorists have gone abroad as visiting scholars and/or as presenters at conferences. Still, there is a trend for young folklorists to get degrees abroad and return to work in China. The role of Chinese folklorists on the world folklore stage is becoming important, whether in voicing their opinions or participating, even leading, international organizations or events, as described below.

Reflecting upon the development of folkloristics in China, Bingzhong Gao points out that the present historical opportunity is based on these four factors: (a) the economic and ideological reform in the 1980s; (b) folklore entering the urban and mainstream life from the rural and marginal groups; (c) folklore becoming the "intangible cultural heritage" in the ideological reconstruction at the state level in China; and (d) the international influence regarding postmodern thoughts, particularly through the UNESCO system (Gao 2008:5).

In Gao's opinion, the central theory and method for folklore studies (mostly folk literature, or folktales) until the 1980s were based on the European "survival" theory, namely, examining the object or literature that survived in text. However, substantial changes began in the 1990s, when folklore studies extended to contemporary texts and material life. Meanwhile, the new generation of folklorists (who earned a PhD in Folklore or Folk Literature in the 1990s) have explored and adopted theories from other disciplines and self-reflected the history of folkloristics in China. The most meaningful progress is that Chinese folklorists have begun a new disciplinary orientation by focusing on "contemporary," "everyday life," and "common people" (Gao 2015a:7). These changes are highlighted in these specific research areas: traditional festivals; folk beliefs; and intangible cultural heritage items.

This paradigmatic shift becomes clear with the rising team of folklorists across China and increasing publications emphasizing "the disciplinarity of folkloristics" in recent years. At present, Chinese folklorists have earned their status by voicing their opinions in public cultural affairs in the ICH movement. For example, based on the suggestions by the CFS in 2005 (via a committee led by the CFS president Liu Kuili), the Chinese central government changed the public holiday system in 2007 by making some traditional festivals to be public holidays with days-off to accord with the traditions that the common people had celebrated for centuries (Xiao 2017).

Development and Contributions

Whether in the public or academic domain, "Chinese folklore" has experienced a transformation from the negative image of being "backward" or "superstitious" to being a "distinctive" or "traditional" part of diverse human cultures. The negative stereotype was developed mainly through the depiction by foreign missionaries or visitors prior to the mid-twentieth century. This depiction was internalized by the Chinese until the 1980s, as is evident in many movies made in China in the 1980s (e.g., the so-called "fifth-generation" directors). Furthermore, the stereotypes of the Chinese tradition and folklore were reinforced by ideological propaganda coming out of Hollywood movies (e.g., the image of Fu Manchu). As the world gets a better knowledge of China and Chinese culture, these images have recently begun to change. Folklore has certainly played a key role in this process.

However, "Chinese folkloristics" is little known throughout the world, as Alan Dundes observed when he visited China in 1990 and subsequently wrote in the preface to the Chinese translation of his work in 2004 (i.e., *The Interpretation of Folklore*; see also, Chen 2017; Hu 2017). Language is indeed a mutual barrier for both Chinese and non-Chinese folklorists; limited face-to-face communication between Chinese and foreign folklorists is also a sad reality. However, there may be other reasons as well including the venues for such communication and the cultural attitudes toward each other. As Francis L. K. Hsu (1973) pointed out about the effect of "white anthropology," there was the assumption among both white and non-white scholars that non-white anthropologists could at best only collect data, but could not analyze that data. As a result, in the volumes edited by European and American scholars on "world folklore/folkloristics" or related to "Chinese folklore/folkloristics," the descriptions lack either critical insight or relevant depth, and often are not written by Chinese experts on the topics. In fact, while major achievements in world folkloristics are constantly translated into Chinese (e.g., the performance-centered approach in Bauman and Babcock 1977), meaningful discussions and high theories explored in China are yet to be known to the rest of the world (Baron 2017). A collection of stories told by the folklorists from China and the United States about their experiences through personal interactions in the past decades, known as "metafolklore," is a meaningful illustration of the benefit of face-to-face exchange (Zhang and Song 2017).

Indeed, "Chinese folklorists have developed various refreshing and creative perspectives" (An and Yang 2015:280), and they are certainly worthy of being recognized as contributions to world folkloristics (Zhang and You 2018). Some of the achievements can be outlined as such:

- Delineating the goals of the discipline: Focusing on current practices by common people in everyday life through folkloregraphy; a departure from the previous "survival" model and "looking down at" (*xiangxiakan*) the folk.
- Distinguishing folkloregraphy from ethnography (Xing 2016): a unique development of the approach to "documenting folklore" in contrast to

"studying folklore" based on Zhong Jingwen's idea (Wang 2016; Gao 2007); a potential departure of the racial/ethnic-centered paradigm.

- Training folklorists through dozens of folklore programs in universities and other public culture departments: non-academically trained folklorists are being recognized as "public folklorists."
- Exerting influence on public education through folklore museums and on public policies through involvement in such social activities as the ICH movement.
- Establishing bachelor's, master's, and doctoral degrees in Cultural Industrial Management (*wenhua chanye guanli*, since 2004) as part of regular higher education, integrating folkloristics, public policies, enterprises, public culture, and cultural tourism.
- Expanding the scope of folkloristics to include and develop the following: video-documenting folklore in relation to visual anthropology; women-folklore (*nüxing minsu*) (Wang 2012; Xing 1995); eco-folklore (*shengtai minsu*) (Jiang 2003); performative folklore; folk culture (Wan 2010) and hometown folklore studies (An 2004).
- Strengthening theories with more systemic views on "mythologism" (Yang 2016), introduction and development of Propp's morphology of folktale (Li 1996; Liu 2010), tale-type (Qi 2007; Liu 2002; Ting 1978; Ting 1974), folk fairy tale (Liu 1985), and folk narrative (Liu 2017; Liu 2010; Lü and An 2006).
- Strengthening interdisciplinary studies by applying philosophical (Lü 2015), semiotic, religious studies, linguistic, and other disciplinary theories and methods; seeking "grand theories" and paradigm shifts (Wu 2015; Liu 2009).
- Localizing international folklore theories such as context and performance, myth studies, ritual studies, and (intangible) cultural heritage studies.
- Transforming folklore studies into a domain of public culture or culture heritage by bringing "everyday life" as the target as well as the means of folklore studies, so that common people become active subjects, rather than passive objects, of folklore traditions.

Engaging in international discourses. In this regard, Chinese folklorists have begun to move from the previous "being-translated" or "translating others" to a stage of "self-translating" through conferences, visits, and non-Chinese publications. These dynamic discourses suggest that the most meaningful change is that Chinese folklorists are beginning to break away from the "self-inferior" mentality internalized through colonialism and racism, and to gain their self-confidence and equal attitude in exchanges about *self* and with *others*.

These aspects reveal the idea of establishing Chinese folkloristics "with Chinese characteristics," which was first proposed by Zhong (1980a). While the academic programs are growing and folklorists begin to participate in national cultural projects and policy-making, a few fundamental questions are still not well clarified or answered: What unique contributions can folkloristics make to humanistic studies, and to the construction of national identity? What are the immediate and ultimate goals for the discipline?

The introduction of ICH to China in 2003 marked a historical turning point. But it was a process that began when China signed the *1972 Convention Concerning the Protection of the World Cultural and Natural Heritage* in 1985. This enabled the process of establishing cultural self-confidence and recovering the inherent self-healing mechanism. The essential expression of this effort is localization (*bentuhua*) through coexistence, a Chinese-characteristic syncretism, rather than only "Westernization" or exclusive "revolution." Certainly, the ICH concept is not an almighty elixir because it, too, is a product of a specific set of cultural values. Although the concept recognizes the potential conflicts (including cultural property during armed conflict) among diverse human cultural values at all levels, one of its core concerns is a "universal value" which is essentially the Western values.

Indeed, the birth of ICH has its specific background through the platform of UNESCO, where different or conflicting cultural values are recognized and negotiated. The roots of UNESCO's ICH programs can be traced back to the "Convention for the Protection of Cultural Property in the Event of Armed Conflict with Regulations for the Execution of the Convention 1954." The Convention also marked the reordering of the world cultural resources during a period of decolonization which is still in the process. Subsequently, UNESCO issued the 1972 Convention, which was based on the notion "universal value," judged from the Euro-centered value system. This system was practiced in the following forty years, while the world changed tremendously in many ways. Critiques of this universal value system from non-Western states and cultures finally resulted in the proclamation of the Universal Declaration on Cultural Diversity in 2001 (taking effect as the Convention in 2005). Its purpose was to rectify the previous universal value system (Labadi 2013, Arizpe and Amescua 2013). Meanwhile, the Convention of Safeguarding ICH was passed in 2003 (taking effect as the Convention in 2006). Thus far, these Conventions are the most important ones regarding human cultures, even though some countries have not joined them (for instance, the United States has not joined the 2001 and 2003 Conventions).

The positive implication of ICH, however, lies in its wakeup call to the Third-World, or developing countries, to gain self-awareness and self-confidence in the world context by recognizing, accepting, and protecting diverse human cultures and by claiming their own traditions with pride. This has been effectively demonstrated through the practice in China. It must be pointed out, nevertheless, that the ICH appeared in China at a historically meaningful moment, or a "heavenly timing" (*tianshi* 天时) as expressed in a Chinese saying. The economic boom provided the occasion for the external force of ICH to be implemented and to awaken cultural self-confidence. Of course, there are numerous problems in carrying out ICH policies, especially in the economic arena, but they do not alter the conclusion that the ICH movement is central in building China's current cultural self-confidence (Wang and Yu 2008; Yuan 2009; Peng 2012; Wang 2012; Kang 2013; Wang 2013a; 2013b; Song 2014; Cai 2014; Huang 2014; Yang 2014; Wang 2015; Chen 2015; Xiao and Chai 2015; Zhang and Zhou 2017).

Specifically, current folkloristic scholarship on oral traditions in China may be represented by the theoretical development in these three areas:

Tale Type

The studies of folktale types (*minjian gushi leixing* 民间故事类型) yielded the earliest fruit in the publication by Antti A. Aarne in 1910, which was later extended by Stith Thompson in 1927 and 1961, respectively, known as the Aarne-Thompson (AT system), which is still further expanded into the ATU system (Uther 2004). In the AT system, Thompson used four sources of Chinese tales to support seventy-two types in his revision of the masterful work (1961), and the four sources included two from Eberhard (1937, 1941), one from D. G. Graham (1954), and one from E. Chavannes (1910–134).

In classifying tale types of Chinese tales, there have been these efforts: N. B. Denny was the first European who studied Chinese folklore by applying the European theories at time, and was the first who studied Chinese folktale types with a similar approach to the Finnish school by setting eight categories and fifteen types (1876:143–145). The next efforts were in the 1930s, when Chinese folklorist Zhong Jingwen, among others, was representative of the efforts during that decade with his unique list of 45 categories/types and the translation of the 70 types from some types of *Indo-European Folktales* (1931). By 1937, German Sinologist Wolfram Eberhard went to China and gathered a number of publications and handwritten records of the tales popular at that time. As a result, he published in German the *Chinese Folktale Types* (1937a), in which he made 12 categories in 215 types, with an additional 31 types in the category of "humor." The Chinese translation of this book was published in 1999 and a revised version in 2017.

Nai-tung Ting played a pivotal role in Chinese studies of folk and fairy tales by introducing the AT Index system to Chinese folklorists in the early 1980s (Zhang and Song 2017). He introduced his own work, *A Type Index of Chinese Folktales* (1978), and immediately inspired Chinese folklorists in several universities as a new path to establish a field between folklore and folklore studies. As a result, Ting's work was translated and published in three editions (Ting 1983; 1986; 2008).

In the following decades, tale type studies in China have cultivated a field that is still growing healthily. For example, in addition to translating works on the topic (e.g., Brunvand's work on urban legend type index, 2016), Chinese scholars have published a wide range of works: specifically on ancient Chinese tale types (Qi 2007, Gu 2014), on the grand collections of folktales in the late twentieth century across China (Jin 2000), on regional tales such as in Shanxi Province (Zhang and Fan 2019), in Taiwan (Hu 2008), and in Ningbo in Zhejiang Province (Cheng 2012). Almost every study set a new system of categorization. For example, recognizing the limit of the AT system and in comparison, Qi has identified more than 500 types (Qi 2007). Without comparing to the AT system, Yuan (2006) has made 12 categories with 549 types (each type with subtypes) to classify Chinese tales. Also, there are also joint projects among Chinese, Japanese and Korean folklorists to identify the common types.

Meanwhile, comparative studies of different systems have demonstrated some meaningful results (Chen 2010). For example, Chen compared the five systems respectively by Zhong (1931), Eberhard (1937), Thompson (1961), Ting (1978), and Jin (2000), and showed that many unique tale types that are not included in the AT system are identified by folklorists of Chinese tales as such:

- "Wolf grandma" as 333C by Ting and Jin, Type 20 by Zhong, and Type 11 by Eberhard
- "Snail girl/wife" as 400C by Ting and Jin; Type 19 by Zhong; Type 35 by Eberhard
- "Wife from other animals" as 400D by Ting and Jin; Type 37 by Eberhard
- "Spouse of man and ghost" as 400E by Gu (2002:238)
- "Snake boy/husband and two sisters" as 433D by Ting
- "Snake boy/husband tragic death" as 433E by Liu (2002:408)
- "Snake boy/husband as ancestor" as 433F by Liu (2002:410)

While some exemplary studies of Chinese tale type (Liu 2002, 2016, 2017) have shown a theoretical framework, the recent trend of paying attention to ICH has led to fewer and fewer publications on tale-type studies. Liu Shouhua, a leading scholar of tale studies in China, has proposed that, in order to establish the field of Chinese tale studies, it is necessary "to treat myths, legends, and folktales as one entity" and "to establish a tale index system different from the AT system" (Liu 2009:76). Clearly, his vision is being testified and implemented, as seen in the way of treating "tales" in this collection.

Motif

In terms of motif, Chinese folklorists' interest began (or rekindled) in the early 1980s with the translation of Ben-Amos's article, "The Concept of Motif in Folklore" (1980; 2018). This concept influenced the studies of folktales, in particular, myths. For example, Chen Jianxian has collected 500 variants of the flood myths from ancient Chinese texts and mapped out their distributions (1996), also compared them with myths from other cultures (2000), and finally proposed to define terms such as "variable motif" and "constant motifs" (2016). Yang and Zhang have compiled the massive *A Motif Index of Chinese Myths* (2013) in reference to Thompson's (1955–1958) motif-index system.

Other motif studies range from concrete examination of specific motifs in specific tales to theoretical debate of the meaning, Chinese equivalent, philosophical function (Lu 2009), and redefinition of "motif" to reflect upon the studies of Chinese oral tradition (Qi and Wan 2019). A preliminary search through the Chinese academic databases shows that there are about 100 research articles on the topic of "motif" in the past 30 years or so.

Chinese folklorists have also well studied Alan Dundes's terms of "motifeme" and "allomotif" (1962:101; 1997: 196; 2007:321), which Dundes wanted to apply "to all folklore genres" (Bronner 2007:317), with the intention to expand the study of motif to include a contextualist perspective (Ben-Amos 1995:75). Similarly, Ben-Amos's new theoretical proposition that "in folklore there are no motifs but symbols" (1995:81) has also stimulated many discussions among Chinese folklorists, along with his ideas like "folklore" and "tradition," which are translated into Chinese (Ben-Amos 2018; Zhang 2019b).

Genre

The interest in genre is characteristic of the folklore scholarship in China. On the one hand, it has been extensively discussed; on the other hand, there is not even a common term to translate or express the idea of "genre." For example, while *leixing* (类型) seems to be better accepted, other terms like *menlei* (门类), *zhonglei* (种类), *xingshi* (型式), *ticai* (体裁), *wenti* (文体), and *wenlei* (文类) have been used in different publications. Indeed, folklore studies as a discipline requires a commonly accepted term to convey the meaning of any concept like genre. However, the confusion is not just a problem in Chinese; it is a problem in folkloristics in general. Besides the issues within

European categorization and its application to other cultures (Ben-Amos 1969), Chinese situation can be seen from these three areas:

There are genres that are used in other cultures but not considered as a genre in Chinese. For example, "tall tale" is not a categorical term or concept in Chinese literature, since it is not common to tell traditional stories as "personal experience" in Chinese culture. Most Chinese approaches would categorize it as joke/humor/anecdote (e.g., Lin 1930, 1938; Eberhard 1937b; Qi 2007).

There are terms of "genre" or "category" used in ancient Chinese literature, but they were abandoned in order to adopt the Western system. For example, "myth" is used today in Western concept by recategorizing traditional "spirit/ghost/strange tales." But, *zhiguai* (志怪 for all kinds of "strange" records/narratives) was commonly used from the seventh to the nineteenth century, while the tale *Yexian* was in the category of *nuogao* (诺皋 for the mysterious phenomenon in Daoist sense) in the ninth century.

There are new "genres" being developed since the early twentieth century when such concepts as "folklore" and "fairy tale" were introduced to China. For example, *tonghua* (children's story) was invented to correlate with the Western "fairy tale."

These situations are exactly at the core of the issue of "ethnic genre" that Dan Ben-Amos discussed in his seminal essay (1969). His concept of ethnic genre can be seen as a lead to the paradigmatic shift in folklore studies in the early 1970s (Zhang 2020a). In studying Chinese folklore, it is necessary to question: To what extent could and should the concepts defined on the basis of European culture and history be applied to Chinese studies? Or, to what extent could and should Chinese construct their own conceptual tools in analyzing Chinese folklore? Efforts to develop "local concepts" (*bentu gainian* 本土概念) in folklore, ethnomusicology, and some other disciplines.

When Dan Ben-Amos tried to apply his Eurocentric training in categorizing folklore genres to his fieldwork in Nigeria in the late 1960s, he realized that it did not work (Ben-Amos 2014). Out of his African experience, he came up with his definition of folklore as "artistic communication in small groups," proposing a context-centered approach to folklore by departing the previous text-centered approach (Ben-Amos 1971, 2014). While this definition has been proved to be a paradigm shift that "dominat[ed] thinking in folklore" in the following decades through the label of "performance theory" (Shuman and Briggs 1993:110), his definition of "ethnic genre" seems to have been buried under the enormous publications on "ethnic folklore" or "ethnic identity" and, thus, his contribution to the paradigm shift has been under-evaluated (Zhang 2020a).

The significance of the concept of "ethnic genre" lies in the fact that it moved away from the text-centered approach to context-centered approach; it is not only a shift in disciplinary method, but, more importantly, in ideology. Therefore, this concept emphasizes the meaning of "native" or "local" as the essence, which also means that one should not simply impose the Eurocentric model of genre classification to other cultures and societies. Of course, limited by historical periods and cultural environment, the term "ethnic" has carried many different meanings, but its idea of respecting the local practice in categorizing folklore forms is essential (Zhang 2020a).

In further discussing "ethnic genre," Ben-Amos writes, "it is possible to consider an ethnic genre as a verbal art form consisting of a cluster of thematic and behavioral attributes and to formulate the relationships between the various elements of the folkloric system in the form of a paradigm" (1969:231). In fact, he has explicitly and systematically argued that there are no "ideal types" in folklore, and that it is necessary to differentiate the naming categories by the folklorists and by the native speakers, rather than using "ideal types" to contrast "natural genres" (1992:20).

Thirty years after developing the concept of "ethnic genre," Ben-Amos considered that "folklorists have taken two distinct directions" in studying the

> indefiniteness of folklore genres and the concept of genre in folklore. . . . The first . . . to construct the concept of genre as a category of analytical classification; the second . . . to conceive of genre as a category of cultural discourse. (1997:410)

These views are directly about folklore genres, but they are fundamentally in consistency with his ideological approach, that is, the Eurocentric ideal types should not be imposed to other cultures where there are different native ways of knowing, categorizing, and expressing, and those should be recognized and respected in studying folklore as part of the society and culture.

While the increasing attention to these key concepts among Chinese folklorists have also led to a confusing situation, in which there are no "standard" terms for most terms or concepts, the next step is clear: the more debate and discourse there are, the greater progress the discipline will make.

CHINESE FOLKLORE AND
FOLKLORISTICS IN PERSPECTIVE

The past forty years of restoration and reconstruction of folkloristics in China can be seen as a move "toward disciplinary maturity" with increasing disciplinary communication between Chinese and international folklorists (Li 2015). However, "many questions have also surfaced in terms of its theoretical discussions, disciplinary practices, and disciplinary orientation" (An and

Yang 2015:274). In discussing the challenges based on the current development, An and Yang take ideological and methodological aspects into consideration: within folkloristic studies, the theoretical orientation began to shift in
the 1980s from previous "class struggle" and "revolution" views in collecting
and studying folk literature to the "perspective on folklore as the everyday
lived culture of the common people of a nationality" (2015:278). This marks
a useful advance for the discipline, that is, people studying people, as seen in
the fact that terms such as "folk," "folk culture," and "folklore" have entered
the public discourse and everyday practice. However, some of the challenges
are also obvious.

Lack of Distinctive Disciplinary Concepts, Terms, Methods, and Theories:
This lack of theorization reveals a lack of understanding of the histories of
those ideas that have European origins. It is encouraging to see that some
efforts are being made to define those concepts with terms/characters that
have historical connections in Chinese culture.

Separation of Academic and Public Folklore Sectors: There is a lack of
connection in both theories and practices, although there is a nation-wide
network of public culture services. Recent movement in safeguarding ICH
enabled some collaborative work on certain aspects, but the curricular in
most folklore programs do not have a relevant component of public or applied
folklore.

Lack of Disciplinary Orientation: From the text-centered to context-centered approaches, Chinese folklorists are now debating: how to do fieldwork
(i.e., between "looking down at" the folk and "looking backward at" the text,
or between "going to the people" and "going among the people"), how to
study "everyday life" (i.e., to take it as the means or the end for the discipline,
to as a platform for interpretation), and how to reconceptualize "folk/common
people" (or "citizen") and "folklore in practice."

Drawing Disciplinary Boundaries: Although the number and size of folklore programs across China are growing, some important areas are yet to
be included in curriculum and research, or in interdisciplinary studies. For
example, musical aspects in festivals and rituals, folklore and mental health
or therapy, folklore and law, and studies on marginalized groups such as the
peasant-workers in the cities.

Broadening the Horizon and Vision: Many younger folklorists have demonstrated their interest in developing international communication and multidisciplinary approaches, but there is a lack of institutionalized mechanism for
sustaining such communication. For example, the recent exchanges between
Chinese and American folklorists have exerted a very positive impact, but
those were largely enabled by temporary grants and individuals efforts
(Zhang and Song 2017).

Clearly, folkloristics in China remains at the periphery of the humanities and social sciences. Such questions are to be reflected upon: its disciplinary orientation (e.g., folk literature versus material folklore studies); importance of folklore to national cultural identity; the separation of folk culture and elite culture; and the tendency to degrade folklore studies. Although the flourishing of folkloristics in China in the past two decades has much to do with the concept of "ICH," which has provided Chinese folklorists a role in reconstructing national identity, this political aid should not be seen as the driving force for the sustainability of the disciplinary studies.

Overall, the practices and impacts of the ICH in China are probably unique in the world; China has appropriated the ICH concepts and policies for its own political, social, and cultural agenda. It happens that this act has been in accordance with the *cultural self-healing mechanism* in Chinese culture and history: traditionalizing, heritagizing, and localizing different cultural expressions. These practices, however, are key to understanding folklore and folkloristics in contemporary China.

Chapter 2

The Inherent Cultural
Self-Healing Mechanism

The previous chapter has depicted a historical and social background for answering the key question in studying China: What has enabled Chinese culture to persist for the past millennia? Scholars have given various answers pointing to factors of the Chinese writing system, political administrative system, everyday ritual practice, and interaction between the official or Great Tradition represented by the elite and the unofficial or Little Tradition represented by the common people. Citing these factors might explain cultural continuity, but not the inherent logic for maintenance of an overarching culture, especially after potentially disruptive social upheavals. Furthermore, the explanations are culture-specific and do not account for the reproduction of cultures outside of China.

This chapter proposes a theoretical framework, which I call *the cultural self-healing mechanism*, in order to provide a logic for the maintenance of certain traditions, and discontinuation of other traditions. This framework helps understand not only the continuity of a specific tradition within a culture but also the rise and fall of human cultures in general. In the following sections, I will first describe the logic of this *cultural self-healing mechanism*, then expound on related concepts, and finally examine contemporary Chinese traditions in practice through the lens of this framework. The remaining chapters of this book will further illustrate this framework with examples of representative forms of oral traditions.

THE OPERATION OF THE CULTURAL
SELF-HEALING MECHANISM

The formation and reproduction of culture is a combination of the internal factors (the existence and continuity of human life) and external factors (the environment for the existence of a social group). Within this premise, the internal factors can be seen to be fundamental to a culture in both spiritual/ mental and material senses; the external factors are catalytic and include both the natural environment and the interactive relations among different groups. Consequently, the reason why culture once existed and then discontinued must be that its internal and/or external conditions were no longer effectively in existence.

Therefore, it is essential to first identify the driving internal factors and functions of the external factors. Subsequently, one can assess the ways that these factors operate through a mechanism inherent to the culture, or to a specific tradition as a part of the whole. To do so, the first task is to determine the logic through this interpretive framework.

The system of *fundamental beliefs and values* that develops in a society drives reproduction of the culture. It embodies cosmological and supernatural beliefs about the universe and reflects the effects of a natural environment upon a group's existence. At the microsocial level, the system comprises normative ethical values that guide interpersonal communication within groups. These fundamental beliefs and values are repeatedly expressed by its members in everyday life. In turn, the group's practices reinforce those beliefs and values through certain expressions as their collective *identity markers* that distinguish one cultural group from another. Some of those expressions function as the *core identity markers* and some as *arbitrary identity markers*. The core identity markers are rooted in fundamental beliefs and values, and thus demonstrate the *vitality* in the transmission of a tradition or a culture. The arbitrary identity markers reveal the *validity* of the strategic practice in the transmission of a tradition or a culture during adaptive interactions with other external factors.

The interrelations of vitality and validity are not rigid or separated by a clearly defined divide, but are often blurred together depending upon the change in internal and external factors. It is in coping with certain specific internal and external factors that some traditions or cultures discontinue or disappear, while some others continue. It is also in this process of adaptation that, meaningfully, new traditions or cultures, or a *third culture*, emerge and thus begin a new stage of the cycle of cultural development. As a result, a tradition or a culture with a long history reveals its *cultural self-healing mechanism* which enables it to survive internal and external upheavals and continue in a new environment.

Related to this framework is the biological principle that human life continues with the "selfish gene" through "memetics" (Dawkins 2006), which passes its vitality through "memes" in a condition of hybridity in order to adapt to and survive new environment. Folklorists have applied this theory to interpret the continuity of folk and fairy tales (Zipes 2008; 2011), and further argued the positive and negative aspects in applying it in cultural studies (Oring 2014a; 2014b). By the same principle, a folk group relies on both its genetic and cultural hybridity for its existence as a human cultural group; no folk or cultural group is continued on the basis of pure "race"/blood or tradition. Furthermore, cognitive factors play a critical role in the generation and perception of cultural practices that are associated with Chinese culture but might not be apparent to non-Chinese observers, for example, the writing system, tonal language, and dialects. The two aspects underlie debates in cultural analysis of whether the *folk* or the *lore* is to be given priority, how *text* and *context* are related, and how *folklore* and *identity* are intertwined.

With these questions as the base for the framework in discussion, I argue that *folkloric identity* (i.e., identity based on shared folklore practices, rather than imposed "racial/ethnic identity" based on the racist notion of pure "race") should be treated as the core of folklore studies (Zhang 2020b), while folklore studies are at "the center of humanities" (Wilson 1988:158). In a broad sense, this framework is also in accordance with the idea of "folklore in practice," which emphasizes a "holistic understanding of culture" (Bronner 2019:3, 76).

FUNDAMENTAL BELIEFS AND VALUES IN CHINESE CULTURE

"China" is a "stream" that always has been changing, and, as expressed in another metaphor, is a "living tree" embodying a "Cultural China," which, philosopher Wei-ming Tu argues, can be analyzed in relation to an ongoing "interaction of three symbolic universes," which are fluid like "streams": geographical China (mainland China, Taiwan, Hong Kong, and Singapore, "populated predominantly by cultural and ethnic China"); peripheral China ("Chinese communities throughout the world" that constitute a minority population in the countries in which they live); and intellectual China (individuals "who try to understand China intellectually" and contribute to discourse about "Cultural China") (Tu 1994:13–14). The leading philosophers of the twentieth-century China consider that the concept of "sustaining/continuing/perpetual" (*jiu* 久) is the sustaining force (as a cosmic belief or ethical life-view) for the long existence of "Chinese culture," which is also expressed through the distinctive Chinese notion of "mind-heart nature" (*xinxing* 心性) as "the reasons why Chinese history and culture have continued so long" (中国历史文化所以长久之理由) (Chang, Tang, Mou, and Hsu 1958). This concept of *jiu* reveals the essence of Chinese culture and is attested by the continuing vibrant traditions that has shaped Chinese cultural identity (Zhang 2017a).

Furthermore, these abstract concepts are expressed through concrete everyday practices. For example, anthropologist Yih-yuan Li, in developing Tu's concept of "Cultural China," examines Chinese cultural identity through daily practices of family concept, diet structure, and fortunetelling that includes various activities in search of auspiciousness and avoidance of inauspiciousness (Li 1995). In this sense, the following six aspects can be summarized as the *fundamental beliefs and values* in Chinese culture, with examples of their everyday expressions:

The Immortality of the Soul (*linghui bumie* 灵魂不灭)

This view of life and death is primarily expressed through the practice of ancestral worship as seen in various rituals and festivals. For example, every wedding, funeral, and the Spring Festival family reunion banquet includes offerings to the ancestors as part of the event, in addition to other expressions of communication with the soul (or spirit, ghost) in everyday life.

The Unity of Man and Nature (*tianren heyi* 天人合一)

This belief shows the naturalistic or cosmic view about the role of humans as part of the universe, and it is further transformed into ethical norms of Chinese culture dominated by the Confucian ethics. The practices in building houses and tombs, as well as in cultivating land and raising domestic animals, show not only the views about the relationship between the living and the dead, but also between the human and nature, as parts of a whole within the universe. The current discourses on environmental and cultural sustainability have inevitably found nurturing ideas from the practices of this belief. Philosophically, this belief emphasizes that humans are integrated with nature in contrast to the dualistic thinking of Western religion and philosophy.

The Confucian "Great Unity" (*dayitong* 大一统)

This ethical concept is implemented into social governance in a polytheist society to maintain social order through inclusive, peaceful and harmonious relations. In everyday speech, *chabuduo* (差不多 almost; not much different) is frequently used, showing Confucian values about integrating different ideas and practices. In other words, instead of insisting on the binary thinking of something being "good or bad" or "black or white," this concept encourages finding a middle ground or the means for coexistence to maintain greater social order and harmony. For example, many religions have been practiced throughout Chinese history, but there has never been one in dominance. Instead, Confucian and Daoist ideas of seeking the "middle/the mean" (*zhong* 中) and "harmony" (*he* 和) have played a central role in living a meaningful life. This aspect also explains why Chinese culture has continued despite the fact that China was at times being split into kingdoms and states or being ruled by non-Han Chinese.

The Emphasis of Harmony with Differences (*he'er butong* 和而不同)

This concept is based on the ideas of yin-yang and the interdependence of the five elements as the naturalistic philosophy, and it further extends to personal and social harmony. This philosophical belief was that the universe was made of Five Elements—metal, wood, water, fire, and earth, while each element had its internal component of yin and yang, and that the changes of the universe was caused by the interaction of yin and yang within each element, and by the supplementary and suppressive relations among the Five Elements. These ideas, according to philosopher Wing-tsit Chan, "go far back to antiquity and to quite independent origins," and "may be regarded as early Chinese attempts in the direction of working out a metaphysics and a cosmology." Chan adds that "no aspect of Chinese civilization—whether metaphysics, medicine, government, or art—has escaped its imprint" (Chan 1963:244, 245). The concept of harmony with differences, according to Joseph Needham, a sinologist of Chinese science and history, has a "central importance for the history of scientific thought in China," and is among "the most ultimate principles of which the ancient Chinese could conceive" (Needham 1956:216, 232). For example, the role of the *yin-yang* master or *fengshui* master (e.g., for ritual timing and location), as a medium of tradition, is indispensable in everyday life. Similarly, the role of matchmaking for marriage also expresses this concept.

The Importance of Following Local Customs (*ruxiang suisu* 入乡随俗)

This ethical concept has informed folklore through the practice of respecting and following local customs, as part of the mechanism of localization. This concept enables people to be adaptive to different local lifestyle and rituals, without imposing one's own idea or practice. This explains why various cultural forms (e.g., dialects/topolects, cousins, local beliefs, local medicine, and local rituals) are distinctive across China, and why, for example, Chinatowns with their common "Chineseness" have taken root in every part of the world, but each place has its own local cultural distinctiveness. In fact, the effort to standardize spoken Chinese only began in the early twentieth century.

The Avoidance of Inauspiciousness (*quji bixiong* 趨吉避凶)

The concept of avoiding inauspiciousness is practiced through *zhanbu* or *suanming* (占卜; 算命 fortunetelling or divination). While in practice it is closely related to the concept of *heerbutong*, it shows a positive effort in seeking changes in life to make sense of everyday actions, rather than holding a pessimistic attitude toward fate (Li 1995). In everyday practice, when one is facing life crisis or choices, obtaining the services of a fortuneteller provides a spiritual or psychological solution. However, when one feels that solution is not ideal, that person usually goes to a different fortuneteller to seek a new fortune. Such a process of seeking fortunetelling itself shows that one wants to make changes to make life more meaningful. It is also seen in the emphasis on education and family in Chinese culture. For example, the protagonists in folk and fairy tales often appear to be in the process of taking Civil Examinations as rites of passage in life, taking adventures to seek their destinies, using matchmakers for marriage, and having children as a marker of happy family life. In contrast, protagonists in European tales would often be on a pilgrimage, searching for treasure or seeking revenge.

THE VITALITY AND VALIDITY IN THE TRANSMISSION OF TRADITION

Traditions that are deeply rooted in beliefs and values of a culture have *vitality*. When a tradition shows its vitality, it tends to be stable in its transmission. In contrast, the *validity* of a tradition shows in its practical usefulness (often seen in popular culture practices). The practical validity vacillates in its adaptation of a tradition, as a strategic help for *vitality*. As a result, the vitality often lies in the *core identity marker* and the validity reveals in the *arbitrary identity markers*.

The question of continuity and discontinuity of traditions is essential to many disciplines. In folkloristics, there has been a general understanding that what determines a tradition to be continued (or, in that sense, to be discontinued) lies in the hands of the practitioners (Brunvand [1968] 1978:1; Toelken 1979:32; Glassie 1989:31; Cashman, Mould, Shukla 2011:2, 5). However, a further question should also be asked: in understanding the role of the practitioners,

> Is it the self-conscious choice of the practitioners, or is it simply situational or pragmatic? Do the practitioners choose on the basis of the temporary validity or vitality of the tradition to their group identity? Or, are they even aware of these differences? (Zhang 2015b:467)

The conceptual relations of traditions may help answer such questions by revealing a certain practice's role as an identity marker in relation to its vitality or validity.

Here is one example of how those concepts are revealed in everyday practice, in which the form of a tradition (validity) may change while the meaning (vitality) remains to connect the practitioners to their fundamental beliefs and values. In 2005, I attended a funeral in a remote village in northeast China. While the local villagers were struggling between obeying the government's law of cremation (i.e., cremation must be carried out in most part of China with exceptions only for certain regions or certain ethnic minorities) and following the traditional practice of earth burial, they gradually developed (or were influenced by others) their localized new tradition. What they did was to obey the law by cremating the corpse, but they also used the traditional dress and coffin and earth burial for the ashes. Specifically, when the body was cremated, some bigger pieces of bones were left on purpose (by controlling the time and temperature). Then, following the traditional rites of encoffining, they identified some pieces of bones to place them in the dress inside the coffin so that the "whole body" was imaginatively encased and buried. In this new practice (but now common in many rural parts of China), the belief in the immortality of the soul is continued, and the Confucian ethics of filiality of not damaging the body is observed, as expressed in the notion of *rutu weian* (entering the earth as peace 入土为安). In other words, the vitality of the fundamental beliefs and values are continued, although certain forms of the rites are changed. Meanwhile, the arbitrary markers or validity aspects are utilized to adapt to the new social and natural environments, such as obeying the law of cremation (Zhang 2009).

CORE AND ARBITRARY IDENTITY MARKERS

It is crucial to differentiate the roles of *core identity markers* and the *arbitrary identity markers*, and their interactive relations since they may be changeable, to explain the role of each expression in the continuity of the tradition. The core identity markers embody the vitality of the tradition, and are rooted in the fundamental beliefs and values, and thus show their durability and sustainability. The arbitrary identity markers reveal their validity in adapting to a new environment, and thus often change strategically. Both kinds of identity markers are necessary in reconstructing and maintaining identities at all levels, and in developing new cultures.

The importance of differentiating them is particularly apparent in safeguarding a folk tradition. For example, in the past twenty years in China, some traditions have been preserved from disappearing with an awareness of their cultural values; some have been rediscovered, restored, or revived from forgotten traditions to living traditions; some are simply disappearing regardless of the efforts or money invested in preserving them; still some have become "new" traditions as the result of cross-cultural hybridity as a *third culture*. Clearly, efforts to safeguard those arbitrary markers will not prevent them from disappearing. The ICH movement in China has shown that some traditions are disappearing (or disappeared) regardless of the efforts to safeguard them. But, the disappeared tradition may be transformed into certain symbolic expressions that can be either a core or an arbitrary identity marker of a new culture.

HYBRIDITY IN CULTURAL CONTINUATION AND THE MAKING OF THE THIRD CULTURE

The process of cultural hybridity is essential to the continuity of a culture. As emphasized in the concept of *folkloric identity*, no folk or cultural groups are pure in "race" and in cultural origin (Zhang 2015b; 2017a). Therefore, accepting the reality of cultural hybridity is the premise in understanding the continuity of traditions. Vitality is gained and maintained by absorbing new cultural elements through strategic localization, or traditionalization. While existing cultures may continue by means of revitalizing their own cultural self-healing mechanism, the result of mixing different cultures is the process of the making of a new culture. This new culture is habitually called with a term combining the known origins, for example, Chinese Americans as a cultural group, like any other diasporic groups, create a distinctive new culture that has integrated different religious, linguistic, biological elements from all over the world, rather than a simple combination of "Chinese" and "American" cultures (Zhang 2015a; 2015b). Thus, we may call it the *third culture*, because we lack proper names for such cultural reproduction.

The development of Chinese culture exemplifies ways that vitality lies in its hybridity by absorbing beliefs and traditions (mixing, for example, the Daoist, Confucian, Buddhist doctrines and ethics for everyday behavior). For example, the current fifty-six nationalities (*minzu*; or "ethnic groups") in China were identified only in the second half of the twentieth century. However, dozens of "cultural groups" once existed and then disappeared in the history of China, including cultural groups from central Asian and Middle East (e.g., groups of Jews came to China throughout the history and were integrated into Chinese culture, even though the existing written records are from the seventh to eighth century). Obviously, they were mixed into the new "Chinese" group which is changing all the time like a stream.

THE CULTURAL SELF-HEALING
MECHANISM IN CHINESE PRACTICES

Upholding the *cultural self-healing mechanism*, a culture, even when being in crises or predicaments through social conflicts, can reclaim its roots through self-awareness of its own fundamental beliefs and values. Then it can regain its self-confidence, and finally recover and revitalize its roots. This self-healing process also means that in surviving a crisis, a culture can effectively absorb new external traditional elements, and thus strengthen its vitality.

In China, from the mid-nineteenth century to the late twentieth century, the same central question had been constantly asked: Could China survive the social changes and become one nation that could be equal to the rest of the world without losing its traditions or identity? It was a pressing question since China was at the edge of becoming fully colonized and divided by being occupied by European powers and Japan during that period. For example, all the traditional festivals were forbidden by the Chinese government in order to promote the Gregorian calendar as part of modernization/westernization in China in the early twentieth century, and those traditional festivals were not fully restored until the early twenty-first century (Xiao 2017).

In this sense, UNESCO's ICH Convention (2003) introduced the concept to China, which thereafter has brought an opportunity for Chinese to reflect upon their own traditions and histories (Zhang and Zhou 2017). As discussed in chapter 1, China enthusiastically adopted this concept and launched a nation-wide movement, although a few developed countries, including the United States and United Kingdom, have not consigned the convention. The result has encouraged Chinese people to regain cultural self-awareness and self-confidence so that they are able to distinguish and hold onto their roots and find paths to grow amid cultural conflicts and interactions with other cultures (Zhang and Zhou 2017). Whether this goal can be achieved is a new test of this cultural self-healing mechanism. Historically, Chinese culture has periods when its mechanism worked and further enriched itself (e.g., during the Mongolian and Manchu dynasties, and there were times that this mechanism was outweighed by other forces, for example, during *xixue* (西学, the idea of Westernization) in the early twentieth century, and during the Cultural Revolution (1966–1976) when all "traditions" were labeled as *fengjian* (封建 superstitious). Today, the operation of this mechanism can be seen at three levels in contemporary China: state, elite, and folk.

At the state level, the national ICH Law was issued in China in 2011. Since 2004, China has actively implemented the idea in economic and cultural policies. As of 2020, forty traditions from China have been inscribed on the lists of ICH by UNESCO. Since 2006, China has celebrated National Cultural Heritage Day (second Saturday in June, first as ICH Day). For the past years, an active network of surveying, listing, and safeguarding has been in action at four administrative levels (national, provincial, city, and *xian*-county). Currently, "(intangible) cultural heritage" is being integrated into the K–16 school education systems with the slogan of "ICH into campus" (*feiyi jin xiaoyuan* 非遗进校园), and the idea of "ICH Studies" (*feiyixue* 非遗学) is promoted as a disciplinary field (e.g., a number of universities offer BA degree in ICH; a national conference on the issue or probability was held in December 2020 in Beijing Normal University).

The past four decades have proved one fact, that is, the socioeconomic development in China has helped Chinese people regain self-awareness and self-confidence through their new understanding of their traditions and returning to their roots. The dilemmas that China had had in struggles between "traditional culture" and "Western modernity," between "socialist planned economy" and "capitalist market economy," and between "authoritarianism" and "Democratic Centralism," have eventually resulted in the current Chinese practices that emphasize "Chinese characteristic" (*Zhongguo tese*) in integrating the tradition into the modern, and the capitalist into the socialist market. Similar examples are also seen in political reform, religious practice, and other areas. Clearly, without this model based on the self-healing mechanism, China's economy would not be at its status as the second largest in the world.

The ideological struggle about Chinese cultural identity is evident in the "searching for the roots" (*xungen* 寻根) movement in 1980s and the ongoing ICH movement in relation to "national identity" (*guojia rentong* 国家认同). In reality, such a struggle is expressed through everyday folklore practices: defending tea as tradition in fighting against coffee; eating in neighborhood restaurants to fight against the Western fast-food chains; wearing traditional robes to restore Han Chinese traditions. However, as seen today in numerous streets, both traditional foods and Western cuisines are popular, both tea and coffee businesses are growing, and all styles of dress are visible in everyday life. Clearly, Chinese people have never been more confident in their own cultural roots over the past two centuries than they are today; they have regained the sense of seeking "equal" status and discourse with the others in international affairs in this globalizing age.

One particular example of what the ICH movement has brought to Chinese traditions is on the change of policies about folk belief (Zhou 2006, 2017; Xu 2010; Hou and Fan 2001). For example, in the current ten categories of ICH on China's official lists (i.e., folk literature, folk music, folk dance, traditional dramas, traditional storytelling and performance [*quyi*], acrobatic and games, folk arts, traditional hand craftsmanship, traditional medicine, and folklore), there is no category of "belief" or "religion." Yet, the self-healing mechanism has enabled the continuity of the fundamental beliefs and values through the inclusion of this category as ICH, treating it with the Chinese characteristic of flexibility by defining and redefining "folk beliefs" as "heritage," rather than "superstition."

An example of strategically adapting to a new environment through the mechanism is the government's handling of the folk temple fair traditions. In a village in Hebei Province, there is the local "temple fair" tradition. The villagers believe that they are the descendants of the dragon, and thus hold sacrificial rites on the second day of the second lunar month. However, this tradition was banned as a superstition during the Cultural Revolution (1966–1976). In the 1980s, it was revived as a local tradition. During the ICH movement, it was considered to be a form of "heritage." The local government rebuilt the temple and expanded it into a cultural museum as well. As a result, one building now has two names: a traditional "temple" and a modern "museum" (Gao 2006). It was through this strategy that this tradition was approved as an ICH item at the provincial level in the category of "folklore" in 2007, and application is being made to recognize it at the state level.

Such practices reveal the operation of the cultural self-healing mechanism. This is seen as a "pragmatic" strategy, or "playing the edge ball" with the government (Li 2014), but it is not an unusual practice throughout Chinese history. In fact, it is such "double-name" or "multiple-name" practices that have exemplified the mechanism of "including" or "co-existing with different cultures."

Throughout the debates in the twentieth century, Chinese elites began to "return" to Chinese fundamental beliefs and values (Fei 1997, 2003), although the idea and effort for total Westernization in China never faded. The mainstream of the elite has come to realize that total Westernization is not the path for China because it is against China's inherent cultural logic, and that only localization and harmonization can be constructive for the future of Chinese culture. This turn marked a new beginning of the cultural self-healing mechanism.

In the process, the elites have continued the practice of getting involved in the making of cultural policies at all levels, particularly in designating or recognizing ICH items, as seen in the revival of traditional festivals in the new "holiday system" since 2007 (Xiao 2017). Chinese folklorists have become a dynamic force pushing the ICH movement forward, while also expanding the scope of folkloristics by meeting the challenges and taking advantage of the opportunities at the same time (Gao 2015b). Their questions remain to be:

Can traditional Chinese beliefs and values coexist with the Western values? Can modern lifestyle and the traditional coexist?

The everyday practices of the common people reflect their degree of awareness and confidence in their cultural traditions during a particular historical period. In other words, when the government provides social and cultural spaces and the elites nurture folk practices, traditions tend to better express their self-confidence and vitality. For example, the Chinese economic reforms that started in the 1980s were highlighted by the slogan of "culture sets the stage, economy sings the drama," which enabled the revival of traditions that had been long suppressed. As this "drama" was near its finale, the ICH movement came on stage, which further legitimated the traditions as valuable heritage. These two "acts" brought the common people in China from local stages to the global stage in demonstrating the vitality of their own local "traditions." Indeed, perhaps the phrase and concept of ICH has never experienced a more popular public "consumption" in other countries. ICH in China is not only a cultural and political term but also a fashion in cultural consumption and cultural tourism.

Many expressions of cultural self-confidence at the folk level have emerged in all aspects of everyday life in the past century. For example, names referring to Westerners have shown such a transformation: from "foreign devils" (*waiguo guizi*) or anything fearful at initial encounters to "distinguished guests" (*guibin*) or "foreign guests" (*waiguo pengyou*) or anything admirable during the self-denial century, and finally, at the beginning of the twenty-first century, to "foreign persons" (*waiguoren*) or "old foreigner" (*lao wai,* as in "Old Wang," a casual way among people for the same status in everyday life) or simply "old American" (*laomei*), "old French" (*laofa*).

The popular "old mother dance" (*dama wu* 大妈舞, a folk dance performed primarily by women in public squares; *dama* referring to mid-aged women) transforming to "square dance" (*guangchang wu* 广场舞, for anyone to join dances in public spaces) is another example. In the 1980s, the waltz dance was a fashion in China, representing "modern" and "advanced" dance, in contrast to the traditional folk dance along the streets. Yet, it took only one generation, from the 1980s until the 2010s, or in the dancers' own generation, from their age of twenties being fans of Western dances to their fifties or sixties being aficionados of the mix of traditional Chinese dance and modern Western music, for transformation to occur. This unique phenomenon reveals the interaction of tradition and modernity and of Chinese and foreign, the syncretism in the Chinese mechanism of self-healing, and the change in public discourse and public space. The increasing popularity of the "*dama wu*" to the reconfiguration of participants as "*guangchang wu,*" being joined by people of all ages and both genders, has vividly illustrated the path that Chinese culture has taken in the past two centuries or so. It even becomes visible as

"China dance" in familial and community spaces outside of China, practiced by both Overseas Chinese and non-Chinese amateurs.

Symbols of Western and modern lifestyle, such as the fast-food chains like McDonalds or Starbucks, also illustrate such a path. From "authentic western food" to "fast food" to "junk food," it reveals the change in Chinese mentality from blindly admiring the West to objectively treating any foreign elements as a "choice." Indeed, to the Chinese who are accustomed to enjoying cuisines from different places, a value placed on "diversity within unity" is evident. "Foreign" foods or drinks are treated as "fashionable" just like other Chinese regional styles. They have simply enriched the diversity in Chinese cuisine and lifestyle. The fact is, while such "foreign" stuff becomes popular, various local and traditional cuisines and drinks are also enjoying a renaissance. Once again, Chinese practices prove that it is wrong to entertain the displacement theory that with the widespread availability of foreign food, traditional cuisine will be in danger. The vitality of Chinese culture lies in the integration of all cultural elements. As seen everywhere in China, for example, the tea cultural events and sales are increasing and widespread while coffee culture and shops (e.g., Starbucks) are also spreading widely.

HARMONIZATION, HERITAGIZATION, AND LOCALIZATION

As a component of the fundamental beliefs and values, the idea of "harmonizing with existent differences" encourages the coexistence of diverse cultures. The concept of Cultural China, as defined by Wei-ming Tu (1994), shows that "Chinese" are a mixture of people with different cultures. Chinese culture has its sustainable philosophical and practical foundation to continue as a system different from that in the West (Chang et al. 1958). As seen in the texts from the Oracle Bone Inscriptions (16th c. BCE–10th c. BCE) and Bronze objects (13th c. BCE–3rd c. BCE), Chinese culture itself has been a constant mixture by absorbing new cultural elements for thousands of years. Indeed, the notion of authenticity is but an imagined empowerment over the claim of those who possess the power of discourse. Chinese culture is by no means a static tradition possessed and maintained by the "Chinese" without contribution from non-Chinese people and cultures. In contemporary China, it is the "folkloric identity" that maintains the tradition by integrating people and cultures of different backgrounds, but not those notions and policies based on "racial identity" or race-based "ethnic identity" (Zhang 2020c).

The success of ICH in China is inseparable from the self-healing mechanism through such a "transformer": heritagization or traditionalization through institutionalization (e.g., governmental organization and school system) and industrialization (e.g., combination economic and cultural interests). In this environment, Chinese culture has developed more healthily through the self-healing mechanism with these two factors that function as supplementary yin and yang: heritagization operates as an effective mechanism in China to revive previously suppressed traditions as a part of spiritual life, whereas institutionalized industrialization enables traditions to continue with solid economic foundation. In Chinese culture, what is "passed down" inherently possesses greater power or authority, or even "authenticity," as in the practice of "ancestral worship." Therefore, heritagization echoes such a cultural logic, and exerts great influence in maintaining the vitality of cultural traditions.

Such a mechanism is also essential to Confucian ethics through the virtue of ritual propriety (*li*). Many gods in Chinese folk beliefs are derived through heritagization of historical figures or incidents, such as the popular God of Treasure (deified Guan Gong, a historical person). Today, the ongoing process of deifying Mao Zedong follows the same cultural logic: temples or shrines are built; Mao's portrait is hung in a vehicle for safety; and souvenirs with Mao image are ubiquitous.

Cultural development is also cultural production, and thus leads to the "culture industry" (or industrializing culture, *wenhua chanye*). In Chinese history, cultural development was primarily dependent upon the self-sufficient localized economic model. "Commercialization" was always a necessary part of everyday practice of traditions. However, industrialization is more than commercialization: it emphasizes the training of the tradition bearers, the producing of traditional art crafts or practicing of traditional arts (performances), demonstrating/performing in public spaces, educating the public on the importance of cultural heritage, and consuming traditions both in economic sense and in cultural sense, that is, gaining self-awareness and self-confidence. The separation of tradition as "pure/authentic," nonprofit, or sacred, distinct from the secular pursuit of profit in producing and consuming "culture," is another dualistic thought. No traditions can develop without being supported by economic interests; traditions have always gone hand in hand with modernity. In fact, encouraging the culture industry may provide a path of survival for disappearing traditions, because commercialization/ industrialization and tourism may provide the economic base for some traditions to sustain.

The continuity and discontinuity of a tradition is determined by its vitality; such vitality shows its validity when the root of the tradition is reasonably recognized. In other words, those traditions rooted in the fundamental beliefs and values maintain their vitality and may endure in more stable forms and contents. Otherwise, those traditions that are based on temporary validity or practicality may be discarded when social and economic conditions are not supportive. As seen in China, some practically disappearing traditions are able to be revived, but others are endangered regardless of efforts from any interests. The culture industry has shown itself to be an effective way to safeguard many traditions in China. It may be said that this industrialization is not the reason for the disappearance of traditions, because even spiritual traditions are developed on the basis of economic conditions.

Localization is the ultimate expression of the cultural self-healing mechanism. In Chinese history, the localization of Buddhism, represented through the "three-teachings-in-one" (*sanjiao heyi*), transformed Chinese culture into a more integrated and inclusive whole. The establishment of the Republic of China by the Nationalist Party (*Guomindang*) in 1912 and the People's Republic of China by the Communist Party (*Gongchandang*) in 1949 are both based on localization of the Western political concepts and structures. The contemporary "socialist market economy," "one country, two systems," and "democratic centralism" all proved to be effective.

To understand the mechanism of localization in Chinese culture, one needs to put each tradition in its own historical context and observe its continuity through its integration of new cultural elements. "Renaming" or "double naming" is one of the concrete examples. Double names provide the condition for coexistence of different practices. This is also inseparable from the linguistic characteristic of multiple homophones uniquely distinctive in the Chinese language, another example that shows the cultural uniqueness and that cannot be understood with the current Western semiotic models.

The possibility of localization has to be based on the cultural connections between the local and the foreign cultural elements. For example, a large number of folktales that were introduced and developed in China by the ninth century through Buddhist teachings became localized as a result of the strategic adaptation: the new forms were practically valid while the essential content and meaning were in line with those in Chinese indigenous tales or legend. Localization in such cases strengthens and diversifies local beliefs and values by bringing in new vitality and validity to the old symbols and meanings.

The localization discussed here refers to acculturation in general, but stresses the regional (or national, that is, Sinification) adaptation. It is a process of syncretism, creolization, hybridization or mixing, regardless of how it is called in different contexts. The central point is, however, there is no "pure" or "authentic" tradition, but all traditions are the results of cultural hybridity. Localization is not to totally reject or accept, but to mingle and thus create a new culture, a *third culture*, because that is the way human cultures have been created and developed.

An everyday example of localization can be seen in the Sinification of the Western Christmas. During Christmas in China, the "apple" (*pingguo*) becomes symbolic because it is homophonous with "peace" (*ping*), and thus it is a "must" gift for the festival. The Christmas "evergreen" tree is now transformed into a "money tree" (*yaoqianshu*), which also has a long history of folklore practice in China, by making it golden in color or decorating it with "gold coins." One may (or not) be surprised to see Santa Claus resembling the "God of Treasure," who has been a popular figure in Chinese folklife. After all, Christmas trees and Santa Claus have a short history both in China and abroad. Similarly, we see such adaptations in other cultural domains, for example, *Guanyin* (Avalokiteśvara in Sanskrit; Bodhisattva of Compassion and Wisdom) was transformed from a male god prior to the Tang Dynasty to a popular Goddess (of Delivering Sons; *songzi* Guanyin) in the widespread folk practice in China.

In conclusion, the interpretative framework of the cultural self-healing mechanism is not only useful in making sense of traditions in Chinese culture but also in understanding different traditional practices in other cultures. What has been proved to be vital is the practice of localization with diversity, but not uniformity or conformity in cultural conflicts and interactions. After all, culture is enriched by its diversity and hybridity, but not by exclusive uniformity. Global communication forces us to question: Is there a universal cultural system that fits all human cultures? Are there possibilities to maintain the diverse human traditions and cultures in harmony but with differences (*he'er butong*)?

Part II

GUSHI

TALES OF CHINESE CHARACTERISTICS

Every society or culture has its own system of defining or naming its ways of oral communication through telling stories, jokes, histories, or experiences. Yet, the dominance of the Eurocentric system of categorizing and defining such folklore forms, or *genre*, in the past two centuries or so have seriously impacted those non-European cultures through colonialistic and imperialistic imposition with a racist ideology. For example, China, at the turn of the twentieth century, in seeking national independence and national equality in international affairs through modernization, officially abandoned many of its own traditions (e.g., the traditional Chinese calendar and festivals; and a failed attempt to replace Chinese character writing system with Romanized alphabetic system) in order to comply with the European systems.

As a result, in literary and folkloristic studies, the Eurocentric "genre" system was adopted in China to recategorize Chinese traditional narratives or literature. Terms that had been used for more than one thousand years such as, *zhiguai* (志怪, strange/wonder tales) and *biji* (笔记, written tales/narratives), were abandoned. Instead, terms like "fairy tale" (*tonghua* 童话; meaning children's stories), "myth," and "folklore" were adopted. In fact, even today, those traditional narratives about gods, legendary figures, or wonder experiences are often categorized differently within Chinese domestic context from that in the international scholarly discourses, a testimony of the idea that Eurocentric categorizations should not be imposed upon, or fully adopted by, other cultures that have their own "ethnic genre" (Ben-Amos 1969).

Gushi (故事; meaning *happenings in the past*) is the most general concept in Chinese for categorizing various forms of storytelling narratives. For example, people use *shenhua gushi* (mythical stories; stories about gods of creation), *chuanshuo gushi* (legendary/passing-down stories), *tonghua gushi* (fairy/children stories), *yingxiong gushi* (hero stories), *xiaohua gushi* (joke/

laughing stories), among others, in everyday life (not to mention many local and dialectic terms), while academic folklorists often use the Western genres such as myth, tale, and legend. While there is no definite boundary among any of those categories, it is here meaningful to explore how the Chinese adopted the Western concept of genre, and how this concept has brought impact to Chinese scholarship which, in turn, affects storytelling in everyday practice.

Within this part, chapter 3 examines the transformation of the term *tong-hua* (fairy tale) in China, and the uses in literary reform, children's education, women's education, and the construction of national identity, and, in particular, how the Brothers Grimm's spirit was localized through promoting *tonghua*. Furthermore, the transformation of folk and fairy tales from the twentieth century to the new social environment in the twenty-first century (Bacchilega 1997; 2013) is discussed. Chapter 4 focuses on the role of matchmaking or matchmaker in a particular tale (Predestined Wife) that has its written records as early as the ninth century, and is still told and practiced in daily life. By applying and developing the historic-geographic method in examining the integration of the traditional Chinese elements and emerging Buddhist ideas, this chapter extends the study of this tale to oral telling in the early twenty-first century.

Through these two chapters, one may understand how the *cultural self-healing mechanism* operates through folk narratives to maintain diversity within unity in Chinese culture and society, how people use tales to adapt to new environment to reconstruct their local and regional identities, and how the vitality and validity of this tale reveal their connection to the Chinese *fundamental beliefs and values* in transmitting and transforming this particular oral tradition. This mechanism is still in operation through the ICH movement in the past two decades in China, which has reinvigorated many folk and fairy tales in the reconstruction of local and national identities by designating/inscribing them as the essence of Chinese traditions with the name of "ICH Items" at international, national, provincial, city, and *xian*-county levels.

Chapter 3

Fairy Tale as *Tonghua*

Localizing Narrative Genre and National Spirit

This chapter first discusses *tonghua* as a literary "genre" by briefly describing: (1) the transformation of the fairy tale from Europe to China at the turn of the twentieth century; (2) its subsequent development in the following century; and (3) the uses of *tonghua,* as well as the questions it raises, in China today. Next, *tonghua* is discussed as a set of specific cultural and historical expressions and, importantly, as something that is more than simply a literary genre, that is, something that transcends its structural limits and offers the hope of living a meaningful life. *Tonghua* is then further examined as a way to construct a new national spirit for a New China in the early twentieth century, with particular focus on the Lin Lan fairy-tale phenomenon. Finally, this chapter argues that, now from a distance of 100 years, Lin Lan be "rediscovered" as the Grimms of China and examined from a cross-cultural perspective to reveal how Chinese tales have been used in the West, and how those tales have created and reinforced stereotypes toward Chinese people and culture.

Examining how the European genre of "fairy tale" was transformed into localized Chinese *tonghua* (童话, children's story) helps answer these questions: how *tonghua*, as a term for a new type of literature, is manipulated as a means to achieve certain ends: namely, a discourse with the West and, at the same time, a discourse within China to revitalize its own tradition; how this process reflects the syncretic and self-healing mechanism that is essential to the continuity of Chinese traditions, despite the impact of colonialism and imperialism; and how a tale's vitality lies in its expression of the fundamental beliefs and values in a given culture.

Once *tonghua* was accepted in China in the early twentieth century, it has been like a genie let out of a bottle, metamorphosing for the past 100 years, and still changing. Although Chinese intellectuals have tried to import the "genre" as it is used in Europe, the current realities have proved that it is not a "genre" at all, but a genie from Europe with several heads stretching to different directions. After all, efforts outside Europe, even within Europe to a certain extent, to define fairy tale as a genre have been "irrelevant" (Ben-Amos 1971:4) and have "failed" (Zipes 2011:222).

THE TRANSFORMATION FROM "FAIRIES" IN EUROPE TO "CHILDREN" IN CHINA

The examination of metamorphosis from *fairies* in Europe to *children* in China has to begin from the formation of fairy tale in Europe. A recent reevaluation of the Italian invention of the form by Giovanni Francesco Straparola (ca. 1485–1558) suggests that his tales also influenced the origin of fairy tales in France (Bottigheimer 2002, 2012). This view, however, has been challenged on the basis that the "wonder-tale" existed "long before Straparola's time" in Europe (Ben-Amos 2010:426), and his tales do not contain many motifs that are now known to be characteristic of fairy tales (Vaz da Silva 2010:398, 419). Indeed, although the Italian and French writers may have institutionalized what we call the fairy tale in the Western world, which in turn had an influence on Middle Eastern and Asian versions of the fairy tale, it is clear that the origins of the fairy tale can be traced back further to the oral traditions of Ancient Asian, Ancient Egyptian, and classical Greco-Roman times (Zipes 2015:xxi). In this regard, the influence of the French term, *conte de fée*, upon other languages, needs to be examined first at semantic level and then at ideological level.

The formation of *contes de fées* in the 1690s in France and the subsequent English circulation of "fairy tales" after the 1750s happened within particular social and religious contexts: these stories were often created by women (of certain social class) as "their resistance to the conditions under which they lived" (Zipes 2011:224). Yet, that such an esoteric practice became a widespread movement in Europe shows that there are deeper and broader reasons for the continuing growth of fairy tales, first in Europe, then beyond. These reasons include: the Reformation in the sixteenth century; the social and familial suppression of women in Europe; concepts of Nationalism from Giambattista Vico (1668–1744) to Immanuel Kant (1724–1804) and Johann Gottfried von Herder (1744–1803); and the British Industrial Revolution from the 1750s to the 1840s, which led directly to the peak of colonization in the late nineteenth and early twentieth century. As a result, even though the French continued developing their *contes de fées*, the Germans their *Märchen*, and the Danish their *eventyr*, it was the English term—fairy tales—that embodied the semantic and ideological meanings and functions, along with the concepts of "folklore" and "nationalism," that, in the early part of the twentieth century, attracted China's attention.

It was an unprecedented period in Chinese history that witnessed the European powers scrambling for China with their opium and cannons; the collapse of the Qing Dynasty (1644–1911) and, with it, the end of two thousand years of the dynastic system of government; the establishment of the Republic of China (1912); and the subsequent New Culture Movement to westernize (or modernize) China (1910s–1930s). To rescue China from being fully colonized and subjugated and to seek independence and modernity, Chinese elites found that *nationalism*, along with *folklore* as its expression (certainly including *tonghua*), could be the catalyst needed to awaken the National Spirit (*minzu jingshen*).

Let us begin with the Chinese term for the "fairy tale." Both *fée* and "fairy" represent a particular image of a female, perhaps with angel-like wings, in a forest; both emerged during Medieval Europe and were/are applied to stories directed at both adults and children. *Märchen* broadly means tales or mythical stories, and *eventyr* refers primarily to adventure stories, although both include stories for children. The Chinese term *gushi* (故事) is the closest to the German and Danish terms for "stories" or "tales." Nevertheless, the new form was named *tonghua*, literally, children's story/stories.

Historically and semantically, the closest Chinese term to "fairy" is *xian* (仙, immortals; a Daoist concept), and tales featuring *xian* as a genre flourished in the third century in China. The earliest detailed definition or description of the immortal *xian* is from the fourth century text by Ge Hong (284–364). In his *Book of the Master who Embraces Simplicity* (*Baopuzi*), he explained the *xian* (after gaining the Dao) to be

> the ancient immortals, who could gain wings and move by flying; they have lost their human nature and have somewhat abnormal bodies, and some are like the sparrow transforming into the clam or the pheasant into the oyster, without acting in the human way. (Ge 1986:52)

The naming process involves not only a decision concerning what a story should be about but also a choice as to what it may be used for beyond direct readers, that is, is the story part of an ideological process that goes beyond literary forms. *Tonghua* was precisely created for this purpose. Interestingly, the Chinese characters for *tonghua*, along with *minsu* (folklore), were directly borrowed from the Japanese. In fact, "folklore" was first translated as *mijian wenxue* (folk literature) and *minxue* (folk/people studies). It was only later that the term *minsu* prevailed. This conceptual struggle about the definition and categorization of these terms is still seen today among disciplinary divisions in China.

In 1909, *tonghua* was first used in China as the title of a series of publications, edited by Sun Yuxiu (1871–1922), in which European fairy tales or *Märchen* were offered as examples. Sun thus created a new category in publications and library categorization. Today he is heralded as the father of "Chinese *tonghua*" (Chen 1984; Wang 2009; Xie 2010; Zhang 2013). His ultimate goal was to promote "child education," as had other intellectuals and writers such as Zhou Zuoren (1885–1967), who was responsible for introducing the term *minsu* to China (1913) and who translated fairy tales by Oscar Wilde, Hans Christian Andersen, the Brothers Grimm, and other authors in the 1910s. By the 1920s, *tonghua* became widely accepted as a new genre of literature. It also aided the extensive New Culture Movement (Li 2014:123) by arousing the awareness of Chinese folk literature. In particular, *tonghua* authored by Chinese writers began to be accepted and welcomed by society, which marked its taking root in China. In particular, *tonghua* produced by Chinese writers were gradually accepted and welcomed by large segments of Chinese, thus establishing it as a subgenre of authored *tonghua* (*zuojia tonghua*) that differentiated it from other subgenres like folk *tonghua* (*minjian tonghua*), literary *tonghua* (*wenxue tonghua*), and children's *tonghua* (*ertong tonghua*).

Clearly, it was because *tong* meant child or children that it was chosen to become part of the Chinese term for fairy tale (*tonghua*) and *Märchen*, rather than *xian*, the third century Daoist term meaning "immortals" (Liu 1985:6; Wu 1992:4); while *hua* meant speech or telling. Thus, *tonghua* was created to promote a social and political agenda, but it also led to an ongoing conceptual struggle.

TONGHUA IN METAMORPHOSIS: LITERARY TONGHUA, FOLK TONGHUA, AND CHILDREN'S LITERATURE

Closely related to the development of folk literature and folklore in China, as described in chapter 1, the developmental stages of the literary form of *tonghua* (Wu 1992; 2007) is not fully in line with the history of other forms. Therefore, it is necessary to describe these stages against ideological and social background in the twentieth and twenty-first centuries in China.

1900s–1920s: Sinification (or, Transforming the Western Fairy Tale into Chinese *Tonghua*)

In addition to translating fairy tales or *Märchen*, Chinese authors also began to write *tonghua*. In form, they imitated European fairy tales; in content, they broadly adapted traditional Chinese myths, legends, and folktales. Beijing

University intellectuals and writers launched the "ballads movement" (*geyao yundong*; collecting folk ballads/songs) all over China, which enabled the birth of folklore studies in China. *Tonghua*, along with *folklore*, became a revolutionary tool for both domestic and international discourses. The publication of the best known indigenous *tonghua*, *The Strawman* (*Daocaoren*, 1922) by Ye Shengtao (1894–1988), marked the first success of Sinification, even though the influence of Andersen's "The Hardy Tin Soldier" was obvious. The first use of the term *minjian tonghua* (*folk tonghua*) in 1927 was to differentiate the newly authored tales from anonymous traditional tales (Liu 1985:6). (The use of "fairy tale" and "literary fairy tale" or "folk fairy tale" in English is a separate issue; see Zipes 2015:xxi; Hanks 2003:63–64, ft. 5).

1930s–1940s: Politicization

With World War II, the Sino-Japanese Wars, and the Civil War in China, political campaigns for "national independence" were the priority for Chinese writers and folklorists. The most representative *tonghua* written during this period is *Dalin and Xiaolin* by Zhang Tianyi (1906–1985). The story is about twin brothers who represent dualities: laziness and diligence, cowardice and bravery, and the ruling and working class; they thus depict both individual and social problems that are still seen as relevant. This tale, although obviously influenced by the Brothers Grimm, is considered a twentieth-century classic, marking the maturity of *tonghua* in China (Li 2014:129–130).

1950s: *Tonghua* for Education

In the early stages of the People's Republic of China (since 1949), social and cultural reconstruction, along with economic rebuilding, became the goal of literary workers, that is, to serve the working class by creating literature for the working class. As a result, the "common people" were praised as the "masters of society" and all kinds of folktales, known to originate from the common people, enjoyed a boost in collection and publication; they were also used as effective ways of propagandizing the new ideology in a New China. This was a flourishing time for writers of *tonghua*. Yan Wenjing (1915–2005) being the most representative among them. His "Dingding's Wonder Trip" (1949), "Earthworm and Bee" (1950), and "Three Proud Cats" (1954) are still highly regarded.

Early 1960s: New *Tonghua*

Writing new *tonghua* became a political task for Chinese writers. Traditional Chinese myths, legends, and tales in general were adapted and re-created as new *tonghua* in order to promote the new political agenda.

1966–1976 (Great Proletarian Cultural Revolution): Disappearing

During this extreme political movement, folk literature—or anything that praised "the masses" or "working classes"—was preserved and developed. *Folk tonghua* were promoted as a means to educate the masses. In contrast, *tonghua* by the intellectuals and educated elite began to be seen as bourgeois and, thus, had to be wiped out.

1980s–1990s: Artistification and Literaturization

During this recovery period, *tonghua* as a *genre* began to be transformed into "high literature," and was increasingly distanced from its previous identification as folk literature. In the 1980s, folkloristics in China was revived and had to re-establish its relationship with folk literature. At the same time, the "searching for roots" (*xungen*) literature and thought movement began to reconstruct Chinese cultural identity at both the national and international levels; this movement influenced all cultural products, such as film, poetry, fiction, music, and language. Conflicting ideas of *Westernization*, *postmodernity*, *globalization*, and *traditionality* complicated the proper placement of *tonghua* in the cultural scene.

2000s–2010s: A Consumer Culture, Merging into the Global Market

One distinctive feature of this period is the transformation of *tonghua*, both oral and written, into various multimedia cultural forms. At the present time, *tonghua* faces yet another transformation and categorization. Whether it is defined as Literature, Folk Literature, Folkloristics, or Folk Narrative, we must transcend disciplinary boundaries in order to understand the mechanisms of its transmission and transformation and the way in which it functions to heal diverse strains in Chinese cultural identity.

If a generalization can be made about the use of *tonghua* in the most recent decade (2010–2020), it is the industrialization through print publication and mass media/animation production (imitating the Disney World), including computer games and e-sports. While there is a strong commercial interest in this trend, and even a public "fear" of corrupting children through the abuse of children's literature, there is also a positive side, that is, the widespread popularity of folk and fairy tales among the young generation from Chinese tradition and from other cultures as well.

DEFINITIONS AND CATEGORIZATIONS TODAY

As outlined earlier, *tonghua* has evolved over the past 100 years. Attempts to define or redefine them, modify their content, and recategorize them have led to confusion in academia, while, at the same time, there has been a greater acceptance of them in popular culture. Looking at the situation of *tonghua* today, we find that: (a) within High Literature (versus folk literature), there is a debate about the relationship between "*tonghua* literature" (which includes the "fairy tale" or "fantasy tale," but whose content is not only about "children") and "children's literature" (whose content is limited to that which is appropriate for children); (b) within folk literature, there is a debate about the distinctions between *tonghua* and "folk *tonghua*"; and (c) within Folkloristics, a debate about the distinctions between "narrative" and "folk narrative," both having *tonghua* as a subcategory. The differing concepts of *tonghua* among these three "fields" make it difficult for *tonghua* to gain academic status and for scholars to obtain resources for research in China. However, the genie's shadows continue spreading in popular and folk culture without those concerns.

In the field of "high literature," *tonghua* has gained a stable position as "children's literature" and is recognized in a section of the China Writers Association, the highest national organization under the central government. The first attempts to write a disciplinary history of *tonghua* resulted in two monographs (Jin 1992; Wu 1992), which affirmed an academic status that *tonghua* had never before had. In addition, "*tonghua* writers" have formed a professional group, most of the members of which were born in the 1950s. This group is becoming increasingly better recognized in China and abroad. The best known representative of this group is Cao Wenxuan, professor of Chinese Literature at Beijing University, who was honored by being given the Hans Christian Andersen Award by the International Board on Books for Young People (IBBY) in 2016.

In the field of "folk literature," *tonghua* is treated with great confusion, although the term has been widely known. In authoritative textbooks for the past thirty years, folk tale, myth, folk legend, and folk ballad are categorized as four parallel genres. Under "folk tale," there are four subgenres: fantasy tale (*huanxiang gushi*), everyday life tale, folk fable, and folk joke. *Tonghua* is treated as an alias of fantasy tale (Zhong 1980:204). Furthermore, the distinction between *tonghua* and *folk tonghua* is drawn clearly here in order to distinguish a large amount of "folk tales" from high literature *tonghua*.

Folkloristics, in contrast, attempts to blur the boundaries between high literature and folk literature, between *tonghua* and *folk tonghua,* and between *tonghua* and other types of "stories" (*gushi*), by promoting the concept of "folk narrative." In an influential textbook, "oral prose narrative" has replaced "folk oral literature" with three subcategories: myth; legend; and folktale and joke (within "folktale," one branch is "fantasy tale," also called "wonder tale" (*shenqi gushi*), "magic tale" (*mofa gushi*), or "folk *tonghua*") (Zhong 2009:247). In the rising field of "folk culture studies," however, *tonghua* is categorized as follows: everyday life tale, folk fable, folk joke, fantasy tale, and folk *tonghua* are all subtypes of "folktale" (Wan 2010:264).

"Folk narrative," as an emerging concept, has achieved more widespread recognition because of its inclusiveness. In the *New Introduction to Folkloristics* (Xing 2016), "folk narrative" has replaced "folk literature." This is a development of recent scholarly efforts: folk narrative is not only used to blur the traditional *genres* but also to emphasize a broader communicative context (Lü and An 2006; Lin 2007, 2012; Liu 2010).

In reality, however, the academic *genre* of *tonghua* has already been broken down by those who originally created it. For example, in an English publication, *Fairy Tales of Chinese Nationalities,* edited by Zhong Jingwen (1991), who is hailed as the father of Chinese folkloristics, the following four "fairy tales" are included: "The Cowherd and the Weaving Girl," "Meng Jiang Nü," "The Butterfly Lovers," and "The Legend of the White Snake." These four tales are acknowledged to be China's most popular "legends," "myths," "wonder-tales," or "fantasy tales." Clearly, they may be considered to be *tonghua* or "fairy tale" in Western discourse, but they are better known, in Chinese discourse, as *shenhua* (gods' stories; myth) or *chuanshuo* (passing-the-telling; another awkward transplant of the Western legend). The *genre* of *tonghua* provides a means of discourse beyond the study of fairy tale, that is, it reflects a desire for the Chinese to keep abreast with the West in search of an equal "national" status and equal discourse in the world. In this sense, the production of *tonghua* in China is not different from the production of *Märchen* in Europe.

Thus far, two facts have become clear: First, the *tonghua* "genre," from the very beginning, is culturally distinctive and is more than simply the "form" it claims to be; it is, rather, a matter of the right and power of discourse. *Tonghua* in China has further proved what Dan Ben-Amos points out: that "the categorization of prose narrative into different genres depends largely upon the cultural attitude toward the tales and the indigenous taxonomy of oral tradition," and that "Thus, in the process of diffusion from one culture to another, tales may also cross narrative categories; and the same story may be myth for one group and *Märchen* for another. In that case the question of the actual generic classification of the tale is irrelevant, since it does not depend on any autonomous or intrinsic features but rather on the cultural attitude toward it" (Ben-Amos 1971:4). Jack Zipes concludes similarly: "Almost all endeavors by scholars to define the fairy tale as a genre have failed. Their failure is predictable because the genre is so volatile and fluid" (Zipes 2011:222).

Second, the transformation of *tonghua* reveals the strategic use of the term *genre* in discourse with the *other* and demonstrates the operation of the inherent mechanism of cultural syncretism, transmission, and self-healing in the continuity of Chinese culture as a whole.

BEYOND GENRE: BELIEFS AND
VALUES IN EVERYDAY LIFE

The issue of defining genre is superficial. The essential matter is, however, the core beliefs and cultural values embodied in stories regardless of how they are categorized. *Tonghua* in China reaffirms this point. Indeed, the fairy tale or *tonghua* is itself a belief, as Zipes points out: "Fairy Tale signifies belief in the supernatural, not the suspension of belief. We all believe in the extra-ordinary of Once Upon a Time. We need to believe. We all dream and breathe through our tales" (Zipes 2011:221). However, to pursue this further, one needs to examine how such a belief, functioning as a means of communication and a process of meaning-making, reveals different belief systems and cultural values in different cultures, and how they operate in cross-cultural communication.

Answering these three questions is necessary to understand *tonghua* beyond the limitations of its *genre*. The first is: What particular Chinese beliefs and cultural values are embodied in tales in general or *tonghua* in particular and how are they different from those of the West? The answer is twofold and depends upon a synchronic view of today's Western and Chinese cultures and a diachronic view of the continuity of Chinese culture as a whole for the past three millennia, at least since the time of the Shang Dynasty's Oracle Bone Inscriptions (sixteenth century BCE). In short, ancient China's animistic cosmos developed polytheist practices, which were characteristically all-inclusive and syncretic; monotheism, however, which was characteristically exclusive, became the dominant worldview in Judeo-Christian Western culture. As a result, Chinese culture contains a large number of stories about all kinds of gods, spirits, ghosts, and immortals. This inclusiveness is essential to the continuity of Chinese culture as a "diversity within unity," which is expressed in these *fundamental beliefs and values* as part of the cultural self-healing mechanism discussed in chapter 2.

The second question is: How do *tonghua,* or folk narratives in a broad sense, reflect continuity and self-healing mechanisms in Chinese culture?

Renaming genres is one of the mechanisms by which "old" ideas can be reaffirmed through "new" forms. For the Chinese, as long as the fundamental beliefs and values remain unchanged (e.g., in a tale), other names or elements of the "form" may be easily substituted.

The third questions is: What conclusion can be drawn by merging the above two questions? *Tonghua* were not meant to transplant European "fairy tales" to Chinese culture; they were, rather, a means to awaken the cultural self-awareness and self-confidence of the Chinese, especially at a time when, as a result of the disdain shown them by the invading colonial and imperial powers, they had internalized the mentality of being "inferior."

Historically, the transformation of all kinds of tales in China also demonstrates what mechanisms are involved in the transmission of Chinese traditions. Let us look at *Yexian* (叶限, ATU 510A), an ancient Chinese tale that superficially resembles "Cinderella," to demonstrate the continuity and vitality of *tonghua* in everyday life. While there is a complete translation by Waley (1963:147–162), here is a summary of the version (about 770 Chinese characters):

> The people of the South tell a story from about a thousand years ago. A chief had two wives, but one died and left a daughter named Yexian. She was loved by her father, but he died only a few years later. Her stepmother was mean to her. Once Yexian caught a tiny fish and kept it in a bowl. It then grew bigger. Eventually she had to put it into a pond. The fish would show its head to Yexian when she came, but never to other people. The stepmother tricked Yexian to get her out of the way, put on her clothes, hid a knife, and walked to the pond. The fish showed its head. By now it was very big. She killed the fish, ate the meat, and buried the bones. When Yexian came back and found no fish, she wailed with grief. Suddenly, a man appeared and told her, "Your mother killed the fish and the bones are under the dung. Get the bones and hide them in your room. They will make every wish you make come true." She followed his instructions and got beautiful clothes and delicious food. Then it was time for a fair. The stepmother went to the fair, but asked Yexian to work at home. Nevertheless Yexian attended in secret with her feather-clothes and gold-shoes. When she was almost recognized by her stepsister and stepmother, she ran away in a hurry and lost one shoe. The shoe eventually was presented to the king. He asked the people around to try it on, but no one could make it fit. It was as light as down and made no noise even when walking on stone. The king then ordered every woman to try it on. Finally, Yexian was found, and the shoe fit her. The king then brought her and the fish bones back to his court, and made her his chief wife. She was as beautiful as a fairy. The stepmother and stepsister were later struck to death by flying stones. One year, the king asked the fish bones for too much treasure, and his wishes were not fulfilled. He then buried the fish bones

along with enormous wealth on the seashore. But when he needed the treasure to suppress a rebellion, everything had been washed away the night before.

Yexian was categorized as *zhiguai* (志怪, strange/wonder/ghost story) in the ninth-century book *Youyang zazu* (*The Miscellaneous Morsels from Youyang*) by Duan Chengshi (803–863). *Zhiguai* is a 2,000-year-old well-known "genre" in literature that matured and gained popularity in the ninth century. Furthermore, *zhiguai* were categorized in Duan's *nuogao* chapter, a Daoist term for summoning ghosts and spirits. The term was first used in *Baopuzi* from the fourth century by Ge Hong (1986), as mentioned earlier, possibly at the beginning of a séance. Thus, this tale had its own *genre* for a long time before it was relabeled as *tonghua*.

The three key motifs in *Yexian* are: magic fish; festivals (or fairs); and shoe-for-marriage (Liu 2017:212). The first shows fish-worship among the people who live on fishing (in contemporary Guangxi, China, and Vietnam), a belief shaped by the mode of production and the geographic conditions of this group of people. This version of the practice of worshipping fish is not seen in other regions (Ting 1974), but versions that are modified to accord with local beliefs and values do appear in other regions. The second motif—festivals—also reveals a particular aspect of social life that is still celebrated in Guangxi, Southwest China, and northern Vietnam; this particular festival is known as *nongdong*, or song-fair, and was mentioned in the original ninth-century text. The third motif exhibits unique Chinese cultural symbolism: the homophonous relationship between "shoe" and "harmony" (same pronunciation, *xie;* different characters). The symbolic relationship between shoe and marriage is also seen in weddings in many regions in China. Thus, these are "tales" that cannot be separated from real life (Beauchamp 2010).

What is of particular interest in *Yexian* is the belief that the fish bone is a representation of the immortality of the soul, which is often seen in the practice of secondary burial. Because of this belief, the tale and the practice it reflects are still alive today in Guangxi where *Yexian* originated. In contrast, when "Cinderella" loses its specific cultural connection to a particular region or group of people, it also loses its connection with current beliefs and enters the world of wonder as a generic expression of the aspiration of girls to "marry up" (Zipes 2011). Thus, equating "Cinderella" and *Yexian* (Li 2016:201) is not culturally meaningful, even though they are both labeled ATU 510A. Cinderella is alive in the wonder-world of books and films (e.g., the Disney versions in 1922, 1950, 2015), but operates distinctly in the world of belief. The plots in the *Year of the Fish* (a film directed by David Kaplan in 2007) and the *Crazy Rich Asians* (a film directed by Jon Chu in 2018) arguably reinterpret the narrative in light of the *Yexian* tradition. While "Cinderella stories" continue in the world of fantasy, *Yexian* is alive in a particular region where local beliefs, values, and lifestyle are reinforced through the tale and related folksong festivals (more discussion on this point in chapter 7).

In summary, the aforementioned three culturally distinctive questions have illustrated how various cultural mechanisms are used in Chinese tales to perpetuate their transmission and transformation. During the nineteenth and twentieth century, for example, the Chinese went through a cultural trauma, losing their self-awareness and self-confidence in facing the colonial and imperial powers, and even internalizing feelings of inferiority as a colonial effect. However, deep in the Chinese tradition, those core beliefs and values continued through traditional tales; the hardship of life was relieved with tales that maintained a sense of cultural "roots." This proves the cultural self-healing mechanism in Chinese history: whether China was ruled by non-Chinese, divided between the European and Japanese powers, or riven by internal chaos, the maintenance of beliefs and values by the common people through everyday folklore practices activated a self-healing mechanism whenever socioeconomic conditions allowed (Zhang 2017a). The metamorphosis of *tonghua* (or folklore in the broad sense) in China provides a precise example of this; it operates as a narrative form that enables the negotiation of cultural expressions to accommodate ideological differences, it reflects discourse at different levels, and it sustains its identity over time, while simultaneously regaining and rejuvenating its cultural vitality.

In the nineteenth and twentieth centuries, when China suffered under the domination of Western colonial and imperial powers, the Chinese were forced to adapt to Western ideas and concepts in order to establish discourse with the invading forces. However, as the Chinese gained self-confidence, their feelings of inferiority gradually disappeared and, eventually, they were able to give voice to their own cultural distinctiveness. They were thus able to construct a new national and cultural identity that facilitated a discourse between the insider and the outsider as equals. The Chinese then began to take pride in their own traditions.

Thus far, the metamorphosis of *tonghua* in China is not only of significance within the fairy-tale world, but also, more meaningfully, leads our attention to deeper cultural issues beyond fairy tale as a genre. This latter point becomes more important in cross-cultural studies.

In accordance with the mechanism of transmitting and transforming culture in China, integrating "foreign" cultural elements as a discursive tool has been an effective way to enhance the vitality of the culture and to activate the cultural self-healing process. *Tonghua*, at the turn of the twentieth century, played an important role in this process: its format provided a new literary genre to help modernize China, and its spirit awakened the Chinese to the value of their own traditional stories at a time when nationalism was a priority. We have also seen that redefining and renaming is often an effective way of revalidating one's own tradition and asserting one's own right to discourse. We have shown that the transition from "fairy tale" to *tonghua* involved two sets of discourses: an external one with the West aimed at establishing equality; and an internal one concerning the construction of children's literature and child education, or even public education, and, through this, the reconstruction of a national identity. It was also a very important means to help promote the "vernacular speech" (*baihuawen*) movement, which greatly simplified the written style of Chinese literature and, to a great extent, the way the Chinese thought about their own culture. Chinese folk narratives are being retold today on the global stage; however, they are being used to achieve different goals from those at the turn of the twentieth century. Today, they are a crucial way to continue and enhance cross-cultural discourse between China and the West.

CHINESE FAIRY TALES IN THE WESTERN EYE

Too often in the text-centered studies of folk and fairy tales is to interpret tales from any culture on the basis of the Euro-centered theoretical framework with such analytical tools as "genre," "motif" or "tale type." This trend began with the lack of non-European texts, but later it excluded non-European texts in the construction of those theories about genre, motif, and tale type. While this trend is changing by including more and more non-European texts, the sources of such texts are often limited to literary text from even centuries ago or through many reprints, as it is often seen in the Chinese tales in English translation, rather than providing tales from the contemporary oral telling.

Some Chinese classics were translated into European languages by the missionaries as early as the sixteenth century when the Jesuits first successfully entered China. By the end of nineteenth century, a large body of Chinese literature had been translated to the West, and influenced many greats minds such as Gottfried W. Leibniz (1646–1716) in his *Sinophile* through his philosophical, linguistic and mathematical works (e.g., binary system), which inspired many further studies. While it is true to say that any introduction or study of Chinese text to the West would broaden the general knowledge about Chinese history, culture and people, some works also created long-lasting racial and cultural stereotypes. For example, in Max Weber's (1864–1920) work on Chinese society and religion, although he correctly noticed a fundamental characteristic that Chinese belief system did not have the Messianic prophecy impacting the meaning of everyday life, his conclusion about Chinese society and culture as a whole based on a sole ruler of capitalism has been proved biased and misleading (Weber 1968).

There was, however, certain pleasant voice tuned to the classic Chinese literature that stirred up a wave of composing in pentatonic scale and echoing the philosophy of harmonious humanism through symphonic performance (e.g., *Das Lied von der Erde* by Gustav Mahler 1860–1911). But this kind of positive influence and integration has not been given serious attention even by professional musicians. Ignoring or diminishing the importance of many scientific inventions from China, including Zhu Zaiyu's (1536–1611) discovery of the twelve equal temperaments, is another example to "justify" the racist Eurocentric superiority.

In terms of folk and fairy tales, the turn of the twentieth century also witnessed a strong European desire for exotic fairy tales from China. As a result, a number of collections of Chinese fairy tales were published during that period. They can be seen as two categories: translations of Chinese texts (regardless of sources) with minimum editing, mixing, or hybridizing; inventive or imaginative tales for a demanding European market to consume Chinese fairy tales.

In the first category, representative collections (still widely circulated, for example, on amazon.com) include: *Some Chinese Ghosts* (Hearn 1887), *The Chinese Boy and Girl* (Headland 1901), *Chinese Fairy Stories* (Pitman 1910), *Chinese Fairy Tales: Forty Stories Told by Almond-Eyed Folk* (Fielde 1912), *The Diamond: A Study in Chinese Hellenistic Folk-Lore* (Laufer 1915), *Gleanings from Chinese Folklore* (Russell 1915), *A Chinese Wonder Book* (Pitman 1919), *The Chinese Fairy Book* (Wilhelm 1921), *Myths and Legends of China* (Werner 1922b), and *Chinese Nights Entertainment: Stories of Old China* (Brown 1922). In addition, there were many similar collections in other European languages such as in German, Greiner (1913), Kühnel (1914), Rudelsberger (1914), and Staden (1914).

After examining those collections by the Europeans, Zhao Jingshen (1902–1985) pointed out (in the late 1920s) that "When Europeans collect Chinese fairy tales, they never collect tales from our common people or children the type of tales such as snake-bridegroom or wolf-grandma, but from the imagined literary books" (Zhao 2003:2541). Zhao is still respected as the pioneer in the studies of folk and fairy tales in China, who, in the late 1920s and early 1930s, translated both fairy tales and theoretical works from the West and wrote a number of articles on methods and theories for collecting and studying folk and fairy tales, and was representative of his generation in the early twentieth century who were well learned of Chinese traditions and Western theories.

The problems of this kind of publications, even in the eyes of Chinese scholars in 1920s and 1930s, showed that (a) the tales were mostly taken from classic texts without the oral element; (b) there was no clear distinction between folktales, fairy tales, myths, and legends, and no identification of regional differences (significant given the diversity in China); and (c) the "Chinese elements" were generalized, sometimes even adopting Western plots to tell "Chinese" stories (Li 2018:34–35). Clearly, these collections were either from sources that were overgeneralized in terms of regionality, temporality, orality, and authority, or from a regional source but with different missionary purposes (Zhang 2020c).

These problems revealed not only semantic or methodological issues but also ideological superiority that the Europeans held over Chinese tales. In this regard, commenting on European collections of Chinese fairy tales (e.g., Pitman 1910; Fielde 1912; Brown 1922), Zhao Jingshen repeatedly made a clear statement that "any collection edited or compiled by Europeans are all fallacious and ridiculous without exception" because those tales were "not Chinese in essence" (Zhao 2003:2535). After examining a number of collections in great detail such as motifs, structures, and sources, Zhao concluded that those tales were "fabricated or modified" (2003:2535). Specifically about Brown's collection, Zhao scrutinized all the 32 tales and concluded that the collection was "horrible through to the end" (糟透了 *zaotoule*) (2003:2543).

In the second category of pure imagination with the label of "Chinese fairy tales," the representative collection can be the tales written by Béla Balázs (1884–1949). Known for his prolific artistic productions, particularly film works, Balázs was once commissioned to write stories as illustrations for a particular Chinese figurative painting style. Out of this "challenge" and his "great interest in Asian art," in 1921 Balázs wrote 16 tales in German in three weeks for the book *Der Mantel der Träume: Chinesische Novellen (The Cloak of Dreams: Chinese Fairy Tales,* 1922), which received "a glowing review by Thomas Mann" and interested Balázs himself to translate the tales into his mother tongue Hungarian (*Csodálatosságok könyve; The Book of Marvels*) in 1948 (Balázs and Zipes 2010:27).

For Balázs, like some German writers who imbued the *Kunstmärchen* (the literary fairy tale) with complex philosophical notions, he wanted to use fairy tales to enable him and his readers to transcend their existential dilemma (Balázs and Zipes 2010:13). Therefore, "Chinese fairy tales" became an effective means to channel personal desire and imagination. Just like Mahler's attraction to the harmonious views on friendship and the relationship between man and nature through classic Chinese poetry, Balázs was more interested in the Daoist idea about transcending from the earthly human relations, and he used those Chinese fairy tales "to experience the bitterness and joys of life and to reach a condition of suspension or liminality in which nothing can be explained rationally but everything can be understood intuitively" (Balázs and Zipes 2010:52).

Similarly, Robert van Gulik (1910–1967) began to make up his own Chinese tales (e.g., a dozen books about *Judge Dee/detective* stories in the

1950s - 1960s) after he translated some classic Chinese tales. And his self-invention of Chinese tales has led to dozens of similar works thereafter all over the world. Clearly, consuming "Chinese fairy tales" has been a lasting trend, as seen in the several versions of the Mulan story from the Disney productions.

No doubt, all the collections of Chinese folk and fairy tales before the 1930s, translated or invented, have substantially shaped the European imagination of the Chinese people and culture. Those publications were the result of characterizing or defining "Chinese" from both domestic and inter-national (European and Japanese) sides. Within China, the early twentieth century was the time when Chinese intellectuals questioned the meaning of being Chinese and the future of China after a long period of being suppressed by the European powers, particularly from the Opium Wars in the mid-nineteenth century till the establishment of the Republic of China (1912). Outside China, the longtime missionary work, joined by other European intellectuals (e.g., Bertrand Russell's *The Problem of China*, 1922), suc-cessfully depicted the stereotypes against the "Chinese" and "China," under the influence of colonialism and the theory of civilization in Europe in the nineteenth century. Eventually, works like *Chinese Characteristics* (1890) by Arthur Smith (1845–1932) illustrated the "European theory of national character" and presented the Chinese character to the Westerners, though with his "immaturity of theory" and "failure to examine his own middle-class American culture" (requoted from Liu 1995:53). No doubt, those collections of Chinese fairy tales before 1930, including other works on folklore in general such as *The Folk-Lore of China: And Its Affinities with that of the Aryan and Semitic Races* (Denny 1876) and *China: In Legend and Story* (Brown 1907), contributed to stereotyping Chinese people and culture through the monotheist religious criteria and civilization theory. Unfortunately, those collections of Chinese folk and fairy tales are still widely circulated today.

The turn of the 1930s was made through a wave in China studies (or Sinology) sprung from academic scholars with different goals from the pre-vious missionary efforts. Two representative works are the *Three Lectures on Chinese Folklore* (Jameson 1932), through which the ninth-century Chinese tale, Yexian, began to be known to the West as the earliest written version of Cinderella (earlier than the known versions, Cox 1892; Rooth 1951), and the *Chinese Fairy Tales and Folk Tales* (Eberhard 1937b). These efforts were surely positive to provide the text of tales from the oral telling, but there were also two shortcomings: lack of context of the telling events, and neglecting the role of the collectors and publishers. For these reasons, the "Grimms of China" has to be rediscovered nearly a century later (Zhang 2020c.)

LIN LAN AS THE GRIMMS OF CHINA:
NATIONAL SPIRIT IN FAIRY TALES

After the introduction of "folklore," "fairy tale," "nationalism," and some other concepts to China at the turn of the twentieth century, collecting, publishing, and studying folklore reached a peak in the 1930s. During this period, folkloristic exchange between China and the West also entered a new stage when, for example, the Chinese version of Cinderella, *Yexian* (ATU 510A), was first introduced to the West by American folklorist R. D. Jameson (1932), in addition to many translations to and from Chinese (some are mentioned later). Also, German Sinologue Wolfram Eberhard (1909–1989), who later emigrated to the United States, visited China and sensed the popularity and importance of the folklore collection there. Specifically, Eberhard got to know Cao Songye (Ts'ao Sung-yeh 1897–1978), a middle school teacher known for his folktale collection in Jinhua, Zhejiang province. Cao provided Eberhard with many collections of folktales, including the Lin Lan series. In particular, Cao gave a number of his handwritten manuscripts of folktales to Eberhard. In return, Eberhard dedicated his *Typen chinesischer Volksmärchen* (1937a) to Cao. In the same year, Eberhard published *Chinese Fairy Tales and Folk Tales* (1937b), which was perhaps the first scholarly translation of folk and fairy tales with references to specific collections of oral tradition in the early twentieth century. Although most of the tales in the collection were from the Lin Lan series, Eberhard made no mention of Lin Lan at all, except that Lin Lan's name was included in the bibliographical sources. Later, Eberhard published another collection, *Folktales of China* (1965), partly based on the 1937 collection, which was reprinted several times. It remains unknown why Lin Lan was not mentioned. For this reason, and for the fact that there has been an enduring interest in Lin Lan in the Chinese world, this essay is intended to "rediscover" Lin Lan, who played the role of the Brothers Grimm of China.

By collecting and publishing folk and fairy tales over 200 years ago, the Brothers Grimm created models for the study of folklore throughout the world. They also fulfilled their ideological goal by contributing to the making of a new nation and connecting its past and present, its elite groups and folk, and its oral and literary traditions. This achievement inspired many scholars in Germany and other European countries to create a field of study at the end of the nineteenth century that corresponded to the aims of the new nation-states. They all had a common wish for their own nations that were in the process of identity-making in the new world. Later, those scholars who introduced "nationalism," "folklore" and "fairy tale"—among numerous other Western terms and concepts—into the newly established Republic of China (1912) contributed to the emergence of Chinese *tonghua*, popularly represented by the Lin Lan series.

In the past century or so, publications in many countries have demonstrated how widespread the influence of the Grimms was and how various folklorists endeavored to follow their example. If we consider that there were "Brothers Grimm" in virtually every Western country, for example, in Norway (Peter Christen Asbjørnsen and Jorgen Moe), Finland (Elias Lönnrot), Denmark (Hans Christian Andersen and Sven Grundtvig), Serbia (Vuk Karadzic), Czech Republic (Božena Němcova), Russia (Alexander Afanasyev), Portugal (Adolfo Cœlho), France (Emmanuel Cosquin), and Italy (Giuseppe Pitrè) (cf. Ranke 1966:xiii; Zipes 2012), it is not surprising that there was also a similar development in twentieth-century China.

However, the emergence in China of stories similar to those collected by the Grimms and other folklorists has rarely been studied or explored. Consequently, this essay will provide a context for understanding the development of the Lin Lan tales in the early twentieth century in China and its role in the continuity of Chinese folk and fairy tales from ancient texts to contemporary storytelling. Here, one must keep in mind that the Chinese senses of "nationalism," "nation," "folklore," and "fairy tale"—among other concepts borrowed from Europe—have been used to form strands of Chinese "tradition" and "cultural heritage" to construct its "national identity" and to cope with cultural, social, economic, and political conflicts with the rest of the world today.

As a result, a wave of publishing folk and fairy tales began in the late 1920s and early 1930s. Lin Lan emerged as the editor of a series of booklets subcategorized as "folktale," "fairy tale," and "funny stories" (*qushi*). These publications served some of the following purposes: the education of women and children, the establishment of folklore studies as a discipline, and the transition from the previous semi-classic language to the common vernacular speech (*baihua*) (e.g., Western punctuation marks were officially adopted in 1920 as a reform of classical Chinese grammar).

Lin Lan should be heralded as "the Grimms of China" for three primary reasons: (a) the influence of the Grimms in the Lin Lan Series; (b) the exemplary dedication to oral tradition; and (c) the social and literary impact from a historical perspective. When the Brothers Grimm began to collect folk and fairy tales with a clear goal of searching for the true voice of the folk and the pride of their culture and history, the Prussian-dominated German Empire was in a crisis that eventually led to the establishment of the German Confederation (1815). It was during the rise of Germany as a nation-state that the first edition of *Kinder-und Hausmärchen* was published (1812–1815; Zipes 2014). Doubtlessly, this helped create support for a unified nation.

In this sense, the Brothers Grimm developed what can be called "the Brothers Grimm spirit," that is, "the Grimms hoped to find great truth about the German people and their laws and customs by collecting their tales, for they believed that language was what created national bonds and stamped the national character of a people" (Zipes 1987:xxviii). This spirit was also part of romantic nationalism that was characteristic of German ideas in the eighteenth and nineteenth centuries. It is this spirit that became a driving force for many countries that were seeking to maintain their cultural traditions by seeking the sources and roots of a national culture. It was precisely for this reason that the Lin Lan phenomenon took place in China.

Lin Lan insisted on recording oral tales from storytellers, that is, the common people (Li 2018:34–35), as seen in the correspondence between the editor and the contributor/collector regarding the tales "The Garden Snake" and "The Snake Spirit" (discussed later). This principle was particularly emphasized even more in the Lin Lan series than in other similar collections. There is clear evidence that the literati at that time, like Lin Lan, knew a good deal about the Grimms' 1815 letter, in which dedication to the original form of the tale was especially emphasized along with the scope of collecting (Denecke 1968:3–4). In this regard, the Lin Lan series was exemplary.

Even from a contemporary viewpoint, the Lin Lan series has contributed greatly to the continuity of oral and literary tradition in China, linking the previous oral and written records to those collected later (particularly in the 1980s–1990s). Through tale type and motif studies by contemporary scholars (Liu 2002; Li 2018), the fairy tales in the Lin Lan series have demonstrated that they not only mediated between the oral and literary traditions but also stimulated the rise of Chinese *tonghua*. For example, the publication of the best known indigenous *tonghua*, *Daocaoren* (Strawman) (1922) by Ye Shengtao (1894–1988), marked the first success of Sinification under the influence of Andersen's "The Hardy Tin Soldier" (Liu 2017).

While a great number of Western *tonghua* (e.g., those by the Brothers Grimm and Andersen) had been translated and introduced to China, there were also many studies and writings by Chinese scholars and writers. For example, Sun Yuxiu established the journal *Tonghua* (Fairy Tale) in 1909 and published 105 volumes until 1924. But Zhao Jingshen had different views about *tonghua* than Sun, which was a reason for Zhao to work with Li at North New Books and eventually led to the publication of the Lin Lan series (Li 2018:3). Some of those Chinese publications have remained as classical studies or tales of *tonghua* in China, represented by the Lin Lan series, which doubtlessly exerted the greatest social impact and enjoyed the greatest popularity among the public (e.g., children). This can be attributed to its low price, multiple reprints, wide distribution (with more than ten distribution offices across the country), and, of course, the local flavor of the language, which emanated directly from the common people. While there were many others who published folk and fairy tales in the early twentieth century in China, Lin Lan emerged at a unique historical moment.

In the late 1920s and early 1930s, the Lin Lan phenomenon appeared due to several factors. The first is the establishment of the publishing house *Beixin Shuju* (North New Books), which became the most influential publisher during the New Culture Movement (Chen 2006). For example, most of the literary writings by Lu Xun (1881–1936) were published there. The second factor is the editor in chief of North New Books, Li Xiaofeng (1897–1971), who was Lu Xun's closest student and friend, and who used Lin Lan as a pen name for some publications. The third factor is the content of the fairy tales and their role in the transmission of the oral and literary traditions in China, which satisfied the social needs at that time.

Specifically, the pseudonym "Lin Lan" was first used on July 12, 1924, with a set of three literary stories written about Xu Wenchang (1521–1593), a historical figure with many literary works and anecdotal stories still popular today. The success of this first attempt encouraged Lin Lan to publish more folktales and fairy tales that led to an "epochal phenomenon in the history of Chinese folk literature and children's literature" (Che 2002:36). Eventually, the Lin Lan series "played a major role in the development of modern folk literature and theory in China" (Gao 2013:79). Furthermore, the Lin Lan series was categorized into three subgenres, *minjian chuanshuo* (folk legends/tales), *minjian tonghua* (folk fairy tales), and *minjian qushi* (folk funny tales), in 43 volumes containing nearly 1,000 tales. Eight volumes out of the series were categorized as minjian *tonghua*, totaling 154 fairy tales. Of course, many tales in "folk legends" can also be seen as fairy tale/*tonghua*.

Certainly, from a contemporary perspective, the division between folk tales and fairy tales could be redefined. All of the tales were contributed by informants who collected them from oral storytelling in different parts of China in response to a call from the publisher (as the Brothers Grimm did in 1815, and as the *Geyao Yundong* [Ballad Movement] from Beijing University did in 1918). Each volume was about 100 pages with approximately 20 tales. The earliest volume was published in 1926, and the last in 1933. "Many of these volumes were reprinted even three times in 2 to 3 years, and most children in urban schools read these tales" (Che 2002:36).

There are also some important social and economic factors that must not be ignored if we are to understand the emergence of the Lin Lan phenomenon. The May Fourth Movement in 1919 certainly awakened the Chinese to reflect upon the domestic history that led to the "backwardness" of China and to being divided and conquered by the Western powers and Japan. Moreover, it stimulated the Chinese to establish greater exchanges with those powers as a means to rescue the Chinese nation. One conclusion the Chinese elites drew was to advance the nation through a "new culture" (represented by Western science, technology, and ideas in contrast to the traditional Confucian values and lifestyle), which was most obviously marked by the new vernacular speech (*baihua*), with which new ideas were promoted through publication.

Massive publication and distribution of literary works were possible during this historical period because it was, indeed, the only time of relative peace for China from the 1840s to the 1940s. Those 100 years were filled with wars, among other problems: the Opium Wars (1940–1860), the Taiping Rebellions (1851–1864), the First Sino-Japanese War (1894), the May Fourth Movement (1919) and the subsequent social Resistances and Strikes, the first Civil War (1926–1928), the Second Sino-Japanese War (1931–1945, starting in the Northeast in 1931 and spreading to the whole of China in 1937), and the Second Civil War (1945–1949).

Clearly, the emergence of the Lin Lan phenomenon was due to many factors, but the most important was the need for what I would call "the Brothers Grimm spirit" in China, which initiated the New Culture Movement, including the Ballad Movement of collecting folk ballads/songs. Today, academics have a revived interest in the Lin Lan phenomenon (Li 2018) and have responded to the ongoing movement of safeguarding Intangible Cultural Heritage (ICH) and the reconstruction of China's national identity in the twenty-first century.

In the Lin Lan phenomenon, the puzzle who was (or were) Lin Lan seems to have been solved, but its symbolism deserves to be emphasized. When the name "Lin Lan" first appeared in 1924, it was clear that it was the pen name of Li Xiaofeng (Cai 1985; Che 2002; Zheng 2006; Li 2018). Li was a student of philosophy at Beijing University and graduated in 1923. He was one of the founders of a publishing house named Xinchaoshe (New Wave Press). Soon after he published those three stories discussed earlier, he changed the name of the press to North New Books and moved to Shanghai. He continued using the pen name Lin Lan to publish other stories until 1925. At the same time, Zhao Jingshen (1902–1984) also wrote some stories about the same historical person (Xu Wenchang) as Lin Lan did, as well as some others based on other traditional figures and tales. In 1928, Zhao Jingshen took charge of the design and publication of the Lin Lan series. By then he had already published some important works about *tonghua* and established himself as one of the most important scholars of *tonghua*. It was their common interest in *tonghua* that brought Li and Zhao close together. They collaborated in translating the *Kinder-und Hausmärchen* by the Brothers Grimm in 1932. In 1934, Zhao published his first book on drama, which marked his change of research interest; after that, he never published anything further on *tonghua*. It was clearly for this reason that the Lin Lan series also ended in 1933 (Li 2018:23–24). Based on this history and personal experience, folklorist Che Xilun (born 1937), who was Zhao's student in the 1960s, reasoned that Lin Lan was the name used by Li and Zhao, along with others involved in the publication of the Lin Lan series by North New Books (Che 2002:37). Clearly, Lin Lan was the name used by a team (Li 2018:25; Gao 2013:79). It seems reasonable to guess that, on certain occasions, Lin Lan was the name used by a team of two or more people, but on other occasions, Lin Lan was the pen name of one particular person (Li 2018:26).

To some extent, the identification of to whom the name Lin Lan referred is no longer as meaningful as understanding the symbolism of Lin Lan in promoting the fairy-tale genre in China and in introducing European fairy tales to Chinese audiences. The latter has greater significance in reflecting upon the roles in the past century of fairy tale, folklore, nationalism, and national identity. It is not baseless to assume that these popular tales played a role for the generations growing up in the 1920s and 1940s to find their sense of cultural roots—and thus to write unique Chinese fairy tales to arouse national pride and to fight in the Sino-Japanese War for national independence in the 1930s–1940s.

What is significant, however, is the Grimm Spirit transformed in the Lin Lan series. Aside from the similarities between the Brothers Grimm and Lin Lan—the spirit of creating a national identity, the principles of collecting folk and fairy tales, and the social and literary impact—there are two differences that deserve mentioning.

One difference concerns religious topics. The Brothers Grimm had clear religious sentiments. To a certain extent, "Wilhelm Grimm (more than Jacob) revised and altered most of the tales over a period of approximately 40 years to make them more graceful and suitable for children and a proper Christian upbringing" (Zipes 1987:xxviii). But that was not the case in the Lin Lan series. Lin Lan, whether as an individual or a team, reflected a Chinese inclusive polytheist tradition. The editors were attached to modernism and nationalism almost as a faith, although some tales expressed Confucian ethical teaching and the Buddhist idea of *karma*.

The other difference is the pivotal role of their projects. Most of the tales in the Grimms' collection had not been published before, although "many of these tales were a few hundred years old before they were gathered and told by the Grimms' informants" (Zipes 2013:xxiii). Therefore, "little did they know that their 'German' collection would transcend their own country and through translations create universal bonds of understanding" (Zipes 1987:xxviii). Indeed, the Grimms did not realize that their "scholarly revolution" led to changes not only in "the social and intellectual attitudes toward folktales," but also in our perceiving "meaning" as inherent in tales that represent "the dynamics of human imagination" (Ben-Amos 2017:105).

The importance of the Lin Lan series also lies in its pivotal role in the continuity of the oral tradition in China in the early twentieth century. As further discussed in chapter 4, many tales in the Lin Lan series can be traced to the early historical records, and can also be seen in the twenty-first century oral telling. In this sense, the foremost value of the Lin Lan series lies in the preservation of those tales in particular regions during a particular time. Besides the social and political impact, these tales illustrate how they "bear the personal and peculiar marks of the storytellers who kept them in their memory for a purpose" (Zipes 2013:xxiii). By sketching the history of collecting oral and literary traditions before and after the Lin Lan series, and by looking at a few tale types, we can better understand the role of the Lin Lan tales in the Chinese context.

Many tales in the Lin Lan series are not only the variants of the previous written records, as discussed earlier, but are also directly related to the continued oral tradition that is documented in the recent collections from oral telling. In addition, there are many interesting and contrasting aspects in terms of the cultural backgrounds between the tales from the Brothers Grimm and that of the Grimms of China. While the Brothers Grimm (and even the Russian) fairy tales are mostly related to activities in forests (Zipes 2011:231), the Lin Lan series depicts the agricultural life in China with tales told in the rice fields or next to the stove. (Although there are also many minority groups in China who are connected with hunting, many of them speak different languages (e.g., Mongols, Yi, Miao, Daur, and Manchu), which resulted in the fact that their tales are often not included in Chinese-language collections.) For example, the protagonists in the Western tales are mostly hunters, traveling princes, or princesses asking questions, but those in Lin Lan's tales are mostly peasants, cooking girls, weavers, or dragon daughters who can build houses (as in the tale "The Dragon Daughter"). The helpers in Western tales are mostly animals found in forests like wolves, deer, and eagles, but those in Lin Lan's tales are plowing cows and domestic dogs or cats. In the Brothers Grimm tales, breaking taboos to obtain treasures reveals a bravery valued in the hunting culture, whereas in Lin Lan's tales, breaking taboos is often related to losing treasure and credibility. Overall, the Lin Lan series reflects the Chinese agricultural mentality (Li 2018:38) and different values due to different religious beliefs, as seen in interpretations of AT 461 by Wolfram Eberhard and Chinese scholars (Chen 2010:73–74; Liu 2016). (For a collection of more than forty fairy tales from the Lin Lan series, see Zhang 2021.)

The academic value of the Lin Lan series lies in its principle of collecting tales without eliminating repetitions or repeated versions. As a result, many tales contain different local dialects characteristic of the farming peasants of different ages and genders from whom the tales were collected (Li 2018:39). Clearly, the tales in the Lin Lan series are easily identified through historical records, and it is reasonable to say that the impact from the Lin Lan series upon the generations growing up in early and mid-twentieth-century China played an important role in the continuation of the oral tradition today.

FAIRY TALES AND THE STEREOTYPES
TOWARD CHINESE CULTURE AND
PEOPLE IN GLOBAL CONTEXT

The goal of rediscovering Lin Lan and the Lin Lan series of folk and fairy tales is to set the narratives in their historical context and analyze their significance. Aside from Chinese social and literary history, there is one more important feature of the series in regard to the introduction of Chinese folk and fairy tales to Western audiences at the beginning of the twentieth century.

As discussed earlier, the introduction of Western concepts such as nation, nationalism, folklore, and fairy tales was seen by the Chinese elites as a means to celebrate the rise of the Chinese nation. Along the way, *tonghua* has also metamorphosed into a unique Chinese genre (Zhang 2018, 2019a), being more of a cultural symbol than an indexical motif, as Ben-Amos (1995) proposes (Zhang 2019b). Interestingly, there was also a wave of publications that introduced Chinese folk and fairy tales to the Western world, though clearly from different ideological perspectives. For example, Béla Balázs's self-invented *The Cloak of Dreams: Chinese Fairy Tales*, mentioned earlier (also in English translation, 2010). Other examples include *Some Chinese Ghosts* (Hearn 1887), *The Chinese Boy and Girl* (Headland 1901), *Chinese Fairy Stories* (Pitman 1910), *Chinese Fairy Tales: Forty Stories Told by Almond-Eyed Folk* (Fielde 1912), *Gleanings from Chinese Folklore* (Russell [1915] 1973), *A Chinese Wonder Book* (Pitman 1919), and *The Chinese Fairy Book* (Wilhelm 1921).

The problems with these translations were obvious, even in the eyes of Chinese scholars at that time. For instance, (a) the tales were mostly taken from classic texts without the oral element; (b) there was no clear distinction between folktales, fairy tales, myths, and legends, and no identification of regional differences (significant given the diversity in China); and (c) the "Chinese elements" were generalized, sometimes even adopting Western plots to tell "Chinese" stories (Li 2018:34–35).

Partly due to these problems, North New Books published their "Zhengqiu Minjian Gushi" (征求民间故事, Call for Folk Tales) under the name of Lin Lan in *Yusi* (语丝) magazine in December 1927 (vol. 4, no. 1) (Li 2018:35), leading to the Lin Lan series. (*Yusi* was the publication of the Yusi Society, a crucial organization in the history of modern Chinese literature, which started in late 1924 and ended in early 1930. Zhou Zuoren was one of the two editors in chief.) The call emphasized: "When recording a tale, please use understandable plain language and write it out as it is, but not to exaggerate or add so that the original truth is lost" (Zheng 2006:107). The series also reflected the prevalent and dominant status of translating and studying (and even writing) folk and fairy tales in the development of folk literature and folkloristics in the 1920s and 1930s in China.

Clearly, in the first half of the twentieth century, nearly all the translations of Chinese folk and fairy tales (as well as collections that included myths and literary tales) were either from sources that were overgeneralized in terms of regionality, temporality, orality, and authority, like those mentioned earlier, or from a regional source but with different purposes. For example, Wolfram Eberhard (1937b, 1965) tried to change the situation by introducing Chinese folktales to the West, but his contribution in this regard also created certain inaccuracies and even stereotypical images of Chinese folk and fairy tales by mixing the genres and motifs and making arbitrary guesses in terms of the origins of some tales (Chen 2010:74; Liu 2016:49).

Wolfram Eberhard doubtlessly played a crucial role in introducing Chinese folk and fairy tales to the West, representing an academic departure from previous missionaries' works because "earlier purveyors of purportedly Chinese folktales to Western audiences either had translated art stories which differed considerably in style and purpose from the true folktale or had Europeanized the Chinese texts" (Dorson 1965:xxix). Richard Dorson wrote that "the one Western scholar who has made the oral Chinese folktale his specialty is Wolfram Eberhard" (1965:xxviii), and he praised Eberhard's *Chinese Fairy Tales and Folk Tales* (1937b), calling it

> a landmark in the history of Chinese folktale studies. For the first time it presented to the Westerners the oral folktale culled from the inaccessible little books and periodicals where Eberhard's Chinese colleagues had recorded their field work and from the unpublished texts of his friend Ts'ao Sung-yeh [Cao Songye]. (Dorson 1965:xxix)

However, in Eberhard's 1937 collection (published first in German and then English), there are 137 tales (60 categorized as "fairy tales" and 77 as "legends, myths, jokes, anecdotes"); 86 of them were from the Lin Lan series. The English collection purports to have been "collected and translated by Wolfram Eberhard," but Eberhard did not explain how he collected these tales. He claims in the introduction that "I have taken them [the tales] down as they were related to me, as nearly word for word as possible, and I have only altered enough to be sure that a fairy tale appears and not a scientific treatise" (1937b:xiv). Throughout the introduction, the name "Lin Lan" is not mentioned once. In Eberhard's 1965 collection, *Folktales of China*, there are 79 tales (43 tales from 19 different volumes in the Lin Lan series), and most of them were selected from his 1937 collection. In the introduction, Eberhard does not mention Lin Lan, but lists "Lin Lan (collector)" in the index and in the bibliography.

Clearly, what Eberhard introduced to Westerners in his collections (1937b, 1965) was largely based on the Lin Lan series. Clearly, it was the value of oral tradition in China that attracted Eberhard so that he claimed: "The present collection of tales is not diluted fare. In them it is the peasant, the child, the old woman, or even the student, who is speaking" (1937b:xiv). Had he introduced Lin Lan properly, the Grimms of China would have been better known to the world today.

There is no doubt that Eberhard's work on Chinese folklore has been influential and well-respected, both within and outside of China, along with his even greater impact upon China studies in general. For example, Eberhard's works have been translated into Chinese. When he passed away, scholars wrote memorial essays even though they did not know him personally (see Yang 1992; Zhong 2001). Outside China, Eberhard delivered the California Folklore Society (now the Western States Folklore Society) Archer Taylor Lecture in 1983 and published many important works on Chinese folklore.

However, it is meaningful to point out that although Eberhard acknowledged his Chinese fieldwork collaborator, Cao Songye, as mentioned earlier, for providing him with the Chinese tales, Eberhard did not explain how he got hold of the booklets from the Lin Lan series. In fact, Eberhard also did not properly acknowledge another "reluctant folklorist" who helped him in the 1940s in Chinatown in San Francisco (Buccitelli 2014:400). Indeed, there have been many examples of "reluctant folklorists" (co-fieldworkers, local collectors, and tradition-bearers) whose contributions to the advancement of scholarship were not properly recognized for various reasons. For example, Anthony Buccitelli has discovered the story that when Jon Lee (1915–1986) was used by Paul Radin and Wolfram Eberhard in the 1940s for the WPA (Work Projects Administration) project, Lee's name was not mentioned at all in the republished *The Golden Mountain: Chinese Tales Told in California* (Lee 1971), even though Lee was the person who collected those tales, and "More strikingly, Eberhard's preface to the new edition omits Lee's name" (Buccitelli 2016:4).

When Stith Thompson wrote his influential *Folktale* (1946), he did not include Chinese tales due to the lack of sources, but he used Eberhard's works as a reliable source when he revised the *Motif-Index of Folk-Literature* (Thompson 1955–1958) and *The Types of the Folktale* (Aarne and Thompson 1961), believing that Chinese tales were mostly repeated through printing and that collecting oral tales only began to take place in East Asia at that time (Thompson 1946:421, n22). This unfortunate and misinformed judgment was clearly based on previous publications of Chinese folk and fairy tales, including Eberhard's works. Had he known of the rich oral collections in China, like the Lin Lan series, when he was working on motifs and tale types in the early twentieth century, he would have had a different view of Chinese tales.

A few decades later, however, Nai-tung Ting used the Lin Lan series for his *A Type Index of Chinese Folktale* (1978).

In conclusion, this chapter surveys the transformation of the European fairy tale to Chinese *tonghua*, and the use of *tonghua* in the past century in China—how it aided in the construction of a new Chinese national identity by creating three different forms from it: literary *tonghua*, folk *tonghua*, and children's literature. With a discussion of the Lin Lan phenomenon in relation to the Grimm Spirit, this chapter also goes on to discuss the use of tales in a global context, where the history of translating and introducing them shows how negative stereotypes of the Chinese were shaped. Fortunately, as public and academic interests in Chinese folk and fairy tales have increased in recent years (e.g., Roberts 1979; Zhong and Lin 1991; Giskin 1997; Beauchamp 2010; Jones 2011; Chin 2015; Zhang 2021), more contemporary tales from China have become accessible to readers from different backgrounds, which will undoubtedly improve cross-cultural communication and understanding.

Chapter 4

The Moon Man

A Tale in Telling for a Thousand Years

This chapter extends the discussion of the continuity of *gushi* (stories/tales) to the specific tale, "Predestined Wife," and examines how this tale has been actively told for over a thousand years. Building upon a seminal study on the migration and evolution of this tale, I argue that previously existing cultural symbols in oral and written narratives are the essential foundation for the "import" of a new tale, and that the *vitality* of a tale lies in its becoming the *core identity marker* of the culture. It thus gains vitality by relating the elements in the tale to the *fundamental beliefs and values* in the culture (Zhang 2014, 2020b).

The first of the following two sections surveys the tale's textual and contextual histories; examines the changes of the tale from the ninth century to the twenty-first century; and discusses how these changes should be seen through the lens of *core identity markers* and *arbitrary identity markers*, *vitality* and *validity*. The second section focuses on the continuity of storytelling in the twenty-first century by looking at one specific storyteller who is representative of the last generation of traditional storytellers and the ICH Bearers in China.

THE TEXTUAL AND CONTEXTUAL
HISTORY OVER A THOUSAND YEARS

Folklorist Archer Taylor's (1959) study of the "Predestined Wife (Mt. 930*)" set a benchmark for the historic-geographic method in the studies of folktales in general and for the tale type ATU 930A in particular. No attempt has ever been made in the past decades to further the study of this tale regarding its symbolism of the key elements (motifs or symbols) or the method used in the study (Yassif 1999:477n; Shenhar 1983:134–154; Schwarzbaum 1968:143–172; Ben-Amos, Noy, and Frankel 2006:359). While the historic-geographic method is criticized for its "technical and methodological faults" (Hodgen 1942:368) and for being unable to "succeed in making sense out of the results of the many separate studies," the value of this approach "as a method, not a theory" (Goldberg 1984:12) has been well recognized and maintained to a certain extent (Thompson 1946, 1955–1958; Utley 1974). It is not enough to only criticize the method for its neglecting the social setting and values of folktales while focusing on the skeletal outlines for constructing a type index, even with the understanding that "the type index is intended as a tool and not a terminus for the folklore scholar" (Dorson 1965:xv); folklorists need to advance it based on its merit by looking at the broad social and cultural context beyond textual context (Ben-Amos 1993, 2014).

In his study, Taylor's goal is not only to apply the method to trace the origin of this tale, but also to examine the wide migration and dissemination of the tale, which is also the goal of some other studies (Brednich 1986:207–211). Taylor finds that forty-four other non-Chinese versions existed in Asia and Europe over a period of twelve centuries, setting an example for scrutinizing the details not only of this tale itself, but for any particular tale type study. Taylor challenges previous conclusions made by Cosquin, for example, that the tale was spread from India to China and all versions of the tale are "ultimately of Buddhist origin" (Taylor 1959:48) and that the interpretation of the Oedipus story is a "change of sex" invented from this type of tale (80), and challenges Aarne that "the tales of a predestined marriage rest upon an Oriental belief, which he [Aarne] regards as characteristically Indian" (81). He also objects to the idea of *Urform* (82), but promotes the idea of multiple transmissions. Taylor's challenges and conclusions remain insightful and inspiring, his questions for later generations are still valid, and his contribution is immense. In fact, Taylor touches upon an essential point in folktale study—different methods should be applied to the studies of tales with different cultural origins and backgrounds. It is in appreciating this enlightening approach that this author explores the deep cultural context for the adaptation and transmission of the "Moon Man" figure in the Chinese tale and society.

Taylor's central questions about "how much older it may be" and "where the tale originated" (Taylor 1959:48), however, seem to have remained unanswered, and thus become the goal of this study. He notices that the tale had been known in China for over a thousand years, and, with his novel evidence and creative analyses, concludes that "in any case, it has been twice carried across the continent of Asia and apparently from China and not from India" (78). He admits, though, that "it is obviously impossible to determine whether the original tale had a religious or a historical import" (81) after commenting that "the earliest Chinese versions are historical or pseudo-historical traditions" (47). Taylor focuses on the elements themselves without further examining the cultural and historical grounding for the formation and trans-formation of those elements (and of the tale itself) in any specific culture.

In continuing Taylor's study of this specific tale and rethinking of the method, this study will respectively look at the Moon Man (or "the old man in the moonlight," *yuexia laoren* 月下老人 or *yuelao* 月老) element in the formation of the tale in the Tang dynasty (618–907); the prototype of this ele-ment in texts since the late Zhou Dynasty (1100–771 BCE); the development of the element and the tale after the Tang dynasty; and the variants of the tale in current oral tradition in China.

The tale "Predestined Wife" first appeared in China with the title "Engagement Shop" (*dinghundian* 订婚店, or Fix-Marriage Shop) in a col-lection *Continued Records of the Strange (Xu You Guai Lu* 续幽怪录) by Li Fuyan (李复言ca. 827–836) (1973), and has been preserved in various texts or oral variants. For example, some of the stories in this collection, including the one in question, were later collected in the encyclopedic *Extensive Records of the Taiping Era (Taiping Guangji* 太平广记) by Li Fang (925–996) (2008, Vol. 159:1142) and eleven other scholar-officials under the imperial order. There are two sources in which the tale is preserved: one is *Taiping Guangji* and the other is in the collection entitled Shuo Fu, and the name of *Xu You Guai Lu* was also known as *Xu Xuan Guai Lu* (续玄怪录). The version in *Taiping Guangji* (chap. 14, Vol. 159) was also collected *Complete Collection of the Four Treasures (Siku Quanshu* 四库全书). The ninth-century version can be summarized as such (Taylor 1959:45):

A young man named Wei-Ku wishes to marry, but searches in vain for a suitable wife. He encounters an old man reading a book in a strange script. The young man can read foreign languages, including Sanskrit, but cannot read this script and asks what it is. He is told that it is the script of the underworld, and that the book is a list of fated marriages. The young man asks whether he will marry the girl he is then interested in, and the ancient tells him that he will not, but that his foot is already bound to the foot of his future wife by a red cord. The girl is now only three years old. The old man takes the youth to see this child, but the youth is very dissatisfied because she seems very ugly and is apparently of low station. He decides to kill the little girl and to escape his destiny and sends a slave with a knife. The slave succeeds only in slashing her forehead. Fourteen years later, the young man has become an official. He marries a beautiful upper-class girl, who always wears a beauty mark on her forehead. After they have been married a year or more, she tells him how she was wounded by a madman when she was a little girl. Then the husband explains it all to her. They live happily ever after. The shop where the young man first met the old man came to be known as the "Fix-Marriage [Engagement] Shop."

Taylor summarizes the essential elements in the tale type as having: (a) a prophesied marriage to a girl of a lower class, (b) an attempted murder with a resulting scar, and (c) the fulfillment of the prophecy with disclosure of the situation by the scar (1959:50). It is mainly based on these three elements that Thompson classified the tale type—AT 930A, which is now known as ATU 930A (Uther 2004).

Taylor did not include the Moon Man element in his summary of the essential elements in the tale. It is possible to discern from his analyses that, first, he treats the Moon Man to be equivalent to the prophecy element, which is in "typical introduction of Mt. 930, a tale [type] about the predestined marriage," considers the traces of the Moon Man to be also available in "Western versions," and finally infers "that it is not an essential and original element" in this tale type (1959:75). He also notes the association of the moon (not the Moon Man) with marriage, arguing that it cannot be the proof "that the tale is a Chinese invention" because this association "is very widely known" (47). Second, Taylor does not compare the Moon Man in this tale with similar "old man" or prophecy elements in tales of the same type, which may be a reason for his somewhat paradoxical reasoning: on the one hand, he thinks the Moon Man is not "a Chinese invention" and that "this belief cannot therefore be used to prove the Chinese origin of the tale" (47), but on the other hand, he notices that the Moon Man element, along with the red cord element, "does not appear to be ideas known in India," but are "characteristically Chinese" (75). As a result, Taylor focuses on other elements (e.g., red cord, scar, hair), hoping for the future findings of reminiscences in order to "have a valuable clue to the history of the tale (75).

However, it is crucial to make a distinction here: The Moon Man element in association with marriage is unique in Chinese culture both before and after the formation of this tale in the ninth century. It is the intention of this study to demonstrate that the Moon Man is essential to the tale, originated from historical text and practice, was used later to convey a religious message, and contains fundamental Chinese cultural values.

Regarding the tale type and motif, it may be worth noting that there is not a tale type for the "predestined husband" parallel to the "Predestined Wife" (ATU 930A), while the related tale types are AT 930 "The Prophecy"; AT 930* "Fate Foretold as Punishment"; AT 930A (formerly 930*) the "Predestined Wife"; AT 930B "Prophecy: At Sixteen Princess Will Fall in Love with Forty Arabs"; AT 930C "Fated Bride Abandoned in Boat"; AT 930D "Fated Bride's Ring in the Sea"; AT 931 "Oedipus" (Aarne and Thompson 1961:325–328). But, there are related motifs such as Motif T22 Predestined lovers; T22.1 Lovers mated before birth; T22.2 Predestined wife; T22.3 Predestined husband; T22.4 Lovers fated to marry each other born at the same time (Thompson 1955–1958, (5):335).

The imperfection of AT-type from AT 930 to AT 949 has been pointed out with tales in other cultures (Racênaitê 2007:101–112), and modifications are made with commonly seen Jewish examples (Shenhar 1983). In his ground-breaking work on the Chinese tale type index, Ting follows the AT types regarding these related tales, while he identifies over 200 distinctive Chinese tale types (Ting 1978:152).

The fact that AT-type does not apply to or include many tales from many other cultures may reveal the historical limitation of Eurocentric cultural orientations in compiling the tale-type index. For example, type AT 930A and motif T22 (predestined lovers) do not exist in West Africa (Clarke 1958), Central Africa (Lambrecht 1963), Madagascar (Haring 1982), the West Indies (Flowers 1952), Australian aboriginal oral narratives (Waterman 1987), and early Irish literature (Cross 1952), nor in Taylor's (1959) rich collection from over ten countries, Bulgaria (Roth and Wolf 1994), Polynesia (Kirtley 1971), or North America (Baughman 1960).

After all, as Robert Georges points out, "the emergence of tale-type as a technical term for a construct, however, is most closely bound up with the development of the tale-type index and the evolution of the historic-geographic method," and "the tale-type as concept and construct would appear to be biologically based," thus, in different cultures there would be different "conceptualization, characterization, and analysis of narrating and narrative, whether or not we acknowledge or reveal that fact by identifying the construct and its conceptual base with a term such as tale-type" (Georges 1983:21, 28). Unfortunately, the recent *The Types of International Folktales* is still criticized for this shortcoming, although the author believes that it "has eliminated or mitigated these faults" such as too much emphasis on male characters, Eurocentrism, and lack of genre distinction (Uther 2004:8–9).

We should now take a close look at the character of the Moon Man in the earliest version in the Tang dynasty in relation to the versions thereafter. This examination addresses this question: Would this tale have continued to become popular in Chinese (official and popular) traditions into the present day without the Moon Man element? The description of the Moon Man in the tale is itself unique. In Taylor's summary, the Moon Man is reading "the script of the underworld, and that the book is a list of fated marriages." According to the original text (translation by Wang 1944:104–106; also Birch 1961:44): The "old man" replied with a smile: "It is not a book to be found in this world. It is a book of the netherworld (*you ming zhi shu* 幽冥之书)" (here, *you* means ghost or ghost-like, and *ming* means the world of the dead). The young man then asked, "How does it happen that you, a man of the other world (*you ming zhi ren* 幽冥之人), have appeared in this one?" The old man replied: "Since it is the duty of officers of the netherworld to govern the destinies of men, how can they avoid visiting their domain? As a matter of fact, the highways belong half to men and half to ghosts (*ren gui ge ban* 人鬼各半); only most men are not aware of it." The young man then asked: "What are your special duties?" The old man answered: "The marriage bonds of the universe." (After the old man pointed out the girl) the young man angrily said: "I shall have her killed before I will marry her." The old man said, "It will be futile for you to try. She is destined to become a titled woman through the merit of her son." With this the old man vanished.

The half-man and half-ghost feature of the Moon Man is apparently emphasized in all Chinese versions and variants, though it becomes more human-like in modern times. This transformed figure (ghost-officer-man) is first seen in the tale as an "old man" and then appears to be patient and gentle, smiling, with all the characteristics of a wise gentleman. In this tale, the Moon Man is a more complex symbol than a prophet in the tale-type of predestined marriage (ATU 930), and thus should not be treated in the same way as a widely known prophecy element.

At a semantic level, in tales of the same type, none shows the same feature of the Moon Man as the "man of the netherworld." For example, in the seven tales in Volume 159 and five tales in Volume 160 in *Taiping Guangji* compiled in the tenth century, the "matchmaker" element was shown differently such as, a dream (*meng* 梦) as the prophecy; a diviner good at physiomancy (*shanxiang* 善相) and leaking secrets; a female *wu*-shaman (*nuwu* 女巫); a monk as the marriage foreteller; a professional matchmaker (*meishi* 媒氏); an expert in divination (*shanyizhe* 善易者); a fortuneteller (*buren* 卜人), and the falling leaves with poems telling the fortune. Specifically, among the similar tales, a dream is the prophecy in "Cui Yuan Zong." In "Wu Yin," which has the same plot as "Engagement Shop," the diviner is a friend who is good at physiomancy and tells the secret after drinking with the marriage-seeking young man. In "Lu Sheng" (also named "Mrs. Tao of Zheng Guo County" in *Xu You Guai Lu*), it was a female *wu*-shaman (*nüwu* 女巫). In "Zheng Huan Gu," there is a dream. In Volume 160, in "Xiu Shi Yang Ji," a monk is the marriage foreteller. In "Li Xing Xiu," it is a dream. In "Guan Yuan Ying," there is a professional matchmaker, an expert in divination, and a fortuneteller. In "Hou Ji Tu," there are falling leaves with poems.

Furthermore, the usage of Moon Man in this study was not used in the tale itself, but in a reference made afterward replacing the previous terms (e.g., *fake* 伐柯; *dabing* 大冰), and is still popular today, along with the general term *meiren* (媒人) for matchmaker, and *hongniang* (红娘, Red Maid) for a female.

At the ideological level, Buddhist ideas reached a peak by the Tang dynasty in Chinese history. However, one important fact was that these ideas were spread by borrowing the existent Daoist stories about ghosts and transformation. It is mainly in the struggle against Buddhist ideas that

Neo-Confucianism was developed by Confucian thinkers, like Zhu Xi (1130–1200), whose interpretation of Confucianism then became dominant in Chinese thought, continuing today. However, Zhu Xi accepted many practices not necessarily in accordance with Confucian ideas, as seen in his quite influential book *Chu Hsi's Family Rituals* (*Zhu Xi Jia Li* 朱熹家礼) (English translation, Ebrey 1991), showing the syncretic nature of Chinese thought. For example, Zhu Xi also advocated the practice of *fengshui*, which was basically Daoist practice by a *yin-yang* master (*yin-yang xiansheng* 阴阳先生).

By now, we see that the Moon Man element contains mostly Daoist characteristics, although the idea of predestined fate is also important to Buddhism. As Taylor notes, the Moon Man is not repeated in the stock of Buddhist tales in China (1959:48), and that the version in India does not have "one old man" but several "learned men" in the tale (48). We also see that the Moon Man is a unique symbol embedded with condensed meanings based on cosmological, historical, ethical, and religious values, and is different from the prophet in tales of non-Chinese origins, and it demonstrates the following fundamental beliefs and values in Chinese culture and history (see also chapter 2): First, the immortality of the soul, which makes it possible to have beliefs in spirits and souls as seen in the massive stories and the practice of ancestral worship in China. Second, the ideas of unity of man and nature, based on the notions of Yin-Yang and Five Elements and the Confucian ethics. These ideas "go far back to antiquity and to quite independent origins," "may be regarded as early Chinese attempts in the direction of working out a metaphysics and a cosmology," and "no aspect of Chinese civilization—whether metaphysics, medicine, government, or art—has escaped its imprint" (Chan 1963:244–245). These ideas have "central importance for the history of scientific thought in China," and "were the most ultimate principles of which the ancient Chinese could conceive" (Needham 1956:216, 232). They are best exemplified in later Daoist ideas and practices and continue in Chinese society through rituals and other events via the medium of tradition like the *yin-yang* Master through rituals, fortunetelling, grave-selecting (or siting, *fengshui*), and "arranging" predestined marriages. Thirdly, the searching for good fortune and avoiding misfortune, which shows a positive, rather than pessimistic attitude toward fate (Li 1995). The widespread belief and practice of fortunetelling in China is also a driving force for the creativity and flexibility of Chinese culture. When Confucian ideas avoided the discussion of afterlife, and Daoist ideas emphasized the natural way in the universe, it was Buddhist ideas that helped explain the wonder of the world of the dead. With different beliefs and values, ghost stories fulfill the function of entertainment, psychological comfort, and education along the way.

In addition, the family values emphasized by Confucian ethics are highlighted in the concept and practice of marriage. This aspect is unique in

Chinese tales. Furthermore, having a marriage with sons was seen as a virtue rewarded by the ancestors, and was also a cause for the good fortune of the offspring. Therefore, a good marriage was both the result of fortunetelling and the predestined fate. In this sense, the fortuneteller, or the Moon Man in this case, as the medium of tradition, reinforces the values and hope that the people live on.

Thus, the Moon Man symbol brings vitality to the tale for its continuity in China for over a millennium. However, this symbol was not an invention in the Tang dynasty, but rooted deeply in history, as shown below.

In *The Book of Songs (Shijing)*, known to be one of earliest texts formed from the eleventh to the sixth century BCE and edited by Confucius (551–479 BCE), there are several songs emphasizing the role of "*mei*" (go-between, or matchmaker) (媒). The word *mei* is related to *mou* (谋; plan, strategy), meaning to use speeches and plots to bring together two families (or family names) (Guo 2010; Xu 1963). The meaning and image of matchmaking are seen in these songs: In *Meng* (氓), there is this part: "It was not that I procrastinated, you had no good go-between; I prayed you not to be angry, and we made autumn the appointed time" (Karlgren 1950:40). In *Fa Ke* (伐柯), the song goes: "In hewing [the wood for] an axe-handle, how do you proceed? Without [another] axe it cannot proceed. In taking a wife, how do you proceed? Without a go-between it cannot be done" (Legge 1898 [1971:240]). In understanding this song, Arthur Waley ([1937] 1960) thought the matchmaker was not necessary in those days. For example, his translation reads:

How does one cut an axe-handle?
Without an axe it is impossible.
How does one take a wife?
Without a matchmaker she cannot be got.

He then comments, "This song represents, I think, the popular view that marriage was very simple matter, and a matchmaker by no means necessary" (Waley [1937]1960:68).

To the contrary, Bernhard Karlgren comments before his translation: "The marriage should follow the rules laid down by tradition, by the constant praxis in the families: an older married person acting as a go-between for the match between the young ones; the wedding ceremony should be combined with the sacrifices demanded by praxis," and his translations reads as such (Karlgren 1950:103):

How does one hew an axe-handle?
Without an axe one cannot;
How does one take a wife?

Without a go-between one does not get her.

It is from then on, *fakeren* (伐柯人) became a euphemism for matchmaker, and even appeared in works a millennium afterward. In *Pao You Ku Ye* (匏有苦叶), the song goes: "If a nobleman brings home his wife, it should be at the time when the ice has not yet melted" (Karlgren 1950:21). It is from this metaphor of ice, there developed the term "*dabing*" (great ice 大冰) or "*bingren*" (ice man 冰人) as another term for a (male) matchmaker, as seen in another valuable work on myths and customs written two thousand years ago (e.g., Ying Shao 应邵 c. 153–196) (1980, vol. 8:454), and as mentioned in the following example from *The Book of the Jin* (Fang 2008).

In *The Book of Zhou Rites* (*Zhou Li* 周礼, Book 2), known to be one of the earliest texts (from the third century BCE) in China, the position is described as such:

> *Meishi* is in charge of issuing marriage agreements to all people. All males and females must register their names and birthdays after they are initiated and have their own names. The law requires males to get married before 30 years old, and females before 20 years old all marriages must present gifts.

This record not only shows the official position was in power and in need but also the enforcement of the related (legal and ethical) law. Here we begin to see the prototype of the Moon Man, who arranged marriages by crossing the boundary of yin (female; other world) and yang (male; this world).

In *The Book of Rites* (*Li Ji* 礼记), it says: "Male and female, without the intervention of the matchmaker, do not know each other's name. Unless the marriage presents have been received, there should be no communication nor affection between them"; "rules of ceremony [ritual propriety] must be traced to their origin in the Grand Unity (*taiyi* the Great Ultimate). This separated and became heaven and earth. It revolved and became the dual force (in nature) (*yin* and *yang*)"; "the ceremony [rites] of marriage is the root of the other ceremonial observances [ritual propriety (*li*)]" (Legge [1885] 1967, Vol. 1:78, 386, Vol. 2:430).

In *Mencius* (*Meng Zi* 孟子), Mencius used this analogy for following the ancient traditions:

> When a man is born his parents wish that he may one day find a wife, and when a woman is born they wish that she may find a husband. Every parent feels like this. But those who bore holes in the wall to peep at one another, and climb over it to meet illicitly, waiting for neither the command of parents nor the good offices of a go-between, are despised by parents and fellow-country men alike. (Lau 1979b:119)

This is also early evidence for shaping the Chinese (Confucian) "face" value in social conduct.

In the early Chinese language, the word for "marriage" (*hunyin* 昏因 or 婚姻) indicates that marriage is an agreement between the father of the groom (*hun*) and the father of the bride (*yin*), and this *hun* also implies "dusk" when yin (female) comes to yang (male) (Xu 1973; Guo 2010). Thus, the father image, or an old man, also became the prototype of the matchmaker in relation to the official position of *meishi* in *Zhou Li*. It is a practice of the idea of yin-yang in the rites of marriage.

In *The Records of the Grand Historian (Shiji)* (1982) by Sima Qian (c. 145–90 BCE), a great Daoist believer, even though he studied under the Confucian Masters Dong Zhongshu (董仲舒) and Kong Anguo (孔安国) (Zhang 1992; Ji 2004; Xing 2005), the story of Zhang Liang (张良 c. 251–186 BCE), who was a historical figure and then deified, was mystified by adding the Moon Man element. The old man image here is a typical Daoist god with power to transform between the human world and the other world, and between day and night. For example, in vol. 1 of the ten-volume *Records of Unique Strange Stories (Duyizhi* 独异志) (1983) by Li Kang (李亢) of the Tang Dynasty, a painter in the Tang dynasty named Han Gan (韩干), who was good at painting horses, was blessed by a man coming from nowhere for an excellent horse, and the man proclaimed himself to be a messenger for the ghost.

Thus far, in reviewing the Moon Man element in its prototypical forms prior to its climax in the "Engagement Shop," we can see these intertwined strands: the yin-yang idea; belief in ghosts (or the immortality of the soul), official authority; authority of "father," ethical code in everyday life, transformation from an unknown man to a well-known man (or creation of a cultural hero), (Confucian) idea of the mandate of heaven, (Daoist and Buddhist) ideas of predestined fates, and rewards to positive efforts to change one's fate. We also see that the Moon Man element transformed in the following progression: the practice function of "an officer" (*meishi* 媒士) in charge of marriage, the wise man (Daoist immortal) in the moon providing supernatural knowledge/power through books as in the tale of Zhang Liang, the man capable of communicating with the netherworld through the symbol of ice, the traveling Buddhist monk who had supernatural power to solve the problems while proving the predestined fates (parallel to the Daoist idea of predestined fate), and, finally, the Moon Man in the tale of "Engagement Shop." It becomes clear that the Moon Man is a great integration of all the elements present and popular in the society. It also proves that a tradition that survives social upheavals must have vitality in its rooting in the fundamental beliefs of the culture.

This sketch of the history of the element before the formation of the Chinese version, in relation to the following millennium, may help clarify Taylor's concerns:

> But it seems to be impossible to say whether it is native Chinese tradition or whether it is a Buddhist exemplum. On the one hand it is a very old Chinese historical or pseudo-historical tradition but has not been found in the stock of Buddhist tales known in China. On the other hand, it teaches a lesson of great importance in Buddhism. (1959:48)

It may also tell that the tale has its Chinese origin, and it was later borrowed to teach the idea of "predestined fate," which was not an import from Buddhism, since many Buddhist tales borrowed or changed existing elements to bring a fresh look to the common people. The climax of such integration of various ideas in tales by the Tang made it impossible to totally divide the Chinese tales between historical or pseudo-historical, and between religious and non-religious.

Furthermore, texts during and after the ninth century have strengthened the symbolic meaning of the Moon Man as a core identity marker of the Chinese culture. Here are some examples:

As a gender contrast, the positive female matchmaker image of *hongniang* was developed and has remained popular since the thirteenth century. *Hongniang* was the name of a girl as a servant maid in a story entitled *Hui Zhen Ji* (会真记) (1982) written by the poet Yuan Zhen (元稹 779–831). The story was seen as a wonder legend (传奇) or a genre of short story in the Tang dynasty. The Tang version of the story became popular because of the idea of free love with a young person as the go-between, rather than a predestined marriage. But the ending of the story was sad in that the two in love did not marry each other, but married separately. With a twist by the playwright Wang Shifu (王实甫 1260–1336) in his *Romance of the Western Chamber* (*Xixiang Ji* 西厢记), the tragedy became comedy, and the lesser-known role of *hongniang* "became so prominent that the play is named after her . . . and has remained in the regional repertoire until the present day" (Wang 1991:10). As a result, *hongniang* (Red Maid) and *yuelao* (Moon Man) are still popular terms today in both elite and folk usages.

In the *History of Love* (*Qing Shi* 情史) by Feng Menglong (冯梦龙 1574–1646), the "Engagement Shop" was retold with the title of "Wei Gu" under the category of predestined love (*qingyuan*). In this book, Feng collected about 900 tales under 24 categories of love, covering a history of two thousand years. Feng also used such idiomatic sayings to highlight the stories in the category of "marriage of life and death," "husband and wife are not determined in this life; they were tied up five hundred years ago," "*Yue Lao* ties up the red cord," and "Ice Man delivers the word" (Feng 1956). Given Feng's renowned status, his retelling has doubtlessly furthered the popularity of this tale.

In the *Strange Stories from a Chinese Studio* (*Liaozhai Zhiyi* 聊斋志异) (1989) by Pu Songling (蒲松龄 1640–1715), one of the most important collections of ghost stories in China, there are 491 tales known as "narratives" (*zhi*) and "strange" (*yi*) categories. The book is seen to have followed the styles of the Jin and Tang dynasties, and is the ultimate retelling of strange tales and ghost stories. By then the Moon Man element was widely used. In the story of Liu Sheng, both the Moon Man and the red cord elements are used. In fact, the Moon Man element began to show both trickster characteristics and those of a worldly figure who could be bribed. In the story of Mao Hu, it mentioned that the marriage was pre-arranged by the Moon Man.

In *Dream of the Red Chamber* (*Hong Lou Meng* 红楼梦) (2010) by Cao Xueqin (曹雪芹 1724–1764), one of the most important novels in Chinese literature, the story of the Moon Man with red cord is retold in chapter 57, reiterating the role of the Moon Man as a god of marriage tying the predestined wife and husband together regardless of where they had been. It was told in a way to remind people of a common saying, showing how widespread the Moon Man element was in folklife.

With these records, we can see that the Moon Man was not only seen as a definite Daoist immortal or god in charge of marriage, as in the *Complete Stories of the Eight Immortals* (*Baxian Quanzhuan* 八仙全传) of the Song dynasty (Wugou Daoren 1937), but also a folk god with a clear image known from the *Six Chapters of a Floating Life* (*Fusheng Liuji*, Shen Fu 1763–1825), in which the Moon Man was "having childish face and crane-like hair, with one hand holding red cords, one hand carrying a staff hung with a book of marriage, and dashing in seemingly clouds and fogs"—an image seen nowadays in the temples (Shen Fu 2002:8).

Ideologically, the tension between Buddhist ideas and indigenous ideas around the seventh through the eighteenth centuries also helped the creation of numerous "strange and ghost" stories based on Daoist ideas or borrowing the forms of Daoist stories. The two great encyclopedic collections, *Taiping Guangji* (2008) and *Taiping Yulan* (1960), both compiled by Li Fang (1960, 2008) under the imperial order only seventeen years after the establishment of the Song dynasty, were certainly aimed at a new direction in the thought of ruling. For example, the Tang dynasty practiced largely cremation due to Buddhist influence, whereas the Song dynasty promoted burial funeral with the intention of reviving Confucian ethical and ritual practices (Zhang 1985:157–247). As a result, the polytheist Chinese culture further integrated different beliefs. In fact, none of the beliefs can stand alone in tales or everyday practices in China. In this respect, Taylor's question about "whether the original tale had a religious or a historical import" (1959:81) seems to be impossible to answer because the historical and religious elements are intertwined from the very beginning.

Through the earlier discussion, these points may be sufficiently proved that: (a) the Moon Man element (which Taylor does not consider to be a key element in the tale type) is essential to the formation and continuity of the tale itself because it is rooted in the Chinese fundamental beliefs and values, though it is not equivalent to the prophecy (ATU 930) element in tales based on other cultures; (b) Taylor's questions regarding the origin of this tale (1959:48) and "whether the original tale had a religious or a historical import" (81) are clarified by tracing the element in its two-thousand-year history in order to reveal how it has transformed into a thick symbol of different ideas; (c) the survival of an element or a tale depends on how or whether it is rooted in the fundamental beliefs and values in a culture, and that what can be adopted into a tale is either modified to fit into the existing system of symbolism or already has similar form or meaning to the new cultural system; (d) the historic-geographic method may still be a useful tool to examine the processes of transmitting and transforming meaning through the "web of significance" (in Geertz's sense, 1973:5) of the elements in a tale so long as they are put in their cultural context.

ORAL STORYTELLING IN THE
TWENTY-FIRST CENTURY

In the long history of folk literature in China, there are two somewhat parallel and interacting strands: the text tradition preserved and rewritten through elite literature and the oral tradition through oral telling/performing. The *Book of Songs* is a classical example (see one translation by Waley [1937] 1960), and the three *Grand Collections of Chinese Folk Literature* (1984–2009) is the most recent example of the text tradition at the national level. The earlier discussion shows a relatively stable text tradition in which the earliest version was reprinted again and again with little change, and from which we can conclude that the Moon Man element, along with the red cord, was the most influential element in the tale, while the scar is the essential link between a prophecy and its fulfillment regarding predestined marriage (only for the sake of tale type). The following discussion will focus on the oral tradition as seen in, (a) the seventeen versions collected through fieldwork in the 1980s in Northeast China (Liaoning Province) and later published in the *Three Grand Collections: Liaoning Volume* (1994); (b) the four versions collected in the region and published separately (Zhang and Dong Ming 1984:558–559; Jiang

1988:114–118; Xu 1989:17–19; Jiang 2007:160–163); and (c) one version collected by this author in 2006 (see the summary later). Overall, the oral telling of the tale has shown its vitality in its adaptation to the local beliefs and values.

In the first group of seventeen versions or variants in the *Grand Collections of Chinese Folk Literature*, the "Engagement Shop" was told by those who were illiterate or semi-literate and who lived in the same locale for several generations, learning the tale from their ancestors. Since Liaoning province was either the destination or pivotal region for the massive migration in the eighteenth through nineteenth centuries, and the origin of the Manchu ethnic group who ruled Chinese during the Qing Dynasty (1644–1911), this historical aspect was seen in most of the versions. Interestingly enough, the Moon Man element is central to the tale (along with the scar element), but the red cord element is not seen in any versions, nor the element of the book of the netherworld. In the local versions there are rocks or earth clods, instead of a knife or needle, used to hurt the girl. This may show that farming in mountainous regions is the mode of production in the northeast, while weaving is common in the south, and the book is not realistic to the peasants' life.

The second group of four versions further reveals these characteristics. The Moon Man is described as an "old man" in three versions, and the "old man under the moon" in the other. Three versions clearly tell that the young man, after the attempted murder, escaped hundreds of miles to the northeast—a possible reflection of their memory of family migration (mostly from Hebei and Shandong provinces) in the past two centuries or so. And the "young man" in all the versions appears to be a peasant, rather than a scholar.

In Hong's (1989) version in this group (Hong Fulai 洪福来, the telling was on July 15, 1985, in Xinbin County, Liaoning), the scar element is unique. It is a lost small toe, unlike other versions (scars on forehead, eyebrow, or stomach). It is meaningful if we relate this element to the region of Xinbin County known as the origin of the Manchu ethnic group. It also echoes the widespread folk belief that the difference between the Manchu people and the Han people (historically the majority in China) is the shape of the small toe. In Chinese history, disguising one's minority ethnic origin was a common practice during wars or social crises. This changed element reveals the unique local culture.

The third case is Tan Zhenshan's (谭振山 1925–2011) oral version published in 2007 (Jiang 2007:161–163). Comparing this oral version with his earlier published versions (in the first and second groups mentioned earlier), the main elements remained unchanged, but other minor elements changed; for example, the name of the young man, the village name of the girl. This is a normal phenomenon in oral telling to face-to-face audiences. As Nai-tung Ting points out in his studies of Chinese tale types, ancient literary versions of the tale types, especially those retold by professional raconteurs, frequently alluded to specific personal and place names in order to arouse interest. Even genuine oral tales are sometimes localized (though rarely with local color), and name individuals (though names such Wu the Loyal and Chang the Third are not much different in purport from Hans or Gretchen). (Ting 1978:10)

On June 20, 2006, Professor Jiang Fan (江帆) of Liaoning University took me and a group of her students to Tan's home in Taipingzhuang Village, Xinbin County, Liaoning Province. She had worked with Tan for more than twenty years by then. He told this tale to us and some neighbor children. Here is a summary of Tan's nearly seven-minute-long telling of the tale (with the title of *yuelao peihun*月老配婚—The Moon Man Matching Marriages—in his own words) that I video-recorded:

A young man named Wang Xiaozhu was poor and lost his parents early. One day he went to a temple and saw an old man who was moving earth clods around. Wang asked why, and the old man answered, "I am the Moon Man, arranging marriages for people. These clods are men and women. When they become husband and wife, they are in pairs." Wang then asked whether he would have a wife. The old man showed him two pieces of clods, one big and one tiny, and said that his wife was now in a cradle in a family in a village twenty miles away. Wang was upset, but went to the village and found the baby in the cradle. He wanted to kill the baby and threw a piece of earth clod at her. It hit the baby's face, and there was blood and crying. He thought he killed the baby, so he ran all the way to a village several hundred miles away. After some years of hard work, he owned a store with some helpers. Now he was nearly forty years old. One day an old woman and a girl were begging in front of his store, and said they were from Shandong where there was a flood, and had to escape to the Northeast. The helpers gave them food. The old woman felt those were good people, and said they had nowhere to go and since her girl was old enough, she wanted to marry her to a good man. The helpers asked their boss, and he agreed. So they got married soon. At the wedding when they blew the candles together, he noticed the scar on her face, and asked how she got it. She told him that she was hit when she was little. Wang then asked her where she lived. Wang was so surprised and admitted he was the person who hit her, and told her the whole story. She said that no matter what she belonged to him, and now they were married, and could not be separated. They then lived happily together as husband and wife.

By now we see that the Moon Man element has been essential to the tale for the past millennium, along with the scar element, but the book and red cord elements have changed into rocks or earth clods that the local peasants deal with in daily life. We can also see that this oral tradition is not parallel to the text tradition, which means the tale has its vitality in the oral tradition among the folk. This divergent oral tradition is meaningful to the local identity, and thus the tale gains its vitality and validity from the local daily practices.

Tan Zhenshan learned all his tales from his uncles and aunts through oral transmission (Jiang 2007; Zhang and Jiang 2021), although he received some school education in rural northeastern China. Some other storytellers were even illiterate or semi-literate. It can be assumed that for his generation in this region, the tale was passed down orally, but it is not known for how long this tale has been orally transmitted. It may be reasonable to assume that there had been interactions of the oral transmission (among those without text access) and text transmission (among those with text access) now and then in the past millennium so that the tale's plot and main elements have been changed little to maintain the traditional beliefs and values, but some minor elements have been adapted to the local customs, which together form the cultural grounding of a tale. Another aspect of the oral tradition is the various expressions of the Moon Man element in public places like parks, temples or caves where fortunetelling continues and tourism prospers, and in media (e.g., films and TV dramas). It is also worthy of scholarly attention to study the role of the internet in transmitting and transforming the Moon Man element and the tale itself in both oral and written forms.

Here, let us take a closer look at Tan Zhenshan as a representative of the traditional storytellers, demonstrating the continuity of oral tradition in China along the changes of the social and cultural contexts.

He was one of the five representative storytellers on the First List of National ICH Bearers in China in 2007. Parallel to the List of ICH items, the national List of ICH Bearers has also been regularly issued since 2006. The First National List of ICH Bearers (2007) includes a total of 226 individual persons under five categories: folk literature, folk games; folk arts; traditional handcrafts; traditional medicine. Among the 32 individuals in the category of Folk Literature, Tan Zhenshan is one of the five who are recognized through "folktales" (*minjian gushi*), while others are singers of folksongs or epics. As of 2018, five lists of ICH Bearers at National Level have been issued. The fifth list issued in 2018 includes 1,082 individuals covering ten categories of ICH.

All of the five storytellers on the First List were from villagers that had the tradition of storytelling among the villagers. Here is the snapshot of the five storytellers when they were recognized on the national stage in 2007:

- Wei Xiande (1923–2009), age of eighty-four, male, Zoumazhen Village, Chongqing, with a repertoire of 1,700 tales, 433 ballads, 947 proverbs.
- Jin Jingxiang (1928–2012), age of seventy-nine, male, peasant of the Geng Village (*gengcun*), Hebei Province; with a repertoire of 380 tales.
- Jin Zhengxin (1927–2009), age of eighty, male, peasant of the Geng Village (*gengcun*), Hebei Province; with a repertoire of 800 tales.
- Tan Zhenshan (1925–2011), age of eighty-two, male, peasant of Taipingzhuang Village, Liaoning Province, with a repertoire of 1,062 tales.
- Liu Defang (1938–), age of sixty-nine, male, peasant of Xiabaoping Village, Hubei Province, with a repertoire of 400 tales.

These individuals were first discovered through the national project of the *Grand Collections of Folk Literature* (Zhou 1984–2009) in the late twentieth century, and then were recognized at local and national levels. Along with this movement, some *gushicun* (story villages) were also discovered as a cultural phenomenon echoing the national effort of reviving traditions. In fact, historically, storytelling as a village tradition was common in China, with a few master storytellers possessing dozens or hundreds of tales in their repertoires. In such *gushicun*, storytelling functions as a distinctive identity marker of the village, as well as an important component of everyday life of the villagers. Currently, among many *gushicun*, these are better known: Geng Village in Hebei Province, Ditian Village in Zhejiang Province, Budun Village and Wujagou Village in Hubei Province.

As one of those *gushicun* (storytelling village), Geng Village (耿村) is representative. In 2006, "Geng Village Folk Tales" was officially recognized as a National ICH item, and Geng Village became an ICH Site under National Government Protection. Borrowing the metaphor of "one thousand and one night tales," a six-volume collection of 1,100 tales highlights the repertoire of the village (Yuan and Liu 2006).

Geng Village is about 30 miles east of the capital city of Hebei Province, and about 150 miles southwest of Beijing. This village was established in the fourteenth century, and now has a population of about 1,200 people. It is legendarily known as the place where Zhu Yuan Zhang's foster father was buried. Zhu Yuan Zhang (1328–1398) was the founding emperor of the Ming Dynasty (1368–1614).

In the survey in 2006, thousands of tales were told by more than 200 individuals, or 20 percent of the village population. From the 1980s till the 2010s, several surveys showed a consistent structure of the age distribution among those storytellers (with a repertoire of a few dozen to a few hundred), that is, each group of the senior, mid-aged, and young (including children of 8–15 years old) storytellers was about one-third of the total storytellers. For many families, storytelling is kept as a family heritage and a mechanism of maintaining harmonious relations among the villagers. Their tales cover a full range of forms/genres and historical periods. More than 200 ATU types have been identified among the tales from the Geng Village. In particular, younger and female storytellers are actively engaged in learning and telling stories (Yuan and Liu 2006:4).

As an individual storyteller, Tan Zhenshan is undoubtedly representative of the storytellers of his generation connecting the twentieth century and the twenty-first century. At the age of eighty-two, he was recognized as one of the five storytellers at national level. He was hailed as "last singer of tales from the agricultural era of China" (Jiang 2007:1) and as a "one thousand and one night" storyteller in modern China (Mao 2011), even though he was not known to most researchers outside China (Zhang and Jiang 2021).

Tan Zhenshan lived his entire life as a peasant in the village of Taipingzhuang, Xinmin County, Liaoning Province. At the age of fifteen, he dropped out of school to become a peasant for the rest of his life and also began his storytelling "career" (though he never made a living on storytelling). Even at a very young age, he would memorize all the stories that he heard whether at home, in school, or on the road. By the time he was in his thirties, he was well known in the surrounding villages as a storyteller.

Tan learned about two-thirds of his total repertoire of 1,062 tales from six closely related persons: his grandmother, his step-grandfather, his uncle, his elder brother, his elementary-school teacher, and a neighbor known as "xia hua jiang" (a man good at telling stories and jokes). Tan also learned a few hundred tales from others such as his maternal uncle and some neighbors. All of them lived their entire lives within the surrounding area, even though Tan's ancestors migrated from Hebei Province to this region at the end of the eighteenth century. His storytelling heritage or lineage clearly shows that Tan's tales are full of local characteristics such as the use of local expressions, accent, references to local mountains and rivers, and aspects of local lifestyle. No doubt, these characteristics partly enabled Tan to stand out among other folk storytellers who were also well known in this region, and some of them had their tales published in the 1980s when they were first discovered (Zhang and Dong 1984; Xu 1989).

As a traditional storyteller, Tan demonstrated his creative talents of improvising based on specific situations (Jiang 2004; Zhang 2014), but his creative changes rarely deviated from the basic rules of storytelling or structure of composition, whether in the sense of "oral formula" (Parry 1928, Lord 1960) or "functions" (Propp 1968[1928], 1984). Regarding the contents of Tan's tales, they are mostly in line with traditional Chinese storytelling: with clear traceable connection of tale types to the ancient versions and with strong emphasis on family ethics. Tan purposely told his tales to be positive and uplifting to his audiences, reflecting his personal ethical view as a peasant. In each of his tales, the protagonist is a kind, upright, and ethical person, traits which largely reflect his own personality.

Like other tales in general, Tan's tales not only reflect the social and political impact, but also illustrate how they reveal this personal identity. The change of Tan's favorite tales also reflected the social changes in China. For example, in the 1980s when China began its social transition through the Open-up and Reform movement, he often told tales like "A Paper Maiden Turned to a Real Wife" (Zhang and Jiang 2021), revealing the ethical and moral problems in marriage. It is still true today that a large number of bachelors, particularly in the rural areas, experience difficulties in seeking marriage due to poverty, imbalance of gender ratio in the population, and Confucian views about marriage and family. Thus, the need for the hope and magic in this kind of tales has always been strong in China.

The characteristics of Tan's storytelling can be summarized as such: (a) a long period of storytelling: Tan told stories as his hobby and specialty for nearly 70 years; (b) a huge repertoire of tales: a total of 1,062 had been recorded during his last years of life (20 more than the 1,042 tales that Jiang (2007) and Chen and Jiang (2010) reported); and (c) a "conversational" style of storytelling without theatrical/performative voices and gestures or any props: he could tell stories for hours in one sitting.

Furthermore, Tan also represented his generation of traditional storytellers who shared these commonalities: (a) being illiterate or semi-literate, or with up to middle school education; (b) living their whole lives in their home village; (c) building up their repertoires from those of family members, relatives, and neighbors, sometimes reaching; (d) making the characters in the tales localized; (e) telling many tales that are about historical figures, who are correlating with orthodox history, and many tales that explain local landscapes or legendary figures, or general ghost and animal tales; and (f) integrating social changes without changing the tale type (though they did not think in terms of "tale type" and "oral formula").

Today, the storyteller commonalities mentioned earlier are diminishing because the rural population is decreasing and those still in rural areas are experiencing age and gender-structure changes. For example, at the end of 2019 urban population exceeded 60 percent of the total population of China; that was an increase of nearly 50 percent from the end of 1949, when the urban population stood at only 11 percent. Today, *kongxincun* (literally, hollow-hearted village) has become a commonly used term for this phenomenon, which was seen everywhere in China; that is, in villages only the seniors took care of their grandchildren, while the middle-aged adults worked mostly in urban cities.

This phenomenon certainly creates challenges for the tradition of oral storytelling in general. As we see from the generation represented by Tan

Zhenshan, those storytellers grew up in the places where they had their stable local "soil" to absorb tales and pass them on to their next generation. With the drastic changes in those contexts, every storyteller and every story lover faces the problem of "how to find ways to survive." Perhaps new media or new means of communication can also bring new life to the traditional tales. For example, recent films such as, *Year of the Fish* (2007), *Crazy Rich Asians* (2018), *Nezha* (2019), *Over the Moon* (2020), and *Mulan* (2020) (in contrast to previous versions), are among many that are based on Chinese folk and fairy tales, and have already helped spread those tales and remind audiences of human cultural diversity. Or, perhaps, we have not yet fathomed how traditional storytelling is finding its way to survive today. However, there should be no doubt that oral traditions will sustain and thrive so long as the humans need to communicate with a sense of identity.

Part III

YANYU

PROVERBS OF STEREOTYPES
AND LIFE-VIEWS

Compared with proverbs in other languages, Chinese proverbs are undoubtedly used at the most frequent level in everyday life by the most members of the society regardless of age, gender, and social status. Furthermore, the number of several million proverbs in the Chinese proverb repertoire is hardly contestable by any others. This fact also shows that there is an intricate system of conceptual categorization of proverbs and related proverbial expressions for collectors and researchers, as well as different notions for users throughout Chinese history. While these systems are surely a headache for any proverb scholar who is attempting to sort through those categorical terms and create a "scientific" chart like the periodic table of chemical elements or a botanic taxonomy, the *folk* who use these proverbs or proverbial expressions in daily communication have their clear understanding of when, where, and how they use which ones.

For example, along with *yanyu* (谚语, proverb), there are also categorical terms like *suyu* (俗语, customary expression/saying), *xiehouyu* (歇后语, two-part proverb), and *yaoyan* (谣谚, balladic proverb; rhyme). In addition, there are such colloquial usages as, *laohua* (老话, old saying), *suhua* (俗话, common/folk saying), and *changyandao* (常言道, often-used saying). Sometimes *minjian* (民间, folk) is added to emphasize the nature of these expressions being from unknown sources, empowering the users themselves with "tradition." While each Chinese proverb dictionary or collection uses one category or another to define its own scope, there has never been one clear definition for any of those categorical terms.

In the national project of *Grand Collections of Chinese Folk Literature* (中国民间文学集成) (1984–2009), three major categories are used: folktales, proverbs, and ballads. Even with the narrow definition of "proverb" (e.g., excluding customary expressions and two-part proverbs), a total of more than seven million proverbs was collected all over China through that project. Recognizing some of the shortcomings of this project (e.g., lack of contextual information), the most recent national project of *Compendium of Chinese Folk Literature* (中国民间文学大系) (2017–2025) was launched in 2017 with the goal of publishing 1,000 volumes in eight years. The intention of this new project is to collect (mostly from published materials) and publish what was missed from the previous 1984–2009 project, limiting the time period from the early twentieth century to the early twenty-first century. In 2019, the first batch of 12 regional/provincial volumes on several categories were published.

Regarding the ongoing national project, it is particularly meaningful to note that in the first plan of the project in 2017, folk literature (*minjian wenxue*) was divided into ten categories: myths, epics, folk legends, folk tales, folk ballads, folk long poems, folk chante fables, folk dramas, proverbs, and folk literature theory. But in the revised plan about a year later in 2018, two new categories were added: riddles (*miyu* 谜语) and customary sayings (*suyu* 俗语). As a result, these two new categories have gained the equal categorical status to "proverb" (*yanyu*). In the previous project (1984–2009), *suyu* was defined as part of "proverb." Regardless of various definitions, one fact is clear: many more proverbial or proverb-like expressions will be collected to enrich and illustrate the grand proverbial repertoire in Chinese oral traditions.

Subsequently, scholars of Chinese proverbs are facing many challenges to develop the field of proverb studies, or paremiology, with relevant theories and methods based on such a large repertoire and changing social context. There are signs that Chinese proverb studies have progressed to consider proverbs not only from linguistic or literary perspectives based on the text itself, but also from folkloristic, sociological, psychological, and other cross-disciplinary views to emphasize the context with which proverbs are used to make sense of everyday life and to help maintain individual and group identities. In addition, other functions and meanings of proverbs are also studied for other purposes such as, teaching Chinese as a foreign language. In this sense, Chinese characters and their phonetic symbols, *pinyin*, are added to the examples in discussion not only to satisfy the need for those who may have an interest in the Chinese language but also to let readers identify the rhymes in those proverbs.

Chapter 5 outlines the developmental history of collecting and studying proverbs in China. Within this broad picture, one striking stroke is not to be ignored: Chinese proverbs in European translations. This has much to do with the issue of stereotyping through proverbs in cross-cultural contact, as tales/*gushi* or other folklore forms do. Applying paremiological methods, chapter 6 focuses on one particular proverb, "Older ginger is spicier," by examining its origin, development, and variation. More importantly, this proverb exemplarily expresses the *fundamental beliefs and values* in Chinese culture. Consequently, four life-views, including the changing attitudes toward aging and old age, are highlighted with representative proverbs.

Chapter 5

Proverbs with Chinese Characteristics

A History In and Outside China

While proverbial expressions have the commonality as the "salt" of human languages around the world, this salt has many nuances. Each of these flavors contains its local specialty, and together they make life diverse and joyful. Those specialties are the verbal reflections of the fundamental beliefs and values, as well as lifestyles in different cultures. In this regard, looking at the history of proverb collection and use in China will help understand the unique characteristics of Chinese proverbs, especially in cross-cultural context.

This chapter first surveys the long history of proverb collection and studies in China, while identifying key sources and developmental stages in relation to social and linguistic changes. Second, it looks at the European translations of Chinese proverbs since the eighteenth century and discusses how they have contributed to the public imagination of Chinese people and culture.

The central argument of this chapter is that there is a dynamic force in the transmission of traditions that is seen through the interaction of literary and oral traditions, while each tradition embodies the two intertwining aspects of vitality and validity. These interactions have also illustrated the operation of the *cultural self-healing mechanism* that is discussed in chapter 2.

Even though the history of proverb collection in China is long, the history of proverb studies is relatively short. The studies of those proverbs in either Chinese or other languages have remained few in number in comparison to studies of other folkloric genres. This short history can be outlined in these three stages:

The first stage of philological works by the missionaries prior to the 1930s, which included a number of translations and studies (Wilkinson 1761; Davis 1822; Perny 1869; Moule 1874; Lister 1874–1875; Scarborough 1875; Dawson-Gröne 1911; Brace 1916; Van Oost 1918; Plopper 1926; Edwards 1926), and with some excellent studies (Smith 1902; Hart 1937);

The second stage includes limited works between the 1930s and 1980s (Chang 1957; Mateo 1971–1972; Eberhard 1967, 1985; Lee 1979, 1981; Ting 1972; Sun 1981; Hermann 1984; Kordas 1987), but with some academic probes from different disciplinary perspectives.

The third stage features a surge of publications since the 1990s, mostly in the forms of collections or dictionaries (e.g., Kordas 1990; Weng 1992; Yan 1995; Paczolay 1997; Lau 1995; Osterbrauck 1996; Wang 1996; Heng and Zheng 1998; Lin and Schalk 1998; Huang 1998; Clements 2001; Rohsenow 2001; Mah 2002; Rohsenow 2002; Herzberg and Herzberg 2012; Jiao and Stone 2014; Zhou 2016), but with some specific topical studies like proverbs about women (Zhang 1992), power (Park 1998), and "face value" in Chinese culture (Yan 1995).

Nevertheless, these earlier works have pried open the lid on a treasure trove of Chinese proverbs, even though there have not been sufficient theoretical studies to establish a "field" of paremiological studies of Chinese proverbs. Even through European translations, one would be mesmerized by this treasure trove, because, as one scholar notes, "In no country does the proverb flourish more abundantly than in China" (Hart 1937:xix). Furthermore, "Even more important, however, is their [Chinese proverbs'] value as exhibitions of Chinese modes of thought," as a missionary in China observed (Smith 1902:6). Indeed, more than seven million proverbs were collected from all over China in the late twentieth century, as will be discussed later.

To establish a framework for this probe, I propose that the developmental history of Chinese proverbs can be seen through four chronological stages, and that these four stages also represent the four major sources of Chinese proverbs, which I would call "the four strands of Chinese proverbs." It may be of interest to compare these four strands with the four major sources of common European proverbs: Classical, Biblical, Medieval Latin, and cross-Atlantic sources along with the growth of modern proverbs (Mieder 2014:32). By "history of Chinese proverb," I consider these stages without following the conventional divisions in the fields of Chinese history (Bai 1980) and Chinese literature (Yuan 2005) inside and outside China (Ebrey 2010; De Bary and Lufrano 1999; De Bary and Bloom 1999). These stages are largely in line with the consideration by Deming An (2008), that is, Pre-Qin (prior to the 3rd c. BCE); the Qin to the Tang Dynasty (3rd c. BCE–10th c. CE), and the Song to the Qing Dynasties (10th c.–20th c.), excluding the twentieth century.

THE DEVELOPMENTAL HISTORY OF
PROVERB COLLECTIONS AND STUDIES

Of course, it is impossible to treat these four stages/sources separately because most of the current proverbs have evolved through different stages and changed in form and/or meaning over time, with some even gaining opposite meanings from their early forms as "counter-proverbs," or being twisted with different words to create different meanings for different purposes as "anti-proverbs" (Mieder 2008:50), as illustrated in this and the next chapter. Considering proverbs as the cumulative results of the transformation throughout these stages helps put them in historical perspective.

Stage and Source One (Classical Period, before the Seventh Century)

While the Oracle Bone Inscriptions (fl. 1300–1000 BCE) contain some phrases that are related to much later proverbial expressions, the overwhelming majority of contemporary Chinese proverbs are from the written classics. It was also the time when writing styles were standardized and the technology of paper-making and printing became mature, and when different schools of cosmic, philosophical and religious thoughts took root, such as Confucianism, Daoism, Buddhism, Legalism, or other schools. For example, more than 8,300 proverbs and proverbial expressions are identified from hundreds of classical works and documents during this period and the following pre-modern period (Wen 1989, first two volumes).

The most significant collectanea during this period include the following, to mention only a few. The *Book of Songs* (*Shijing*), which is known to be edited by Confucius (551–479 BCE) contains some proverbs that are still used today. For example, these two proverbs from the chapter of Folksongs (*feng*):

一日不见, 如三秋(兮). Yí rì bùjiàn, rú sānqiū (xī).
A day without seeing (him) is like three autumns!
投我以木桃, 报之以琼瑶. Tóu wǒ yǐ mù táo, bào zhī yǐ qióngyáo.
When I am presented with a peach, I return a jade pendant.

This second expression was transformed into a more literary form in a different piece in the chapter of Greater Odes (to the Kings by the literati):

投我以桃, 报之以李. Tóu wǒ yǐ táo, bào zhī yǐ lǐ.
Present me a peach, I return a plum.
(He who gives me a peach shall be rewarded a plum from me.)

As time went by, this form further evolved into the unique proverbial expression in the fixed-idiom form of a four-character (*chengyu*) phrase, as in this one:

投桃报李. Tóutáo bàolǐ.
Receive a peach, return a plum.

Still further, more variants are developed from this metaphor, and they contain more ethical meaning than in the earlier songs of love:

人敬我一尺, 我敬人一丈. Rén jìng wǒ yì chǐ, wǒ jìng rén yí zhàng.
He who respects me one inch will be respected ten times more by me.
滴水之恩当以涌泉相报. Dīshuǐ zhī ēn dāng yǐ yǒng quán xiāng bào.
A favor of a drop of water is to be returned with a flowing spring.

Some recent studies have paid attention to those classics as sources of proverbs (Wang 2015; Sun 2013; Huang 2015; Yue 2015; Xu 1984; Wang 2010). *Disquisitions* (*Lun Heng* by Wang Chong 27–97) and *General Record of Customs* (*Fengsu Tongyi* by Ying Shao ca. 153–196) (1980) are two such classics (Liu 2009; Wang and Gong 2014). *Commentary on the Water Classic* (*Shui Jing Zhu*, by Li Daoyuan ca. 466–527) particularly recorded many regional customs and weather-related proverbs (Xu 2009).

Proverbs related to agricultural production and weather, however, undoubtedly form the majority of the entire Chinese proverb repertoire, given that the history and culture of China are substantially based on agriculture. It is interesting to relate this point to one definition of proverbs which emphasizes metaphor (Dundes 1984; Mider 2006), to the extent that a "proverb" without metaphor should not be seen as a proverb. The metaphorical meaning of a proverb is also determined by the context of using it (Mieder 1996, 2006). An example of this point is how Wolfgang Mieder peels through the origin and use of "No Tickee, No washee: Subtleties of a Proverbial Slur" (Mieder 1996) by emphasizing the context of using a proverb, rather than looking at the text only.

In the four most important agriculture books, that is, *Book of Fan Shengzhi* (*Fan Shengzhi Shu* by Fan Sheng Zhi 氾胜之 fl. 33–7 BCE), *Essential Techniques for People's Welfare* (*Qimin Yaoshu* by Jia Si Xie 贾思勰 fl. 533–544), *Book of Agriculture* (*Nong Shu* by Wang Zhen 王祯 1271–1368), and *Complete Book of Agriculture and Administration* (*Nong Zheng Quan Shu* by Xu Guang Qi 徐光启 1562–1633), there are numerous weather- and agriculture-related proverbs and proverbial expressions (Han 2015; Tian 2009). For example, in one of the four books, *Qi Min Yao Shu* of the sixth century, we find not only agriculture proverbs based on experience and wisdom, but proverbs infused with Confucian ethical values as well:

耕而不耢, 不如作暴. Gēngér búlào, bùrú zuòbào.
Plowing without harrowing is worse than damaging.
耕锄不以水旱息功. Gēngchú bùyǐ shuǐhàn xīgōng.
Plowing and hoeing, shining or raining.
顺天时, 量地利, 则用力少而成功多; 任情返道, 则劳而无获.

Shùntiānshí, liángdìlì, zé yònglì shǎoér chénggōng duō; rènqíng fǎndào, zéláoér wúhuò.

Following the celestial timing and measuring the earthly advantage, there is more success with less strength. Following emotional mood against the Way, hard work yields no harvest.

Also from one of the key Confucian classics, *Mencius* (Mencius ca. 372 BCE–289 BCE), are these examples of integrating values into those sayings:

五谷者, 种之美者也; 苟为不熟, 不如稊稗, 夫仁亦在乎熟之而已矣.
Wǔgǔzhě, zhǒngzhīměi zhěyě; gǒuwéi bùshú, bùrú tíbài, fūrényì zàihū shúzhī éryǐ yǐ.
It is wonderful to grow the five chief grains, but if they are not ripe, they are worse than other low-level grains. So is the virtue of humanism, its value lies in its maturity.
天时不如地利, 地利不如人和. Tiānshí bùrú dìlì, dìlì bùrú rénhé.
Fortunate timing is not equal to advantageous location; advantageous location is not equal to human harmony.

Regarding family life as a key venue for social and ethical education in China, there has been a long history of "Family Books" (*jia xun*) as a category of Chinese literature and moral teaching. For example, *The Family Book of the Yans (Yan Shi Jia Xun)* by Yan Zhitui (531–591) used many proverbs by quoting "the ancients say" or "the proverb goes" (Yan 2011). In his preface, he noted that similar "family books" have been many, but he still wanted to write one for his own family, even though it may seem repetitious of the old sayings, such as:

屋下架屋, 床上施床. Wūxià jiàwū, chuángshàng shīchuáng.
Build a room within a room; set a bed on top of a bed.

In talking about the importance of teaching young children to love learning and be ethical, he first quoted Confucius's words:

少成若天性, 习惯如自然. Shàochéng ruòtiānxìng, xíguàn rúzìrán.
Teach the young a habit (of loving learning), their habit becomes natural.
and then, quoted an ancient "proverb":
教妇初来, 教儿婴孩. Jiàofù chūlái, jiàoer yīnghái.
Teach a wife when she first enters the house, teach children when they are babies.

In punishing young children for their wrongdoing and to make them remember the lesson, he said that bamboo sticks could be used to spank them:

父母威严而有慈, 则子女畏慎而生孝矣.
Fùmǔ wēiyán ér yǒucí, zé zǐnǚ wèishèn ér shēngxiào yǐ.
Strict and compassionate parents make children respectful with awe and filial.

This idea was later developed into:

慈威并济方得良子. Cíwēi bìngjì fāng dé liángzi.
Compassion and strictness together bring up a good son.

Today, these expressions are still common, with a more colloquial sentence structure:

严父出孝子. Yánfù chū xiàozǐ.
A strict father brings up a filial son.
棍棒底下出孝子. Gùnbàng dǐxia chū xiàozǐ.
A filial son grows out of sticks.

To encourage learning, he quoted the proverbs from a story written four centuries earlier:

Duke Ping of the Jin State (fl. 6th c. BCE) once asked Shi Kuang, a sagely master of music, "I am 70 years old. I have a desire to learn, but I am afraid it is too late."
"Why not hold a lamp?" replied Shi Kuang.
"How dare a minister make fun of his master?" said the Duke.
"As a blind man, how dare I make fun of my master? I have heard that 'To love learning at a young age is like the sunshine at sunrise. To love learning at mid-age is like the sunlight at noon. To love learning at old age is like walking at night with a lamp.' Walking at night with a lamp or without a lamp, which is better?"
"Good advice, indeed!" said the Duke.

Therefore, those three lines have become popular proverbs. Along with these variants that are still commonly used are:

幼而学者, 如日出之光. Yòu ér xuézhě, rú rìchū zhī guāng.
Learning as a young child is like the light at sunrise.
老而学者, 如秉烛夜行. Lǎo ér xuézhě, rú bǐngzhú yèxíng.
Learning as an old man is like walking at night with a lamp.

Overall, the classics of this period are one of the four major sources of proverbs in China. The collection, categorization, and application of proverbs during this period are in line with the use of other forms of oral traditions (e.g., folksong, legends, myths, jokes) as ways of educating and reforming (*jiaohua* 教化) the folk with Confucian humanistic virtue (*ren* 仁), and observing the reactions of the folk to the rulings of the governments by "observing the fashions" (*guanfeng* 观风), "listening to the music being played" (*lingyin* 聆音), and "inspecting governance" (*chali* 察理).

Stage and Source Two (Pre-Modern Period, 7th–19th c.)

The separation of this stage from the previous one does not indicate any discontinuity of the proverbial tradition, but is solely done for the sake of emphasizing the widespread use of "folk literature" (*suwenxue* 俗文学) from the seventh century on, which is considered here as another major source of Chinese proverbs. This term is used to refer to the widespread use of non-classical Chinese in writing as well as in forms (genres) other than orthodox poetry and prose (Zheng 1938:1). In fact, the Chinese term *suwenxue* is also translated as "vernacular literature." In the Chinese context, vernacular literature was first about the nonofficial language (e.g. nonliterary spoken style in grammar and vocabulary), as discussed here. Subsequently, it also implied the genre/form and content which was not orthodoxy. In Chinese, *su* is often interchangeably used as a noun and an adjective as in "folk" literature, "vulgar" or "customs," without the implication it has in European history.

This change is evident in the popular use of semi-classical grammar and vocabulary, written records of everyday and/or strange stories, which laid the foundation for the development of fiction writing in Chinese. Printing technology and social mobility were also among the factors that should not be ignored. As a result, official and nonofficial written records during this period contained numerous proverbs and proverbial expressions.

Extensive Records of the Taiping Era (Taiping Guangji) and *Imperial Reader or Readings of the Taiping Era (Taiping Yulan)*, both formed during the tenth century, collected nearly all literatures before the Song Dynasty (960–1279). The former contains the well-known tale of Chinese Cinderella (Waley 1947), *Yexian* (ATU 510), first recorded in the ninth century. The proverbs quoted in these two grand collections include:

一饮一啄, 系之于分. Yīyǐn yīzhuó, xì zhī yú fēn.
A bite or a drink, all predetermined.
一鸡死, 一鸡鸣. Yī jī sǐ, yī jī míng.
One chicken dies, another crows.
不救蚀者, 出行遇雨. Bú jiù shí zhě, chūxíng yù yǔ.
He who does not save the eclipse will be caught by the rain.

君子不镜于水, 而镜于人; 镜于水见面之容, 镜于人则知凶吉.

Jūnzǐ bú jìngyúshuǐ, ér jìngyúrén; jìngyúshuǐ jiànmiàn zhīróng, jìngyúrén zé zhīxiōngjí.

A man of virtue does not use the mirror of water, but the mirror of people. The mirror of water reflects a face, the mirror of people tells fortune.

This last proverb also shows a custom that continues today: people would bang the gangs or pots when there is a sun eclipse, believing that it would scare away the dog that is biting the sun. Thus, the translation can be: "He who does not bang the gang to save the eclipsed sun will encounter rain when going out."

Besides such encyclopedic collectanea, there are also some specific collections in this period that contain proverbs from the classics and contemporary variants or new ones. They are representative of the development from classical literary idioms to folk sayings or proverbs popular then, and that are still used today:

女爱不敝席, 男欢不敝轮. Nǚ ài bú bìxí, nán huān bú bìlún.

Women's love wears out before the mat is worn out, men's love wears out before the wooden wheel gets rotted out.

恭敬不如从命. Gōngjìng bùrú cóngmìng.

A better respect from a guest is to submit to a host.

马异视力, 人异视识. Mǎ yì shìlì, rén yì shìshí.

Strength distinguishes horses, experience tells apart people.

远亲不如近邻. Yuǎnqīn bùrú jìnlín.

Relatives afar are less beneficial than neighbors nearby.

忠言逆耳利于行, 毒药苦口利于病. Zhōngyánnìěr lìyú xíng, dúyào kǔkǒu lìyú bìng.

Loyal words are harsh to ear but good for behavior, strong drugs are bitter to mouth but good for health.

树怕剥皮, 人怕伤心. Shù pà bāopí, rén pà shāngxīn.

Trees are afraid of skin-peeling; people are afraid of heart-hurting.

若要好, 大作小. Ruò yàohǎo, dàzuò xiǎo.

To do well, do big as if small

(To get a thing done well, one needs to lower his status or ignore one's status.)

远水不救近火. Yuǎnshuǐ bù jiù jìnhuǒ.

Water from faraway can't extinguish a fire nearby.

嫁鸡随鸡, 嫁狗随狗. Jià jī suí jī, jià gǒu suí gǒu.

Marry a rooster, follow a rooster; marry a dog, follow a dog.

树高千丈, 落叶归根. Shùgāo qiānzhàng, luòyè guīgēn.

No matter how tall a tree is, its leaves fall to its roots.

衣要新好, 人要旧好. Yī yào xīn hǎo, rén yào jiù hǎo.

New clothes are good, old spouse is good.

千里送鹅毛. Qiānlǐ sòng émáo.

Go a thousand miles to deliver a goose feather.

The *Expanding Knowledge Sayings* (*Zengguang Xianxen* 增广贤文) of the late sixteenth and the early seventeenth century contained nearly 1,000 proverbs. Unfortunately, there is no contextual information for each proverb in this collection. But many of those proverbs are still used today, and many were translated into English (Perny 1869). Some examples include:

难合亦难分, 易亲亦易散. Nánhé yì nánfēn, yìqīn yì yìsàn.

Hard to be friends, hard to be apart; easy to be together, easy to be apart.

狗不嫌家贫, 儿不嫌母丑. Gǒu bùxián jiāpín, ér bùxián mǔchǒu.

Dogs don't see their owners' poverty; sons don't see their mothers' ugliness.

枯木逢春犹再发, 人无两度再少年. Kūmùféngchūn yóu zàifā, rénwú liǎngdù zài shàonián.

Dried trees sprout when spring returns; people can't be young again.

平日不作亏心事, 半夜敲门心不惊. Píngrì búzuò kuīxīnshì, bànyè qiāomén xīnbùjīng.

No wrong doings all the time, no fear at door knocks at night.

Ancient Proverbs (*Gu Yao Yan* 古谣谚) of the nineteenth century by Du Wenlan may be the most important collection and study of proverbs during this period. It is also the most frequently cited work on ancient Chinese proverbs. It contains a total of 3,300 proverbs and proverbial expressions (including ballads and rhymes) extracted from 860 ancient books with references (Du 1958). Some examples include:

钱无耳, 可使鬼. Qián wú ěr, kě shǐ guǐ.

Money can drive devils.

豹死留皮, 人死留名. Bàosǐ liúpí, rénsǐ liúmíng.

What is left behind by a leopard when it dies is its skin, what is left behind by a man is his reputation.

端午晴干, 农人喜欢. Duānwǔ qínggān, nóng rén xǐhuān.

A dry day on the fifth of the fifth moon is a farmers' joy.

好事不出门, 恶事行千里. Hǎoshì bù chūmén, èshì xíng qiānlǐ.

Good things don't get out of the house, bad things travel a thousand miles.

While there are numerous proverbs recorded in many anthologies (Wen 1989), the attention from those collectors or even researchers is mostly on the text or the intertextuality of the proverbs (An 2008:585). Rarely does it touch on the broad context of how the proverbs are used.

Stage and Source Three (Modern Period, Twentieth Century)

The pivotal change in the Chinese language (e.g., standardization of pronunciation, new grammar, new vocabulary, new fonts and low cost of printing), and thus also of literature and arts, is the movement of promoting *baihua-wen* (*baihua* for folk or oral speech, *wen* for writing, that is, writing literature as it is spoken in everyday life, rather than in traditional classical Chinese) in the early twentieth century. This change was part of the New Culture Movement that revolutionized Chinese traditional beliefs and values and gave birth to modern folkloristics in China as well (Zhang 2018). As a result, this period also generated a large number of new proverbs and variants of traditional proverbs, being the third major source of Chinese proverbs. They are also vital in connecting the past and the present.

Baihuawen, in contrast to classical written style, was promoted to use folk or oral speech in writing as a new genre. Although "*baihuawen*" is often translated into "vernacular," it was fundamentally about the reform of writing style, while spoken style had a much longer history of being "vernacular." *Baihua* had been used to mean common speech in contrast to "official" and classical style, while *wen* referred to writing. In fact, *baihua* began from the Tang as seen in the non-orthodox writings (as a marker between the first and second stages discussed earlier). By the early twentieth century, with massive publication of new literature, *baihua* (or *baihuawen*) had become standard in speaking and writing, and largely formed the current "common speech" (*putoghua*) or "Mandarin."

This linguistic transformation is widely seen in the parallel use of the fixed idioms as proverbs and folk sayings. For example, the classical literary form of

孤掌难鸣. Gū zhǎng nán míng.
Single palm [is] difficult sounding.
 was transformed into:
一个巴掌拍不响. Yīgè bāzhang pāi bù xiǎng.
One palm claps no sound (You can't clap with one palm) (cf., It takes two to tango).

Chinese paremiology began in the early twentieth century with the publication of a few specific studies of proverbs (Guo 1925; Xue 1936; Yue 2019; Chen 2019:28). However, most decades of the twentieth century in China witnessed wars and social instability, when all academic activities entered a traumatic period. It was in Taiwan where a prolific paremiologist Zhu Jiefan (朱介凡 1912–2011) spent his lifetime compiling an eleven-volume ethnographic collection of Chinese proverbs, containing some 52,000 proverbs (Zhu 1989; Guo 1997).

China's economic reform in the late twentieth century also positively influenced the development of Chinese folklore studies (Zhang 2018). At least two dozen dictionaries or collections were published in the last two decades of the twentieth century (Chen 2019:30). A six-volume collection of proverbs from Chinese classical literature included more than 20,000 entries (Wen 1989), and later a one-volume dictionary contained 15,000 proverbs (Wen 2011). However, the sources of these works are limited only to the classics and well-known authored literature.

One important paremiological issue of this period involves the definition and "author/creator" of proverbs by various scholars. According to an authoritative linguist, *yanyu* (proverb) is seen as a typical type of *suyu* (popular/vernacular/nonliteral saying) (Lü 1987:1), and, along with *xiehouyu* (two-part proverbs) and *guanyongyu* (fixed folk and proverbial phrases), is called *suyu* (Wen 2004:1). This view is widely accepted in the fields of linguistics, literature, and folkloristics. Similarly, in regard to the authorship of proverbs, the representative view in those academic fields is that "proverbs do not have clearly identified authors, and are created collectively by the folk" (Wen 2004:9). The most influential textbook of folkloristics emphasizes that "proverbs are collectively created by the folk" (Zhong 1998:310), which is also the notion stated in other major textbooks in Chinese folklore studies. This view is in clear contrast to what has been argued since the 1930s by paremiologists such as Archer Taylor and Bartlett Whiting who argue that "proverbs are not created by the folk but rather by an individual" (Mieder 2014:28).

The unprecedented collectanea of proverbs in Chinese history is the *Grand Collection of Chinese Proverbs*, as part of the trilogy of the national project (i.e., folktale, ballad, and proverb, total of 298 volumes) directed by Zhou Yang (1984–2009). This proverb collection (in 30 provincial volumes) contains a total of 7,180,000 proverbs (Ma 1984–2009). This number reflects the narrow definition of proverb used in this project, that is, it excluded *suyu* (customary saying/catch phrase 俗语), *geyan* (maxim/aphorism 格言), *chengyu* (fixed idiom/phrase 成语), and *xiehouyu* (two-part proverb/riddle 歇后语), not to mention those were seen as too politically sensitive or too erotic in content.

Naturally, there are some shortcomings to this project. One serious problem is that there is little contextual information about the users and the situations in which those proverbs were used (Chen 2019:33), not to mention anything about the origin or history of those proverbs. Clearly, this remains a task for current and future paremiologists—a challenge that is now being met!

Stage and Source Four (Contemporary Period, Twenty-first Century)

The problem of the previous text-centered collections of proverbs without contextual information is now dealt with by another ambitious national project, *Compendium of Chinese Folk Literature* (*Zhongguo minjian wenxue daxi*), launched in 2017 by the China Federation of Literary and Art Circles. It is expected to be completed in eight years with 1,000 volumes covering such genres of folk literature as ethnic myths, legends, tales, ballads, proverbs, epics, folk operas, and narrative and singing texts. This *Compendium* includes written and oral materials from the past century. The intention is to collect what was not included in the previous *Three Grand Collections*, with a guiding principle of "improving text with annotated context" by collecting information about the time and region of the use, meaning in use, along with related images, to comprehensive contexts (Chen 2019:34, quoting Deming An's words).

Obviously, the *Compendium of Chinese Folk Literature* is an effort of "looking backward" by reviewing the past. For example, a review of the studies in the past 40 years specifically on ancient proverbs lists dozens of publications on the topic (Zhao 2009:122; Ma and Zhao 2019). Another review on proverb studies in the past seventy years reveals that a disciplinary framework for "paremiological studies" is taking shape (Li 2001:30), as well as that of "history of Chinese proverbs" (Fu 2018:117).

Two characteristics of proverb studies in this period can be generalized here: in an academic sense, we see the shaping of paremiology based on folk literature and folklore studies. In a practical sense, we find the wide use of counter-proverbs and anti-proverbs as well as new proverbs, along with those standard or traditional ones, by means of media technology of computer and internet. This latter aspect also constitutes the fourth source of Chinese proverb repertoire. In this regard, the dramatic social and economic changes in the past four decades or so in China can be seen through the similarly drastic change in proverbs.

The use of anti-proverbs in Chinese proverbs is uniquely popular and fashionable because of its linguistic characteristics, that is, a higher percentage of homophonous (and/or tonal) words in Chinese than in any other languages. For this reason, a large number of symbols in Chinese culture are related to the homophones. For example, apples (*pingguo*) are used as gifts to mean "peace" (*pingan*) due to the sound-meaning connection of *ping*. Such uses of anti-proverbs are getting even more popular in commercial advertisements and media reports through the platform of internet:

一鸣惊人 Yì míng jīng rén (míng = bird singing)
To amaze the world with a single sound (act, feat). (Or, to become famous overnight.)
一明惊人 Yì míng jīng rén (míng = clear; bright)
To surprise people (oneself) with a clear vision. (Anti-proverb: An advertisement of a medical product of eye-drop.)
随心所欲 Suí xīn suǒ yù (yù = to desire)
To follow your heart as you desire. (A Confucius saying about being at seventy.)
随心所浴 Suí xīn suǒ yù (yù = to shower)
To follow your heart to shower. (Anti-proverb: An advertisement for shower equipment.)

Ironically, such anti-proverbs are often seen as "abusing" or "misusing" traditional proverbs. There have been times when the governments tried to ban the use of such fixed idioms or proverbs. But the uselessness of those official rules proves that anti-proverbs have their vitality because they are a dynamic part of the language.

In 2020, the COVID-19 pandemic changed the world in many ways. Such a historical event is certainly most instinctively reflected in the use of anti-proverbs or fixed idioms (or folk rhymes called *shunkouliu* 顺口溜 to be further discussed in chapter 7 on ballads/*geyao*) not only in everyday life but also in official uses. For example:

义不容辞 Yì bù róng cí (yì = righteousness)
Justice can't tolerate one's dismissal of duty.
疫不容辞 Yì bù róng cí (yì = pandemic; epidemic)
Anti-proverb: Pandemic won't let itself be ignored.
仁至义尽 Rén zhì yì jìn (yì = righteousness)
Humanism arrives, righteousness/justice is fully served/fulfilled.
仁至疫尽 Rén zhì yì jìn (yì = pandemic; epidemic)
Anti-proverb: Humanism arrives, pandemic completely is to end.

In addition, there are also some other characteristics of the use of "new" proverbs in recent decades: the adoption of foreign proverbs through loan translation; even by the national spokesmen, government newspapers, and TV broadcasters. For example, the most important newspaper/news media in China often use the proverb "One picture is worth a thousand words" (一图胜千言) with a "foreign" (or exotic) taste. However, the origins of the proverb in English has been traced to the 1920s (Mieder 1989:6, 1990:208), and studies show it to be from a Chinese proverb, Hearing something a hundred times isn't better than seeing it once (百闻不如一见) (Stevenson 1949:2611). This circle of "new" proverbs is another feature of the third and fourth stages/ sources.

Contemporary proverb studies in China have continued those conventional topics: (a) proverbs studies as a field (An 2008; Wen 2000; Xu and Li 2016); (b) proverbs of weather (Wang 2018) and agriculture (Li 2016); (c) proverbs in classics (Zhao 2009; Ma and Zhao 2019; An 2017); (d) compiling collections/dictionaries from different textual sources (Wen 1989; Wen 2002; Zheng and Jiang 2008, Wen 2011); (e) proverbs of certain philosophical or religious ideas (Liu 2004, 2014; Li 2005).

In addition, new topics are being studied: (a) the attitudes toward females in ancient proverbs (Zhang 1992; Geng 2005; Wang 2006); (b) proverbs of the minority groups in China (Li 1995) like Kazakh (Yuan 2013), Mongolian (Mei 2018), Tujia (Lei 2006), Tibetan (Zhaxihuadan 2011), Uygur (Fu and Chen 2014); (c) proverbs in Chinese dialects (Zhang 2012; Hu 2015); (d) proverbs in teaching Chinese as a foreign language (Shen 2011; Wang 2012); (e) proverbs of occupations like medicine (Luo and Lin 2008), handcrafts (Pang 2017), and martial arts (Peng 1988; Cui 2008); (f) proverbs used by contemporary political leaders like Deng Xiaoping and Xi Jinping (Feng 2001; Li 2015).

In proverb studies, there has been an effort to establish a "paremiological minimum" (Mieder 1992), which, by means of statistical investigation and survey, highlights the most frequently used 300 proverbs as the basis of paremiological studies. Clearly, the academic attention to current new proverbs and proverbial phrases is insufficient, because the emergence of new proverbs and proverbial phrases are not just linguistic or sociological issues, but also related to the fundamental beliefs and values in Chinese culture. For example, traditional expressions such as, "More sons, more happiness" (多子多福), "Raise sons to prepare for old age" (养儿防老), and "Marry a rooster, follow a rooster; marry a dog, follow a dog" (嫁鸡随鸡, 嫁狗随狗) are being replaced by current ones such as: "Get engaged with the white-haired" (白发相亲, older parents as matchmaker for their mid-aged child), and Twilight love (黄昏恋, older widows or widowers get remarried). Some "new" expressions in the twentieth century are already outdated and in the twenty-first century replaced by yet "newer" ones. For example, words for "senior/nursing homes" (老人院; 养老院; 敬老院) have become everyday words.

A GLIMPSE OF CHINESE PROVERBS IN TRANSLATION

This sketch of the state of interest in Chinese proverbs would seem incomplete without quickly skimming through addressing the short history of translating Chinese proverbs into English. This reality has more cultural than linguistic implications. For example, the proverb "No tickee, no washee" reflected a "translated" sentence structure from Chinese, while embodied a "rich" history of how early Chinese immigrants were viewed in the United States, and how such racial stereotypes are still out there (Mieder 1996). Therefore, translation is a double-edged sword: it can bring new ideas, but it can also perpetuate long-lasting stereotypes.

The history of European translations of Chinese classics (which contain proverbs) can be traced back to the Jesuit missions to China, represented by Matteo Ricci (1552–1610, Li Ma Dou 利玛窦 in Chinese). Indeed, the "studies of China," or Sinology, has a history of at least five centuries (Honey 2001). However, systemic translations of dozens of Chinese classics were carried out during the entire nineteenth century by the missionaries from Europe and the United States. One representative of this period is James Legge (1815–1897, Li Ya-Ko 理雅各 in Chinese), whose translations of *The Chinese Classics* (1861–1872) (including *The Analects* and *Book of Songs*, which contain many proverbs) are still widely used.

Specifically on Chinese proverbs, many missionaries collected and translated them as their "side-interest," but with the goal of better understanding Chinese minds through such folk expressions. Most of such translations were published in the nineteenth century (Cui 2019). For example, Joseph de Premare (1666–1735), a Jesuit from France, translated and edited the *Book of Rites (Liji)* into *Notitia Linguae Sinicae* (completed in 1728, and published in 1831), which contains at least four hundred proverbs or proverbial expressions. James Wilkinson's four volumes of *Hau Kiou Choaan or the Pleasing History* (1761) includes many proverbs with commentaries. The true identity of James Wilkinson is not clear, but it is suspected that Thomas Percy published under the name of Wilkinson, as examined from English literature (Min 2010:312).

By the nineteenth century, Robert Morrison (1782–1834), Protestant (later Presbyterian) missionary from Britain, compiled *A Dictionary of the Chinese Language* (1822), which included more than one hundred proverbs. John Francis Davis (1795–1890), British diplomat and Governor of Hong Kong, influenced by Morrison, compiled *Hien Wun Shoo. Chinese Moral Maxims, With a Free and Verbal Translation* (1823), which included 201 maxims and proverbs.

Paul Hubert Perny (1818–1907), Catholic missionary from France, compiled *Proverbes Chinois, recueillis et mis en ordre* (1869), which contained more than 441 proverbs and proverbial expressions, or translation of the Chinese proverb book (*Zeng guang xian wen*, a collection of proverbs and rhymes for children, formed during the sixteenth century), with Chinese text, and an additional 183 proverbs without Chinese text. Justus Doolittle (1824–1880), Presbyterian Board of Shanghai, *Vocabulary and Hand-book of the Chinese Language: Romanized in the Mandarin Dialect* (1872, 2 vols.), which contained about 700 proverbs and couplets.

Among these missionaries, William Scarborough, English Wesleyan Methodist missionary, not only compiled *A Collection of Chinese Proverbs* (1875, 1926 rev.), with a total of 2,720 entries, but also first categorized, indexed, and offered a preface for a comprehensive study of Chinese proverbs. Calvin Wilson Mateer (1836–1908, Presbyterian missionary from the United States, spent twenty-five years compiling *A Course of Mandarin lessons based on Idiom* (1892), which included about 200 proverbs and phrases.

Arthur H. Smith (1845–1932), missionary of the American Board of Commissioners for Foreign Missions, compiled *Proverbs and common sayings from the Chinese: together with much related and unrelated matter, interspersed with observations on Chinese things-in-general* (1888–1902), containing nearly 2,000 proverbs and proverbial expressions. Smith's collection also classified Chinese proverbs and proverb-like expressions under such headings as "parts of body," "weather" "the old villager" (pp. 272–275). Those entries were either from the Classics and Standard Books of each dynasty or from some folk usages that he heard directly or indirectly. Smith's discussion about the history, value, variation, and translation of Chinese proverbs is still valuable.

Before the 1900s, there were also other publications related to Chinese proverbs that had varying impact on the later studies (Bouvet 1697; Moule 1874; Lister 1874–1875). In particular, Joachim Bouvet (1656–1730), Jesuit missionary from France and well-known as a pioneer researcher on the *Book of Changes (Yijing)*, collected fifty-one proverbs and phrases to correlate the Chinese concept of *tian* (sky, heavens 天) to Christian "heaven" and "Lord." The Chinese version of his writing is called, *Kou kin king thien kien* (古今敬天鉴), with several variants due to hand-copying.

During the 1910s–1920s, there were also a number of collections of proverbs published. For example, Dawson-Gröne's *Ming Hsien Chi* (1911) with 170 proverbs, Albert J. Brace's *Five Hundred Proverbs Commonly Used in West China* (1916), and Joseph Van Oost's *Dictons et Proverbes des Chinois Habitant la Mongolie Sud-Ouest* (1918). Although not directly about proverbs, Marcel Granet (1884–1940) scrutinized the *Book of Songs* (which is the origin of many proverbs) in his *Fêtes et chansons anciennes de la Chine* (1919). Evangeline D Edwards's *Collection of Chinese Proverbs (in Mandarin)* (1926). Clifford H. Plopper (1885–1965) published *Chinese Religion seen through the Proverb* (1926) and *Chinese proverbs* (1932). The former book provides comprehensive translations and analyses of 2,448 proverbs. "In fact," he exclaimed by first quoting a saying, "'the genius, wit, and spirit of a nation are discovered in its proverbs.' Of the peoples of all lands, perhaps, the Chinese most clearly express themselves in this way" (Plopper 1926:1).

The 1930s marked a decline of missionary studies of China in general, while academic studies grew, as in the studies of Chinese folklore by Euro-American scholars. Henry H. Hart's (1886–1968) *700 Chinese Proverbs* (1937) provides no Chinese text or any contextual information, though there is "old age" in the Index.

These pioneering works on Chinese proverbs are still meaningful in many ways. For example, "In regard to the translations," Scarborough states,

> it may be remarked that in the few cases the vulgarity of the proverb has not allowed of a literal rendering; and that in many others I have refrained from translating the Chinese by an equivalent English proverb, thinking that a literal translation must be more interesting, while at the same time it could not fail to call up to the reader's mind English, French, or other equivalents. (1875:ii)

One issue in dealing with these early works is about the ideology and intent behind them. Based on the wisdom of his predecessors, Arthur Smith pointed out, "It is difficult to equal in English the compactness and forces of a Chinese proverb at its best, and to surpass it, is quite out of the question" (1902:13). This is not only a philological issue, but also an ideological one in relation to Christianity, as seen in some of the key terms or concepts in translation. One of these concepts is the Chinese word *tian* (天). In the polytheist Chinese culture, there is no one almighty god in heaven, but there are many and often not necessarily related gods and spirits in the *tian* (sky). If this concept is translated to "heaven" in Christian sense, the impact is certainly unmeasurable. However, in those missionaries' works like Smith's (1902:7), "Heaven" is used to translate *tian*:

千算万算, 不如老天一算. Qiānsuàn wànsuàn, bùrú lǎotiān yísuàn.
A thousand or ten thousand reckonings of men are not equal to one reckoning of
  Heaven.
Similarly, in Perny's (1869:1) work:
谋事在人成事在天. Móushì zài rén chéngshì zài tiān.
L'homme propose, le Ciel dispose. Home Proponit, Dues disponit.
In the Chinese mind, the concept of *tian*, as in many proverbs, can be understood as
  such:
谋事在人成事在天. Móushì zài rén chéngshì zài tiān.
Literally, planning things is up to the human, but the completion is up to non-human
  factors.

Indeed, when Chinese use the proverb, People take food as the utmost importance of life (民以食为天), it is always about making a living by having enough food, rather than "people take food as Heaven."

As for the topic of old age, Scarborough created a section in his collection for "aged men" with eighteen proverbs, and one of those is the very proverb we now will tackle (1875:210):

薑桂之性, 愈老愈辣. Jiāng guì zhī xìng, yù lǎo yù là.
The older ginger and cinnamon are, the more pungent their flavor.

In conclusion, this chapter presents some problems in the construction of paremiology in China. It thus is expected to draw attention from interested students and scholars and to stimulate further studies on Chinese proverbs in a more global context. After all, "Chinese proverbs are literally in the mouth of everyone, from the Emperor upon his throne to the woman grinding at the mill" (Smith 1902:7). This observation remains true: "Those who have not examined the proverbial sayings of the Chinese are surprised at the richness of the language in this respect" (1902:i). What is significantly different from Western culture, however, is the veneration of age and the great respect for elderly persons in Chinese culture. Thus, Chinese proverbs are a treasure trove waiting to be further explored, especially as an appreciation for Chinese proverbs grows significantly in the context of today's enhanced global communication. Knowing more about the attitudes toward old age and aging found in older Chinese culture will surely help our own self-cultivation of body-mind-heart (*xin* 心) as we all age at different paces.

Chapter 6

Older Ginger Is Spicier

Chinese Life-Views in Proverbs

Following the general survey in the previous chapter, this chapter focuses on one particular proverb about old age and aging and uses it as a lens through which to probe the essence of Chinese culture. It first outlines the history of Chinese proverb collections and studies, then examines the specific proverb, "Older ginger is spicier" (Jiāng shì lǎo de là 姜是老的辣; all translations in this chapter are mine otherwise noted), through its origin and development, and subsequently concludes by connecting the proverbs about old age and aging to the four life-views, and analyzing them against the background of the Chinese polytheist/inclusive belief system and its proverbial expressions in everyday life. The following discussion is divided into five sections: the concepts and proverbs of old age and aging; the origin of the proverb in question; the transformation and variants of the proverb; contemporary uses of the proverb, and the four life-views reflected in Chinese proverbs in general.

CONCEPTS AND PROVERBS OF OLD AGE AND AGING

Semantically, the word "old" (*lao* 老) in the Oracle Bone Inscriptions (fl. 1300–1000 BCE) is depicted as a (humped) man with a cane, as shown in the images below, along with the word/image of "spicy" (*la* 辣). In an annotated short dictionary formed in the early Han Dynasty, there are several different words to mean different old age, for example, *lao* is used to explain another word, *die* (耋), and, along with these terms/symptoms, yellowish hair (baby hair-like) grown after white hair (*huangfa* 黄发), tiny teeth grown out after losing teeth (*niche* 齯齿), age spots on the back (*taibei* 鲐背, humpbacked (*gou* 考)—terms for the age of 80–90 years old, to refer to one with longevity (*shou* 寿). Also, *lao* was interchangeable with *kao* (考) which is

123

another word for "father" (*fu* 父) (still in use for the late father, particularly on gravestones).

According to a number of records in the early classics, the word *lao* referred to the age of seventy and above, as in *Discussing Writing and Explaining Characters* (*Shuowen jiezi* 说文解字), the earliest Chinese dictionary compiled by Xu Shen (许慎 ca. 58–147). This usage is consistent with several other classics before his time. However, there were also different definitions: "old man" (*laonan* 老男) meant men above sixty years old, "old women" (*laonü* 老女) meant women above fifty years old, as seen in the *Book of Guan Zi* (Guan Zi 管子, 5th c. BCE–3rd c. BCE).

The evolution of the character "old" in Chinese writing shows its image/writing has become more and more abstract and symbolic, but the connotation remains little changed. Similarly, the character "spicy" (*xin* 辛; *la* 辣) has also gone through such a process (see figure 6.1):

In several classics before the third century BCE, "*lao*" was also used as a verb in addition to a noun and an adjective, in the way of "*lao lao*" to mean

Figure 6.1 The changes of the Chinese characters meaning "old" and "spicy." Top Line: The change of the character lao (Old 老, contemporary writing/printing) from Oracle Bone Inscriptions (Two Images on the Left; 3,300 Years Ago), to Cleric Writing (Third Image from Left; 2,000 Years Ago), and to Standard Writing (Image on the Right; 1,000 Years Ago). Bottom Line: The change of the character xin (Spicy 辛, contemporary writing/printing) from Oracle Bone Inscriptions (Two Images on the Left; 3,300 Years Ago), to Cleric Writing (Third Image from Left; 2,000 Years Ago), and to Standard Writing (Image on the Right; 1,000 Years Ago). *Source*: Created by Juwen Zhang.

that people should respect the old and the old should behave as they are expected. The *Book of Guan Zi* explains the term as such: What *lao lao* means is that there should be offices at local and state levels to take care of the affairs of older adults. Those who are above seventy years old should have one son exempt from drafting and receive meat for three months in a year from the government. Those who are above eighty years old should have two sons exempt from drafting and receive meat every month from the government. Those who are above ninety years old should have the whole family exempt from drafting and receive wine and meat every day from the government. Therefore, the *Book of Rites* also emphasized to "Promote *lao lao*, the folk will practice filiality (*xiao*, respecting parents/elders) as a fashion."

While longevity (*shou*) is a key term in Chinese, the *Book of Guan Zi* further defined it to mean "high *shou*" for 120, "mid-*shou*" for 100, "low *shou*" for 80. Today, the character *shou* is a must at all birthday celebrations (e.g., in writings, decorations for gifts or food/cake) for those who are above the age of sixty (although it is not rare to use the word to refer to those who are fifty and above).

What has been most popular and influential in terms of proverbial expressions of age may well be Confucius own self-reflection, as transmitted by his disciples in *The Analects* (论语 2.4), which is still commonly used today:

At fifteen, I had my mind bent on learning. At thirty, I stood firm. At forty, I had no doubts. At fifty, I knew the decrees of heaven. At sixty, my ear was an obedient organ *for the reception of truth*. At seventy, I could follow what my heart desired, without transgressing what was right. (Legge 1861:10–11)

Most importantly, the message behind this narration is about how to cultivate oneself (*xiushen* 修身).

Given that Confucian ideas have been dominant in Chinese thoughts and values, and that Confucius is believed to have died as the age of 73, and his most important follower Mencius (372–289 BCE) died at the age of 84, this saying is more popular in everyday life:

七十三, 八十四, 阎王不叫自己去 (七十三, 八十四, 阎王不叫自己死).

Qīshísān, bāshísì, yánwáng bújiào zìjǐ qù (qīshísān, bāshísì, yánwáng bújiào zìjǐ sǐ).

At seventy-three or eighty-four, even if the King of Hell does not summon, a man will go himself. (At seventy-three or eighty-four, even if the King of Hell does not summon, a man will die himself.)

The aforementioned proverbs are clearly expressions of folk beliefs. Another expression is the belief in the God of Longevity (or Old Age Star, *shouxing* 寿星), one the Three Stars Shedding Light (三星高照), along with the God of Auspiciousness (or Happiness/Good-Fortune Star, *fuxing* 福星) and God of Prosperity (in improving social status, *luxing* 禄星). The images of these Three Stars are seen almost everywhere inside houses, on daily utensils, in all kinds of prints like posters, and, of course, as statues in temples.

Obviously, the meaning of "old" or "longevity" has transformed over time. For example, the proverb "Three/four generations under one roof" (三/四世同堂) was a marker of "a complete and happy life" (*shou*). But it has changed along with the change in family structure or kinship relations in modern China, not to mention the impact of the one-child (now two children) per-family policy in the past four decades. In fact, the traditional sense of old age is being replaced by modern legal concepts, including the concept of "retirement" (though the majority of Chinese population is still in rural areas).

It is meaningful to note that it was only in the past a few years that China changed its legal retirement age for women from fifty to fifty-five, and men from fifty-five to sixty, except for certain occupations to extend a few more years, for example, full professors in universities can retire at sixty-five, but professors with lower ranks must retire at the age of sixty. The legal age for retirement in China since 1978 was: fifty for female physical workers; fifty-five for female nonphysical workers; sixty for males. The new law since 2015 revised it and planned to gradually extend the age to sixty-five all males and females by 2045. Thus, the new concept of "aging" (*laolinghua* 老龄化) has also become an everyday term.

Here is a brief outline of some of the proverbs relating to specific age, even though "age is just a number."

Fifty as Old

When Yan Zhitui (颜之推 531–ca. 597) in the sixth century quoted the following ancient proverb, he continued by saying that "since I am now more than sixty, I have no concerns of any kind about my life":

五十不为夭. Wǔshí bù wéi yāo.
Fifty is not an early death. (Death at fifty years old is not considered premature.)

This mention of the proverb seems to be the earliest written record, but it also reflected to this typical concept during those centuries, as in these two uses by, first, the famous Tang poet Wang Wei (701–761) wrote in his fifties:

老年惟好静. Lǎonián wéi hào jìng.
In my old age, I enjoy only quietude.

And second, Bai Ju Yi (772–846), another famous Tang poet, used at least twice in his poems, even before he reached his fifties:

五十不为夭, 吾今欠数年. Wǔshí bù wéi yāo, wú jīn qiàn shù nián.
Fifty is not early death, and I have several years to go.

Of course, Confucius's saying of "at fifty knowing the mandate of fate/ heavens" is still influential. In rural areas, the fiftieth birthday celebration as *shou* with a village-wide feast for a man (within family for a woman) is still common.

Sixty as Old

The importance of "sixty" as old, or even as a completion of a life, originated from the naturalistic cosmic view or philosophy. From this early cosmic view there developed the ancient numerological system for calendric or chronological purpose. In this system, the combination of two sets of units (e.g., ten celestial stems and twelve earthly stems) makes a total of "60," which is then a complete cycle, and it repeats in the same combination. Within this system derived the twelve Chinese zodiacs, still essential to the Chinese everyday life. Therefore, sixty-year-old is seen as a completion of the *rites of passage* for human life. This notion was historically related to Daoist and Buddhist concepts of staged transformation of life. Today, this notion is seen in the most popular celebration of "old age" or "*shou*" in China (and Japan, Korea).

Currently, many local and traditional concepts of "old age" have gradually adapted to their national laws which, in turn, are influenced by the international conventions set by the United Nations, drawing a line of sixty-five-year-old for counting the population of "aging." For example, according to the UN document, "World Population Aging 2019: Highlights": "Globally, the share of the population aged 65 years or over increased from 6 per cent in 1990 to 9 per cent in 2019. That proportion is projected to rise further to 16 per cent by 2050, so that one in six people in the world will be aged 65 years or over."

With this line, as of 2014, China's "old aged" group took 15.5 percent (e.g., 212 million) of its total population, the highest percentage among all countries in the world, and by 2040, it is estimated that the percentage of the group of sixty-five and above will increase to 30 percent. The establishment of the China National Committee on Aging shows the seriousness of this situation in China. This problem is also clearly shown in everyday proverbial expressions, challenging traditional notions in both positive and negative senses.

The terms like "*huajia*" (花甲, gray-haired at sixty), "*ershun*" (耳顺, ear-in-tune at sixty, in Confucian sense), and "*huanli*" (还历, restart the cycle of the calendar) are metaphorical uses for this age, while these proverbs are common:

五十岁不交钱, 六十岁不交言. Wǔshí suì bùjiāo qián, liùshí suì bùjiāo yán.
Don't deal with money at fifty, don't talk too much at sixty.
六十不赴宴, 七十不留宿. Liùshí bù fù yàn, qīshí bù liúsù.
Don't attend banquets at sixty, don't sleepover at seventy.
六十岁学吹打, 心有余力不足. Liùshí suì xué chuīdǎ, xīn yǒuyú lìbùzú.
To learn to play trumpet or drum at sixty, sufficient desire with insufficient strength

Seventy as Old

In the Confucian *Book of Rites*, there is a saying referring to age and status: "One can carry a cane at home at fifty, in the village at sixty, in the capital city at seventy, in the imperial court at eighty."

人过七十古来稀. Rénguò qīshí gǔlái xī.
People over seventy are very few since ancient times.
人生稀有七十余, 多少风光不同局. Rénshēng xīyǒu qīshí yú, duōshǎo fēngguāng bùtóng jú.
There are only a few who live beyond seventy, customs and times are ever changing. (Trans. by Dawson-Gröne 1911:37).
七十不留步, 八十不留饭, 九十不留坐. Qīshí bù liúbù, bāshí bù liúfàn, jiǔshí bù liúzuò.
A man at the age of seventy should not be kept in a visit; at eighty, should not be kept for a meal; at ninety, should not be kept for a sit.

In current folk expressions, seventy to eighty is also called *zhongshou* (mid-longevity), in contrast to fifty to sixty as *xiashou* (low-longevity), and eighty and above as *gaoshou* (high-longevity) or *dashou* (great longevity), though there are other sayings as well, while some classical terms for higher age are rarely used, except for *baisui* (100 year old). But a general proverb for old age goes like this:

风烛残年. Fēng zhú cán nián.
A candle in wind, a broken year ahead.
(One at an old age is like a candle in the wind, even without a complete year to live.)

Also, in everyday life, the expression "white happiness" (*baixi*) is used for a death of old age, in contrast to "red happiness" (*hongxi*) of a wedding.

The common use of "someone is 'old'" (*laole*) in certain contexts is also a euphemism for "death." Of course, the "old age" has meant different things throughout history, especially the life expectancy of the Chinese, along with the world population has increased dramatically in the past century. For example, according to "Our World in Data" (https://ourworldindata .org/grapher/life-expectancy?year=2015) and United Nation's "Population Division," the life expectancy of human beings from mid-1500 to 1900 was under fifty years, but thereafter, the world average is over seventy years by the early twenty-first century. In Old China, seventy could be indeed "rare" a century ago, but the average life expectancy in China is now above seventy.

Clearly, views and attitudes toward old age and aging are changing in all cultures. For example, in contemporary American society, as shown in the proverb "age is just a number," the belief that "staying young" in important with "denial of the natural aging process" seems to be prevalent (Mieder 2020), meanwhile the mentality of "youth-centered" culture remains strong (Bronner 2016). At the end of 2020, the political leadership in the United States seems uniquely, if not ironically, illustrated both "age is just a number" and "older ginger is spicier" with these age numbers: the president was at the age of seventy-four; the president-elect (Joe Biden) at seventy-eight; speaker of the House (Nancy Pelosi) at eighty; senate majority leader (Republican Leader, Mitch McConnell) at seventy-eight; senate Democratic Leader (Chuck Shumer) at seventy; House Democratic Leader (Steny Hoyer) at eighty-one; and the forerunners of the presidential election were at seventy-nine (Bernie Sanders), and seventy-one (Elizabeth Warren).

In contrast, however, even though "immortality" is an important part of Chinese thought, Chinese proverbs show a mentality and practice of "staying old" or having a "white happiness" as the auspicious ending of this life and a good beginning of the next. Contrary to the pessimistic view in "You can't teach an old dog new tricks," the Chinese "Older ginger is spicier" praises the wisdom of the aged and encourages the young to long for the respect and power at the golden age.

Today, "retirement" (*tuixiu* 退休) is a new concept related to different ages in different occupations. For nonagricultural population, this concept has replaced the traditional "50," "60," or "70"—usually in the proverbial expression "Stating old and returning home village" (*gaolao huanxiang* 告老还乡, that is, announcing one's entering the "old" age and thus "retiring" from offices to return to home village). This is also in accordance with the family values of "Falling leaves returning to the roots" (*luoye guigen* 落叶归根). Currently, those who are "retired" in most cities are given a certificate/ID-card by the governments, so they can enter parks or take buses for free. Today, what may be fascinating to a visitor to China is to see countless "old people," whether early in the morning or other times in tree shade, whether in neighborhood parks or along streets, whether playing chess or cards or *majiang*, playing musical instruments, singing, dancing, exercising, or playing with their grandchildren. Clearly, "old age" and "aging" mean very differently even between generations in modern China.

THE ORIGIN OF THE PROVERB

With the contexts drawn earlier, this section focuses on the origin and context of our proverb, "older ginger is spicier," in order to prepare for the following discussion about how the Chinese cultural roots are reflected in proverbs about old age and aging.

The earliest written record of this proverb, according to various dictionaries (Zhu 1985:560; Song and Duanmu 2001:365), is from the official history book of the Song Dynasty (960–1279), *The History of Song* (*Song Shi*), written and revised during 1343–1345, with a story as such (Tuo 1985): The well-known minister Yan Dunfu (晏敦复 1120–1191) was an upright official. He was once bribed by the most notorious corrupted prime minister in Chinese history, Qin Hui (1090–1155), to support an agreement forced by the invading northern state, but Yan blatantly rejected it by saying that "I am never to be involved in any conspiracy to destroy my country, not to mention that I have the nature of ginger and cinnamon, the older the spicier."

Thereafter, the expression carried the virtuous meaning of being "direct," "straight-forward," "loyal and righteous," and transformed into a proverb:

姜桂之性, 到老愈辣. Jiāng guì zhī xìng, dào lǎo yù là.
The nature of ginger and cinnamon, the older the spicier.

The description of the "spiciness" as the nature of ginger and cinnamon can be traced to the Han Dynasty (221 BCE–220 CE):

夫薑桂因地而生, 不因地而辛. Fū jiānggui yīn dì ér shēng, bù yīn dì ér xīn.
Ginger and cinnamon grow in soil, but their spiciness does not change because of different soils.
夫薑桂同地, 辛在本性. Fū jiāng guì tóng di, xīn zài běnxìng.
Ginger and cinnamon grow from the same place, and have their common nature.

The term for "spicy/spiciness" in these two earlier texts was *xin* (辛), but in the proverb by Yan was *la* (辣). Semantically, *xin* is more literary, and *la* is also used to mean "double" *xin* as shown in the images of the characters. Today, *xinla* is often used as one word to modify nouns like "irony/satire" or "speech/writing."

Perhaps two reasons can be drawn to explain why the version used by Yan has been considered as the earliest written proverb, and cited the most in proverb collections. One is that Yan's version revealed a metaphorical context, that is, his integrity and personality being intolerant of the corrupted deed; the other is the fact that he was facing the most notorious traitor in Chinese history. Clearly, this origin also shows the vitality of this proverb, that is, its underlined ethical values in a metaphorical expression.

THE TRANSFORMATION AND VARIANTS OF THE PROVERB

The transformation of this proverb can be seen in three forms or stages. The first is the simplified sentence with only one part of the original two-part proverb, or a condensed simple sentence. This is consistent with the format of the fixed idiom (*chengyu*) in a four-character structure, and is also in consistent with the two-part idiom (*xiehouyu*), that is, using only one part so that the reader/listener is expected to understand the hidden meaning. For example:

姜桂之性. Jiāng guì zhī xìng.
The nature of ginger and cinnamon (Liu 2000:528).

The second is to directly describe or compare a person to the old ginger, a change from literary to vernacular/oral usage:

姜是老的辣. Jiāng shì lǎo de là.
It is the older ginger that is spicy (or spicier) (Dong 2005:156).

The third transformation is by adding the adverb "*hai*" (还, or *jiu* 就, *also, still, indeed*) so that it brings a rhetorical effect by saying:

姜还是老的辣. Jiāng hái shì lǎo de là.
Indeed, the older ginger is spicier (or, nevertheless, the older ginger is still spicier) (Hu and Fu 2006:83).

This usage implies the speaker admits that he/she is not as "spicy" as he/she thought since now there is an older/wiser person in front of him/her. In other words, context is required to determine the meaning, as proverbs often are "double-bladed."

Thus, over those centuries, the "idea of [its] traditionality" of this proverb, as "the single, and the most crucial, element that empowers proverbs" (Ben-Amos 1995:20), is affirmed. Thereafter, other variants are also created:

姜桂之性, 到老愈辛. Jiāngguì zhī xìng, dào lǎo yù xīn.

As for the nature of ginger & cinnamon, they get more bitter with age.

姜桂之性, 老而愈辣. Jiāngguì zhī xìng, lǎo ér yù là.

The nature of ginger and cinnamon, older it gets spicier it is.

菫荼易地味不甘, 姜桂到老性愈辣. Jǐntú yì dì wèi bùgān, jiāngguì dào lǎo xìng yù là.

Ji-herb and *tu*-vegie (are bitter and) don't get sweet in different places; ginger and cinnamon get spicier as they get older.

薑桂之性, 至老不移. Jiāngguì zhī xìng, zhì lǎo bù yí.

The nature of ginger and cinnamon, no change as they get old.

One thing is clear from these examples is that this proverb was used to praise one's virtue and integrity of being loyal to the country, persistent in pursuing learning and serving the society, and intolerant to unvirtuous deeds. However, a twist was gradually made to emphasize the wisdom or experience an old person may have, with good or bad intention, as seen in the following examples, showing the very nature of proverbs being "double-bladed."

CONTEMPORARY USES OF THE PROVERB: CONTINUITY AND RENOVATION

In the recent comprehensive collection of folk sayings with 100,000 entries, including 13,000 categorized as "proverb" (*yanyu*), the variants of our proverb are listed here (Wen 2004:421). Unfortunately, this huge collection does not provide any other contextual information except the "naked" proverbs, although his earlier compilations provided the sources of the proverbs (Wen 1989). Of course, there are proverb dictionaries without including this entry (Cui 2007). Note how "cinnamon" is gradually dropped from modern uses:

姜桂之性, 愈老愈辣. Jiāngguì zhī xìng, yù lǎo yù là.

The nature of ginger and cinnamon, the older the spicier (*la*).

姜桂之性, 愈老愈辛. Jiāngguì zhī xìng, yù lǎo yù xīn.

The nature of ginger and cinnamon, the older the spicier (*xin*).

姜还是老的辣. Jiāng hái shì lǎo de là.

Older ginger is indeed spicier.

姜老姜辣, 蔗老蔗甜. Jiāng lǎo jiāng là, zhè lǎo zhè tián.

Old ginger is spicier; old sugar cane is sweeter.

姜是老的辣, 醋是陈的酸. Jiāng shì lǎo de là, cù shì chén de suān.

Old ginger is spicier, older vinegar is sourer.

姜是老来辣, 茶是后来酽. Jiāng shì lǎo lái là, chá shì hòulái yàn.

Old ginger is spicier, longer sit tea tastes bitter.

姜越老越辣, 藕越老越粉. Jiāng yuè lǎo yuè là, ǒu yuè lǎo yuè fěn.
Old ginger is spicier, older lotus roots are squishier.
姜在地里长, 土里要干爽. Jiāng zài dì lǐ cháng, tǔ lǐ yào gānshuǎng.
Ginger grows in soil, the soil should be dryer.
姜里老的辣, 沟葱白儿长. Jiāng lǐ lǎo de là, gōu cōng bái er zhǎng.
Old ginger is spicier, scallions in ditches have longer white stems.
姜是老的辣, 梅子嫩的酸, 夕阳也晒人. Jiāng shì lǎo de là, méizi nèn de suān,
    xīyáng yě shài rén.
Old ginger is spicier, younger plums are sour, twilight can also be scorching.
姜是老的辣, 酒是陈的香, 辣椒还是老的红. Jiāng shì lǎo de là, jiǔ shì chén de
    xiāng, làjiāo háishì lǎo de hóng.
Old ginger is spicier, older liquor has better aroma, red peppers have to be older.
姜老辣味大, 人老经验多. Jiāng lǎo là wèi dà, rén lǎo jīngyàn duō.
Old ginger tastes spicier, older people have more experiences.
姜老味辣, 人老胆豪. Jiāng lǎo wèi là, rén lǎo dǎn háo.
Old ginger tastes spicier, older people have more guts.
 Among these current variants, there are probably the most frequently used:
姜是老的辣. Jiāng shì lǎo de là.
Old ginger is spicy. (Older ginger is spicier.)
姜还是老的辣. Jiāng hái shì lǎo de là.
Older ginger is indeed spicier. (The old ginger is spicier after all.)
姜是越老越辣. Jiāng shì yuè lǎo yuè là.
The older the ginger, the spicier it is. (The older the ginger is, the spicier it gets.)

In one recent survey, for example, about the use of Cantonese proverbs and
idiom in Guangzhou, this usage was collected (Hua 2010:43):

蔗要老来甜, 姜要老来辣. Zhè yào lǎo lái tián, jiāng yào lǎo lái là.
Sweet sugar cane needs to be older, spicy ginger has to be older.

This shows not only dialectical use but also related to regional lifestyle or
modes of production. For example, eating sugar cane is common in the South,
but not a custom in North China. Similarly, one can see from the aforementioned list that some are clearly related to local modes of production like
vinegar production or tea growing.

The variants about sugar cane, vinegar, wine, pepper, or scallion clearly
show the local modes of production and lifestyle. They further prove the
proverbiality of our proverb here, showing its versatility in adapting to different regional, dialectic, and occupational contexts. It also shows that a
proverb's vitality lies in its adaptation to a new social environment. Here are
some rather modern variants, and even in counter-proverb or anti-proverb
sense:

姜是老的辣; 葱是嫩的香. Jiāng shì lǎo de là; cōng shì nèn de xiāng.

Old ginger is spicier, younger scallions are tastier.

姜是老的辣; 辣椒可是小的辣. Jiāng shì lǎo de là; làjiāo kěshì xiǎo de là.

Old ginger is spicier, but smaller pepper is spicier.

姜是老的辣; 腕是老的大. Jiāng shì lǎo de là; wàn shì lǎo de dà.

Old ginger is spicier, elder celebrities are cooler.

姜是老的辣; 情是旧的好 (老婆还是原装的好). Jiāng shì lǎo de là; qíng shì jiù de
   hǎo (lǎopó háishì yuánzhuāng de hǎo).

Older ginger is spicier, older love is better. (Older ginger is spicier, first wife is
   better.)

Other variants do not use the "ginger" part, but clearly show the "old age"
and "aging" related connotations (more examples in the following section):

老将出马, 一个顶俩. Lǎojiàng chūmǎ, yīgè dǐng liǎ.

When an old general mounts a horse, one is better than two.

(An experienced hand can get twice as much done.)

初生牛犊不怕虎. Chūshēng niúdú búpà hǔ.

Calves have no fear of the tiger.

老汉不提当年勇. Lǎohàn bù tí dāngnián yǒng.

Good old man does not brag about his youth.

人老不值钱, 拖累讨人嫌. Rén lǎo bù zhíqián, tuōlèi tǎo rén xián.

Old men are worth nothing, but burdensome and annoying.

门神老了不捉鬼. Ménshén lǎo le bù zhuō guǐ.

Old door gods catch devils no more.

长江后浪推前浪, 一代更比一代强. Chángjiāng hòulàng tuī qiánlàng, yídài gèng bǐ
   yídài qiáng.

The latter wave of the Yangtze River pushes the former wave, each generation
   grows stronger.

长江后浪推前浪, 后浪把前浪推到沙滩上. Chángjiāng hòulàng tuī qiánlàng,
   hòulàng bǎ qiánlàng tuī dào shātān shàng.

The latter wave of the Yangtze River pushes the former wave, the latter wave
   pushes the former wave onto sand beach.

And some phrases about the wisdom, devotion, and cunningness of the
old age:

老姜 Old ginger—old age with experience

老狐狸 Old fox—sly, cunning

老油条 Old oil stick—slippery, sly, crafty

老江湖 Old vagrant—experienced with survival skills

老小孩 Old child—old people behave like children

老奸巨滑 Old wicked and super sly
老骥伏枥 Good old horse at work—old people at work with high aspiration
老当益壮 Older but even stronger—with great aspiration

By now, "older ginger is spicier" has become ever more popular and diverse, though the original political and ethical implication is often overweight by the practical and experiential implication. All of these changes also revealed the changed history, language, and family and social values, particularly, attitudes about old age and aging.

Here are a few examples of using this proverb in certain social and political contexts, but there are numerous uses by the common people in everyday life as well as in literature. A report in the most important newspaper in China, *People's Daily* (August 15, 2016), which reprinted a story from another influential newspaper, *China Youth Daily*, about a village head who used the senior villagers to solve one problem, among others:

> It was close to the Spring Festival in 2015. There were two brothers quarreling hard on the issue of splitting household property and their neighbors could not easily ease or remedy the situation no matter what. They then went to the village head who had an idea. He gathered a few older people who had good reputation in the village because he thought the brothers would at least care about their "face" (*mianzi*). They went to the brothers and began to chat. "The older ginger is indeed spicier." Soon the two brothers felt ashamed and guilty of themselves, and compromised with each other. The problem was solved.

Interestingly, the book, *Conversations with Clint: Paul Nelson's Lost Interviews with Clint Eastwood, 1979–1983* (Kevin Avery, 2011), due to the fact that Clint Eastwood is seen as a great master in the film world, is translated into 姜就是老的辣 (*The Older Ginger is Indeed Spicer*) (2015).

FOUR LIFE-VIEWS REFLECTED IN CHINESE PROVERBS

As "older ginger is spicier" has transformed into the status of a traditional or standard proverb, its proverbiality of duality and agility became more obvious. It can be positive to praise one's wisdom and prudence as one is getting older (though the idea of moral integrity in the original context has been changed); it can also be negative to indicate one's cunning and scheming. As seen in the aforementioned examples, being old at a certain age meant specific respect and treatment from family and society in ancient China. Today, the changing meaning of the number of ages has blurred the specific social behavior, but those proverbs still reflect fundamental beliefs and values of

Chinese culture. I argue that the following four life-views are well reflected in old-age-related proverbs.

The concept "life-view" (*rensheng guan* 人生观, or view of human life) is a direct translation from the Chinese expression. This usage, though not common in translations, is used by philosopher Thomé H. Fang in his *The Chinese View of Life* (1956), in which he examined this view in a systematic interpretation regarding how it was effective in the shaping of Chinese culture, and how it was different from other views of life in the Western philosophies. In fact, "life-view" can also be understood to mean "view of living a life" (*shenghuo guan* 生活观) or "view of (all) lives" (*shengming guan* 生命观) from Chinese perspectives.

Therefore, I use "life-view" in this discussion to convey the Chinese perspectives, which are really about the views or attitude toward how to live a life, but are not necessarily related to the religious "pro-life" view, nor to the concept of "value of life" used in economics, social, and political sciences. This "life-view" is not equivalent to the ethical concept of value (values) for human actions, though it is heavily influenced by Confucian ethics. "Life-view" indicates the difference between this practical philosophy of "living a life" (生活 *shenghuo*; 过日子 *guorizi*) in Chinese culture and the concepts used in folkloristic studies such as "worldview," "folk idea," and "folk fallacy" (Dundes 1971). It echoes the idea from Dundes about studying "human thought, rather than follow a natural history model of the collection and classification of items somehow devoiced from contemporary life," as Bronner (2007:179) has interpreted.

Dundes defined "folk ideas" to be "traditional notions that a group of people have about the nature of man, of the world, and of man's life in the world" and thought that "other terms" could be "more appropriate than 'folk ideas'," but his point was to emphasize "the task of identifying the various underlying assumptions held by members of a given culture" (1971:95, 96). The effort here to identify "life-views" in Chinese culture can be seen as a step toward that direction, without using the unclear terms like "worldview" or "thought."

Entering the World (*rushi* 入世)

This concept embodies these beliefs and values in Chinese culture: (a) the immortality of the soul (*linghun bumie* 灵魂不灭), as practiced in ancestral reverence/worship; (b) the belief in seeking harmony while maintaining differences in personal life and interpersonal communication (*he'er butong* 和而不同), as practiced in the concepts of yin-yang and five-elements; (c) the ethics and practice of following local customs (*ruxiang suisu* 入乡随俗), as practiced in being inclusive of different lifestyles and adaptive to new environment in everyday life. This concept emphasizes Confucian values that a person should strive to enter and service the society as a useful member by studying the classics, passing the exams, and holding offices in the government. It encourages a person, especially a young man regardless of family background, to study diligently and be optimistic toward life and reality, and promotes the idea that education is the only ladder to elevate one's familial and social status. These examples are clearly positive toward old age and aging:

活到老, 学到老. Huó dào lǎo, xué dào lǎo.
Live to an old age, learn to an old age.
活到老学到老, 一生一世学不了. Huó dào lǎo xué dào lǎo, yìshēng yíshì xué bùliǎo.
Live long and learn on, much to learn in one life.
(cf. Life is short, art is long.)
蚂蚁爬树不怕高, 有心学习不怕老. Mǎyǐ páshù búpà gāo, yǒuxīn xuéxí búpà lǎo.
Ants are not afraid of high trees, the will to learn is not afraid of old age.
不怕人老, 就怕心老. Búpà rén lǎo, jiù pà xīn lǎo.
Old age is not fearful, old heart-mind is fearful.
树老果不多, 人老心不老. Shù lǎo guǒ bù duō, rén lǎo xīn bùlǎo.
Old trees yield less fruit, old people have young hearts.
人怕老心, 树怕老根. Rén pà lǎo xīn, shù pà lǎo gēn.
People are afraid of getting old at heart, trees are afraid of getting old at roots.
人老志不衰. Rén lǎo zhì bù shuāi.
People get old, but ambition doesn't weaken.
人穷莫泄气, 人老莫丧志. Rén qióng mò xièqì, rén lǎo mò sàngzhì.
Poverty should not deprive ambition, old age should not deprive aspiration.
世无老而不学之理. Shì wú lǎo ér bù xué zhī lǐ.
There is no reason in the world for the old aged not to learn.
年龄长一岁, 责任重一分. Niánlíng zhǎng yī suì, zérèn zhòng yī fēn.
One year added to age, one share added to duty.
明珠尽出老蚌. Míngzhū jìn chū lǎo bàng.
Bright pearls are all from old oysters.
人老智多, 树老根多. Rén lǎo zhì duō, shù lǎo gēn duō.
Old people are wiser, old trees have more roots.
(树老根多, 人老话多. Shù lǎo gēn duō, rén lǎohuà duō.
Old trees have more roots, old people have more words.)
姜老辣味大, 人老经验多; 酒陈味香, 人老识深. Jiāng lǎo làwèidà, rén lǎo jīngyàn duō; jiǔchén wèixiāng, rénlǎo shíshēn.
Older ginger is spicier, old people are more experienced; aged wine is aromatic, aged man is sagacious.

Of course, there are twisted ones with dubious meanings, as counter-proverbs or anti-proverbs:

有志不在年高, 无志空活百岁. Yǒuzhì búzài niángāo, wúzhì kōng huó bǎisuì.
With ambition, one can be young, without ambition, one hundred years is empty.
松树越老越青, 人越老越精明. Sōngshù yuè lǎo yuèqīng, rén yuèlǎo yuèjīngmíng.
Older pines become darker blue, older people get smarter (which may be either
   positive or negative).
后生可畏. Hòu sheng kě wèi.
The later born is to be awed.
小人手多, 老人口多. Xiǎorén shǒu duō, lǎorén kǒu duō.
Little people have too many hands, old people have too many mouths.
狗老咬人痛, 人老还击狠. Gǒu lǎo yǎo rén tòng, rén lǎo huán jī hěn.
Old dog's bite hurts more, old man's revenge hits harder.
人老无能, 神老无灵. Rén lǎo wú néng, shén lǎo wú líng.
Old people are incapable, old spirits are inefficacious.
冷铁难打, 老竹难弯. Lěng tiě nán dǎ, lǎo zhú nán wān.
Cold iron is hard to strike, old bamboo is hard to bend.
树老生虫, 人老无用. Shù lǎo shēng chóng, rén lǎo wú yòng.
Old trees get bugs, old people have no use.
人老珠黄不值钱. Rénlǎo zhūhuáng bù zhíqián.
Old people are like yellowed plants, they are worthless.
老而不死是为贼. Lǎo ér bùsǐ shì wéi zéi.
Living old without virtue is harmful.

This last proverb is from the Confucian *Analects* (*Lun Yu*), and the context
of this usage is in this story:

> Yuan Rang was squatting on his heels, and so waited the approach of the
> Master, who said to him, "In youth not humble as befits a junior; in manhood,
> doing nothing worthy of being handed down; and living on to old age—this is
> to be a pest." With this he hit him on the shank with his staff. (Translation from
> Legge 1861:156–157)

Overall, thinking about the experience of "entering the world" is essential
to the Chinese because it provides an opportunity to emphasize education
and love of learning as a path not only to improve individual status but also
to maintain a harmonious family and society. This explains the continuity of
the state-wide examination system that has continued more than a thousand
years till today.

Exiting the World (*chushi* 出世)

Since seeking immortality is essential to Daoist practice, beliefs and customs
related to seeking an elixir conferring immortality has been an important part.

This concept expresses a Daoist notion that "nonaction" (*wuwei*) is the Way of living a life being an element in the universe, and also related to a Buddhist idea of separating from the human world of desires. Since seeking immortality is essential to Daoist practice, beliefs and customs related to seeking elixir has been an important part of Chinese medicine or early alchemy, and many ways of exercises, not to mention folklife in general. This life-view complements the *rushi*-view when one fails to be successful to "enter the world" so that one can retreat to the mountains away from the worldly world as a transition. It is largely based on the fundamental belief in the unity of humans and nature (*tianren heyi* 天人合一), as practiced in housing, diet, festivals, arts, and other areas. Proverbs of this life-view are sometimes seen as cynical or transcendental:

少而寡欲颜常好, 老不求官梦亦闲. Shǎo ér guǎyù yáncháng hǎo, lǎo bù qiúguān mèng yì xián.
Less desire at a young age makes you look healthy, no desire for office at old age makes your dream relaxing.
告老还乡. Gào lǎo huán xiāng.
Announce old age so as to return to home village.
百年随时过, 万事转头空. Bǎinián suíshíguò, wànshì zhuǎn tóu kōng.
A hundred years slip in a blink, ten thousand things disappear when you turn your head.
老年惟好静, 万事不关心. Lǎonián wéi hào jìng, wànshì bù guānxīn.
At my old age, I enjoy only quietude; ten thousand things are out of my concern.
劳其身者长寿, 安其乐者短命. Láo qí shēn zhě chángshòu, ān qí lè zhě duǎnmìng.
Laboring your body makes your life long, indulging your pleasure makes your life short.
人不可不知有生之乐, 亦不可不怀虚生之忧. Rén bùkě bùzhī yǒu shēng zhīlè, yìbùkě bù huái xūshēng zhīyōu.
One must know the pleasure of life, but must not forget the concern about doing nothing in life.
人生知足何时足, 到老偷闲且是闲. Rénshēng zhīzú héshí zú, dàolǎo tōuxián qiě shìxián.
There is no contented life if one is not content in life, a leisure taken at old age is a leisure indeed.

The Next World (*laishi* 来世)

This view expresses that hoping for a better future or better life for the descendants is the way to overcome current hardship, and that everything unpleasant or undesirable now will change to be pleasant and desirable in the next life or in the next world. This view has a close connection to the

Buddhist view, as well as the Daoist original thought. But Confucian practical ethics is also integrated into this idea, as in connecting *fengshui* burial to the prosperity of ethics in a family. Today, this idea is also seen in these expressions/phenomena: "little emperor" (小皇帝 meaning the central role of a child in a family in contemporary kernel families); "little sun" (小太阳 same meaning as the earlier); "expect a son to become a dragon" (望子成龙); "expect a daughter to become a phoenix" (望女成凤).

This can be seen as a step further of "exiting the world." It is related to the belief in the immortality of the soul and the transformation of life. Therefore, many such proverbs are related to death, so as to psychologically prepare people for their old age and aging, not necessarily a negative view.

今天脱下衣和袜, 不知明天穿不穿. Jīntiān tuōxià yīhéwà, bùzhī míngtiān chuānbùchuān.
When you take off pants and socks today, you don't know if you will put them on tomorrow.
人老无用, 物老出古, 禽兽老了成精. Rén lǎo wúyòng, wù lǎo chū gǔ, qínshòu lǎole chéng jīng.
People age and become useless, things age and become antiquities, beasts and birds age and become sprites.
长江一去无回浪, 人老何曾再少年. Chángjiāng yī qù wú huí làng, rén lǎo hécéng zài shàonián.
The river waves never go backward, people can never be young again.

The following common expressions about old age and death show different Chinese beliefs and values. For example, these often indicate traditional Confucian values:

老了 (Someone) . . . is old/gone/dead.
走了 (Someone) . . . left/gone.
作古了 (Someone) . . . became ancient/ancestor.
入土了 (Someone) . . . entered the earth/buried/completed funeral.
去世 (Someone) . . . left the world.
谢世 (Someone) . . . bid farewell to the world.
百年(之后) (Someone) . . . (reached; after) a hundred years.
落叶归根 . . . fallen leaf returning to the roots.

These have the Daoist implication that death is a transformation to immortality:

升天 (Someone) . . . ascended to the sky.
登仙 (Someone) . . . climbed mountain peak (to be an immortal).

仙去 (Someone) . . . left to become immortal.
仙逝 (Someone) . . . died to become immortal.

These have obvious Buddhist influences that the "west" is where Buddha/ nirvana is:

西去了 (Someone) . . . went to the West.
上西天了 (Someone) . . . went to the West Sky.
驾鹤西归 (去) (Someone) . . . returned (left for) the West on the crane.
见阎王了 (Someone) . . . went to meet the King of Yama.

There is also this expression for death among those who are the communist party members or people in government offices:

去见马克思 To go to meet with (Karl) Marx.
去见马克思了 Went to meet with Marx.

Passaging the World (*dushi* 渡世)

This life-view reflects one of the fundamental beliefs and values in Chinese culture by seeking auspiciousness and avoiding inauspiciousness (*quji bixiong* 趋吉避凶), as seen in the practice of fortunetelling. On the surface, it may seem to be fatalistic or cynical view about life, but, essentially, it is a positive and active belief and behavior to live a meaningful life in this world, often by such expressions as, "seek good luck" (求好运), "seek life of good fortune" (求福命) or "cumulate good deeds/virtue" (积善积德) (the theme is shown in ATU 461, and is widely told in China with many variants, see Liu 2016).

This view can be interpreted differently from philosophical, religious, and cultural perspectives. However, its essence lies in the Confucian view of living a meaningful life in this world, that is, one should strive to do good deeds, to enhance familial and societal harmony, and to pass the inherited virtues to the next generations. The most influential Confucian idea on this is his words, "[I am only] a transmitter and not a maker, believing in and loving the ancients" (*The Analects*; English translation from Legge 1861:59).

Daoist view of life echoes this, emphasizing that one's life is but one of the myriad things in the universe, and thus one's deeds should be in accordance with the movement of nature, but not to be against it. By not doing anything (to change what the universe is), or nonaction (*wuwei*), one fulfills the meaning of life by doing everything (a life is supposed to do). In practical life, one seeks "long life" or "immortality" by retreating from worldly affairs, but maintaining harmonious relations with the universe and leaving it as one once entered. Similarly, Buddhist ideas also took root in this system of fundamental beliefs and values in Chinese culture, because the essential goal of practicing Buddhism is to help the passage of all lives from this work to the other world, widely used as *pudu zhongsheng* (普渡众生) in Chinese (in which *du* means to transit/passage).

In fact, as shown in the model of *rites de passage* (van Gennep 1909), old age and death are one of the three stages of the life cycle that all human beings go through from "separation" to "margin" and then to "aggregation" (departing the world of the living and entering the world of the dead). Thus, one's life from birth to death is a long marginal transition (Zhang 2012).

Clearly, this *dushi* life-view is related, at various degrees, to the *rushi*, *chushi*, and *laishi* views. When living a life becomes too harsh, people would believe that life is to pass through a stage and pave way to *laishi* for the good of their next generations. This view is sometimes negatively expressed as dilly-dallying the world (*hunshi* 混世), as shown in the proverb:

好死不如赖活着. Hǎo sǐ bùrú lài huózhe.
A good death is not as good as making a shameless living.
 But, the counter-proverbs for this are:
雁过留声, 人过留名. Yàn guò liú shēng, rén guò liú míng.
Wild geese leave their sounds as they fly over, people leave their names as they
    pass by.
积善积德, 必有余庆. Jīshàn jīdé, bìyǒu yúqìng.
Cumulate goodness and virtues, there must be more to celebration in the future.

Since life is good but short, there have developed various ways to prolong or better this life. All kinds of "art" or "technique" (术 *shu*) of fortunetelling have thrived as ways of seeking auspiciousness and avoid inauspiciousness (*quji bixiong*). In addition, the *dushi* life-view also reflects the other fundamental beliefs and values in Chinese culture: following local customs (*ruxiang suisu* 入乡随俗) as a practice of the Confucian idea of seeking harmony while maintaining differences (*heer butong* 和而不同). After all, Confucian ethics is a practical philosophy about living a life in this world, as seen in these proverbs (particularly about dealing with aging, old age, and death):

家有一老, 黄金活宝. Jiā yǒu yī lǎo, huángjīn huóbǎo.
An old person in a family is the golden living treasure.
牛老角硬, 人老艺精. Niú lǎo jiǎo yìng, rén lǎo yì jīng.
Older bulls have harder horns, older people have finer skills.
不听老人言, 吃亏(苦)在眼前. Bù tīng lǎorén yán, chīkuī (kǔ) zài yǎnqián.
If one does not listen to the old aged, one will eat losses (bitterness) before his own
    eyes.

树老半心空, 人老事事通. Shù lǎo bàn xīn kōng, rén lǎo shì shì tōng.
Old trees are half-hollowed, old people know everything.
老马识途. Lǎo mǎ shí tú.
Old horses know their roads.
吃过的盐比你吃过的饭都多, 走过的桥比你走过的路都多. Chīguò de yán bǐ nǐ
chīguò de fàn dōu duō, zǒuguò de qiáo bǐ nǐ zǒuguò de lù dōu duō.
(The old man) has eaten more salt than the food you have eaten; walked over more
bridges than the road you have taken.

In "passing the world," cultivating body-mind (*yangsheng* 养生) is an
ancient idea mostly influenced by the Daoist concept of seeking immortality. Chinese medicine, martial arts, and even diet systems are all related to
this concept. As one can see in any neighborhood in China, there are old
people—of course, there are always young people as well—doing all kinds
of exercise such as *taiji* and modern dances. Naturally, there are thousands of
proverbs and proverbial expressions about cultivating life/health (Peng 1988)
like these:

能动能静, 所以长命；动则体壮, 练则寿长. Néngdòng néngjìng, suǒyǐ
chángmìng; dòng zé tǐ zhuàng, liàn zé shòu cháng.
Combine action and inaction, one gets a long life. Action makes the body strong;
exercise makes life long.
饭后百步走, 能活九十九. Fàn hòu bǎi bù zǒu, néng huó jiǔshíjiǔ.
Walking a hundred steps after a meal makes you live ninety-nine years old.
一日三笑, 人生难老. Yí rì sān xiào, rénshēng nán lǎo.
Three laughs a day, one's life won't be old.
一日三恼, 不老也老. Yí rì sān nǎo, bù lǎo yě lǎo.
Three exasperations a day, one gets old before old.
遇事不恼, 长生不老. Yù shì bù nǎo, chángshēng bùlǎo.
Not to be irritated by anything, you will never be old.
笑一笑十年少. Xiào yí xiào shí niánshào.
Laugh often, you are ten years younger.
笑口常开, 青春常在. Xiào kǒu cháng kāi, qīngchūn cháng zài.
Frequent laughing keeps you young forever.
老来忙, 寿命长. Lǎo lái máng, shòumìng cháng.
Keep busy as you age, your life will be long.
今年笋子来年竹, 少壮体强老来福. Jīnnián sǔnzi láiniánzhú, shàozhuàng tǐqiáng
lǎoláifú.
This year's bamboo sprouts will be bamboo next year, a strong body at a young age
brings happiness at old age.
千斤难买老来瘦. Qiānjīn nán mǎi lǎo lái shòu.
You can't buy slimness in old age with a thousand gold.

山中易找千年树，人中难找百年翁. Shānzhōng yì zhǎo qiānnián shù, rén zhōng nán zhǎo bǎinián wēng.

It is easy to find a tree of a thousand years old in the mountain, but it is hard to find a man of a hundred years among humans.

蚂蚁爬树不怕高，有心锻炼不怕老. Mǎyǐ pá shù búpà gāo, yǒuxīn duànliàn búpà lǎo.

Ants are not afraid of the height of trees; exercise is not to be limited by old age.

人老不以筋骨为能. Rén lǎo bù yǐ jīngǔ wéi néng.

Old people can't show off muscles.

筋长一寸，寿长十年. Jīn cháng yīcùn, shòu cháng shí nián.

An inch longer in tendon, ten years longer in longevity.

生命在于运动. Shēngmìng zàiyú yùndòng.

Life lies in movement (exercise).

Recognizing aging and identifying others who are old, whether people or animals or trees, are the most humorous way for old people to adapt to reality, and to prepare themselves for the next steps. Proverbs are thus best in drawing the analogies to comfort the aging people:

人老猫腰，树老焦梢. Rén lǎo māo yāo, shù lǎo jiāo shāo.

Old people have cat's backs, old trees have dried tops.

树老根多，人老话多. Shù lǎo gēn duō, rén lǎohuà duō.

Old trees have more roots, old people have more words.

马老腿慢，人老嘴慢. Mǎ lǎo tuǐ màn, rén lǎo zuǐ màn.

Old horses have slow legs, old people have slow mouths.

人老先从腿上多. Rén lǎo xiān cóng tuǐ shàng duō.

People first age from legs.

树怕空，人怕松. Shù pà kōng, rén pà sōng.

Trees are afraid of being hollow, people are afraid of getting loose.

In fact, the "passing the world" is more about dealing with social life than family life. Even those who are tired of social life would find ways to keep happy family life as a way of having good fortune or auspiciousness (*fu* 福, or *xingfu* 幸福) so that old age would not be miserable. One proverbial expression is *tianlun zhile* (the destined happiness of enjoying family love and joy with children/grandchildren around 天伦之乐), reflecting the Confucian values of family:

老婆孩子热炕头. Lǎopó háizi rè kàngtóu.

Being on a warm bed with wife and children around.

患病需要好医生，年迈需要好老伴. Huànbìng xūyào hǎo yīshēng, niánmài xūyào hǎo lǎobàn.

A sickness needs a good doctor to cure, old age needs a good old partner.

不怕年老, 就怕躺倒. Búpà nián lǎo, jiù pà tǎng dǎo.

Old age is not scary, laying down is alarming.

树老怕空心, 人老怕冷清. Shù lǎo pà kōngxīn, rén lǎo pà lěngqīng.

Old trees are afraid of being hollow, old people are afraid of being lonely.

人老疼孩儿, 猫老嚼孩儿. Rén lǎo téng hái'ér, māo lǎo jué hái'ér.

Old people dote their children, old cats eat their kittens.

要求子孝, 先敬爹娘. Yāoqiú zǐ xiào, xiān jìng diē niáng.

To have filial sons, to respect your parents first.

敬老得富, 敬田有谷. Jìnglǎo dé fù, jìng tián yǒu gǔ.

Respect the old, you get rich; respect the fields, you get grains.

To end this section, an anti-proverb of "older ginger is spicier" may be of interest. In a 1961 film about the civil wars in the early twentieth century in China, *Red Guards on Honghu Lake* (洪湖赤卫队) (dir. Xie Tian 谢添, 112 min. The opera of the same name was premiered in 1958, and was rearranged again for public performance in 2012), there is a scene where a coded sentence is to be spoken by a guerrilla member disguised as a street *erhu* (two-string instrument) performer in order to connect with a covered communist party member. That sentence is:

人老了弦也调不准了. Rén lǎole xián yě diáo bù zhǔnle.

An old man can't even tune the strings.

(Or, as one gets old, he can't even tune a string instrument.)

This proverbial expression became very popular all over China in the 1960s through 1980s, along with the popularity of film. It is also like a coded line for the generation growing up during that period and is often used during gatherings among them. I, who learned this expression as a child, have gained a deeper understanding of it, both physically and metaphorically as I have grown older. In fact, I find myself using it more and more frequently whenever I mishandle or drop something here or there, not to mention mess-ups in playing musical instruments. Naturally, variants of this metaphorical expression have emerged over time, and none of those uses are necessarily related to tuning a strong musical instrument. For example, in a statement, it is to admit or emphasize that an old person can no longer tune accurately, or function properly:

人老了, 弦也(都)调不准了. Rén lǎole, xián yě (dōu) diáo bù zhǔnle.

An old man can't even tune/think/do the job!

In question form, it is to doubt an old person's functionality:

人老了, 弦都调不准了(吗)? Rén lǎole, xián dōu diáo bù zhǔnle (ma)?

As an old man, can you not tune/think/do the job?

And in question or rhetorical from, it is to challenge the denial of an old person's capability:

人老了, 弦真的调不准了吗？ Rén lǎole, xián zhēn de diáo bù zhǔnle ma?
As an old man, can you really not tune/think/do the job?

In conclusion, this chapter argues that proverbs express a culture's fundamental beliefs and values. To support this argument, it offers an interpretive framework that, (a) draws a broad picture of the history of collecting, using, and studying proverbs in China as a way to enforce core Chinese values; (b) gives a brief history of how Chinese proverbs were translated; (c) contextualizes the meaning of "being old" in Chinese culture and history by presenting the origin and development of a specific proverb about age: "older ginger is spicier" and examines a number of proverbs about old age and aging from four life-views.

Part IV

GEYAO

BALLADS AND STORIES WITHOUT WORDS

As discussed in the previous parts, none of the categorical terms for oral narratives has a clear definition. Among them, *geyao* (歌谣, folksongs and ballads) may be the one that is least clear because it contains word/text, singing/ chanting, and music/musical-instrument-playing as one entirety, and because it is often segmented and separated into either text-only or music-only form by collectors and researchers. As a result, *geyao* is the least studied category though it enjoys a relatively higher popularity due to it is role in everyday life and in "folk literature" as seen in the national projects of the *Grand Collections of Folklore Literature* (1984–2009) and the *Compendium of Chinese Folk Literature* (2017–2025). In literature or folk literature (or folklore), *geyao* is essentially treated as text, while in musicological (or ethnomusicological) studies, *geyao* is often categorized as *folk music* with emphasis on musical composition and style.

While the field of *geyao* studies is rather underdeveloped in China, discussing Chinese *geyao* in a non-Chinese language is even harder because it involves dialects, variations of tones in chanting/singing (in contrast to speaking), translations, and diverse musical notation systems. Today, with video-documenting technology and improved methods, this challenge seems to be manageable at least in terms of recording the use or performance of *geyao* as an event.

When the context of using/performing *geyao* in everyday life is stripped into either a text-only or music-only subject matter, it is *disciplinarily* separated into verbal/textual or nonverbal/musical *material/target* for researchers themselves. The practitioners, however, continue their uses of *geyao* as a whole in any form and situation to fulfill their purpose—to establish interpersonal communication and to maintain their personal identity, as seen in different "faces" in performing arts in contemporary China (Gibbs 2020; Cen and Cen 2020).

In reality, *geyao* is inseparable from folksongs and folk music, the use of traditional musical instruments, and, certainly, the specific situations (i.e., when, where, and who said what to whom). Even when singing or chanting *geyao* as children's rhymes or adults' entertainments (e.g., at drinking/feast table) without conventional "musical instruments," objects and body parts are commonly used as "musical instruments," for example, in chopstick-drumming, hand-clapping, or foot-stomping, although such "musical instruments" (including unique vocal/tonal variation from the human throat) are often ignored.

Undoubtedly, since the Kunqu Opera (昆曲, a local storytelling/drama form in south China) was inscribed as UNESCO's Representative Human Oral and Intangible Heritage Masterpiece in 2001 (China's First National Intangible Cultural Heritage List in 2006), followed by the *Guqin* (古琴, seven-string zither) in 2003, the Uyghur Muqam (mukamu 木卡姆) and Mongolian Folk Long Song (*changdiao* 长调) in 2005, and the epic *Gesar* (格萨尔) and some other epics and local music performance in 2009, traditional musical performances have gained a boost in public awareness in China. Similarly, with governmental support and the impact of tourism and trade, traditional musical instrument production has also improved in both quality and quantity.

However, we are still far from the "ideal" situation where text formation, music playing, and musical instrument making, along with the practice/performance of the practitioners, can be taken as one entity and studied with a holistic view in realistic and historical contexts. When these components are treated as separable and independent targets, they are simply used for other purposes held by the researchers, rather than for the understanding of the tradition itself in particular context. Respecting the actual "context" is to respect the tradition itself and avoid manipulating it for other purposes.

With these ideas, chapter 7 first surveys the development of *geyao* in Chinese history, and then looks at the contemporary practice by the common people in daily life, trying to present *geyao* as a combination of text/words, singing/chanting, and music/music playing. Chapter 8 focuses on the developmental history of the clay-vessel flute, *xun* (埙), as a musical instrument, an ethical symbol, and an identity marker at individual, regional, and national levels. To illustrate how this instrument plays a role in multicultural communication, this chapter ends with a reflection upon my own practice of making, playing, and teaching of this instrument in a multicultural context, hoping to shed light on our understanding of how a tradition continues and gains its vitality and validity, how a new culture, *a third culture*, is being developed, and how the practice of tradition shapes individual identity in living a meaningful life.

Chapter 7

The Trilateral Trajectories
Oral, Literary, and Musical Traditions of Ballads

Chinese *geyao* (歌谣), ballads/folksongs, present a set of paradoxes to us: they were the major part of the earliest written records, but they are now understudied in folk literature. Although they have been the richest source for all other literary genres in the history of Chinese literature, they are hardly practiced in its full sense (i.e., integrating words/chanting, actions/dances, music, and musical instrument playing) in everyday life among the majority Han Chinese (but not so in many minority groups with their own languages in China). Furthermore, among non-Chinese publications on Chinese oral tradition, *geyao* seem to be the least researched in both quantity and quality. For example, the earliest specialized collection of *geyao* in modern sense only began in the sixteenth century with the *Ancient and Current Folk Ballads* (*Gujin fengyao* 古今风谣) by Yang Shen (杨慎 1488–1559) (Tian 1957:72). The purpose of this chapter is to redress the imbalance in scholarly consideration of *geyao*.

To understand *geyao* from their early forms to the current situation, this chapter first provides a background by looking at the change in definition and literary characteristics, and then examines the current scholarship with examples from popular uses. In this process, this chapter argues that the prevalence of ballads in early China prior to the Tang Dynasty (618–960) was, among other factors, largely due to the integration of word/text and music, whereas after the rise of the elite *shi*-poetry (*shi* 诗) in the Tang and the *ci*-poetry (*ci* 词) in the Song Dynasty (960–1279) when the Neo-Confucianism began to dominate the entire society and culture thereafter, *geyao* began to be further separated for the use of text/word/content by the elite while the music aspect was neglected. This separation is most obvious in the Han Chinese practice after the Song Dynasty, that is, the literary and art aspects of *geyao* have been over-emphasized and "edited" into elite literature, taking *geyao* out of their practical context. As a result, the nature of *geyao* as the most direct and flexible expressions of common people's dissatisfaction, resistance, and hope has been downplayed through the "historical" lens (i.e., this aspect is often distanced by talking about those collected in the history, but not those used in contemporary life). But among many non-Han Chinese groups, however, ballads/folksongs have remained not only prevalent, but also crucial for everyday communication in reconstructing and maintaining their group identity as "minorities" in China, especially through the form of epics (Bender 2006b; 2016). (Unfortunately, the examples here are all in Chinese, but not translated from other languages.)

GEYAO IN CHINESE AND BALLAD
IN EUROPEAN DEFINITIONS

Unlike the fairy tale (*tonghua*) and proverb (*yanyu*) discussed in the previous chapters, *geyao* may have the most resemblances to "ballad" in its original definition. In Europe, *ballad* has its roots in the Latin "dance" or *ballare*. The word developed through the medieval Scottish dance songs or "*ballares*," and the medieval French *chanson balladée* or *ballade* for "dance songs" (Apel 1972:70–72). In China, *geyao* is a combination of two words or concepts, *ge* (歌) meaning singing or song, and *yao* (谣) meaning speaking/chanting in rhyme. In classical Chinese over two thousand years ago, singing a tune (*qu* 曲) with musical instruments playing (*yue* 乐) is called *ge*; without instruments playing it is *yao*. This relationship between *ge* and *yao* has been the dominant concept in Chinese folk literature and folk music collections and studies until today. Indeed, "It is this apparently simple yet superbly artful way of telling a story in song that is the essence of balladry" (Moreira 1997a:83).

Furthermore, in the ancient Chinese concepts, singing was an advancement of speaking in rhythm and rhyme, and the combination of singing and dancing (*wu* 舞) was an elevation from singing alone, but the combination of singing, dancing, and music-playing (*yue*) was the highest stage of expressing emotions, a distinctive feature of Chinese traditional *geyao*. Of course, music at that time referred to the "official" music, especially with the influence of Confucian ethics. As a result, the relations and tensions between Confucian propriety or rites (*li* 礼) and proper music (*yue*) and between *ya* (upright/ elegant 雅) and *su* (popular/folk/vulgar 俗), have been the central dynamic forces in the continuity of Chinese culture.

The development of regulated metrical poetry further separated the literati's refined upper-class works (*ya*) from the lower-class songs or ballads known as the folk ways (*su*). This distinction ultimately made the Tang and

Song Dynasties (7th c.–13th c.) the pinnacle of Chinese poetry (*shige*; combining *shi*/poem and *ge*/song), meanwhile folk songs were further looked down upon by the elite, although individual collectors and composers never stopped taking advantage of folk songs and ballads.

The term *geyao*, as the combination of folksongs and folk ballads, is still used today, as seen in the three unprecedented national projects: the *Grand Collection of Chinese Folksongs* (1979–2009), the *Grand Collection of Chinese Ballads* (1984–2009), and the ongoing *Compendium of Chinese Folk Literature* (2017–2025) (to be further discussed later). In this sense, the term folk songs and folk ballads are used interchangeably in Chinese folk literature studies, as is the case in this chapter, especially in talking about the ancient periods when *ge*/song, *yao*/ballad, *shi*/poem were closely related.

CATEGORIZATION OF BALLADS

While the Chinese *geyao* and the European-based *ballad* both point to a form of verse or narrative set to music, and both terms emphasize the "song" part, in studies, however, there is often the separation of the folksong music (as a part of musicology) and folksong verses or narratives (as a form of literature). This presents a methodological issue for many collectors and researchers because, in practice, these categories are not easily separable for the practitioners. Even in the simplest form, like in one or two verses, a ballad has a formulaic musical pattern with emphasis on certain structure or rhyme of words, and thus it is a "narrative song that is characterized chiefly by concentration on a single episode, dramatic development through dialogue and action, and objective tone and that is structurally rooted in repetitive verbal patterns and tight, balancing scenes" (Moreira 1997a:81).

In the best-known collection of *geyao* prior to the twentieth century, *Ancient Ballads and Proverbial Expressions* (*Gu Yao Yan* 古谣谚), Du Wenlan (杜文澜 1815–1881) collected about 3,300 ballads from more than 860 books, with citations and contextual information, but "folksongs" were not included. The 100 chapters in the collection are divided into two parts: one related to the imperial life, and the other to the life of the common people. This collection is now seen as the earliest *geyao* study in China.

In the unprecedented *Grand Collection of Chinese Ballads* (1984–2009), *geyao*/ballad is "considered from literary perspective, and consists of the words in folksongs and the folk ballad" (Jia 1997:8). In this *Grand Collection*, as seen in the *Hainan Volume* (1997) with its regional characteristics, ballads are categorized into eleven types (each with subtypes) based on content: preluding songs; ancient songs; work songs; current political situation songs; revolutionary songs; ritual songs; love songs; everyday life songs; overseas

Chinese' homesickness songs; historical legend songs; and children's songs (see an example of the song "I still want to make friends with you" in the later part of this chapter).

However, according to the most influential textbook compiled under the guidance of the folklorist Zhong Jingwen, who was one of the most active scholars in collecting and studying ballads in the 1920s, *geyao* are categorized into six types based on the *content* and the *audience*: work songs (劳动歌); ritual songs (仪式歌); current political songs (时政歌); everyday life songs (生活歌); love songs (情歌); children's songs (儿歌), while regional and dialectical differences are recognized (Zhong 1980:240–276). Similar categorization is also used in some other textbooks (Huang 2013; Duan 2018), and in the later national *geyao* collection projects.

THE DEVELOPMENTAL HISTORY OF GEYAO COLLECTION AND STUDIES IN CHINA

While the definitions of *geyao* in China and ballad in English are similar, and while they also share a similar structure, *geyao* may be more complicated than ballads in many ways due to the linguistic distinctions of the tonal Chinese language and the single-syllable character. However, this chapter is not meant to focus on the stylistic and linguistic comparison, but to look at the developmental history of *geyao* as an oral tradition.

The following outline is based on the most recent collective effort of three decades that resulted in the *History of Chinese Folklore* (Qi and Lü 2019). Since many historical and social aspects are closely related to the previous discussions about Chinese folklore and folkloristics in general, and folktales and proverbs in particular, the following will avoid repetition and highlight the most important ideas and contexts on *geyao*.

Stage One (Before the Second Century BCE)

Though the earliest written examples of ballads appear in the *Book of Documents* (*Shang Shu* 尚书), from the tenth century BCE, a large number of ballads only began to be recorded beginning in the sixth century BCE. The most important representative work is the *Book of Songs* (*Shi Jing*). Sima Qian (ca. 145 BCE– ?), author of the first history book in China, *The Records of the Historian* (*Shi Ji*), believed that Confucius (551–478 BCE) was asked to select from more than three thousand folksongs to edit the *Book of Songs* which eventually contained the current 305 songs/poems. There are three categories of songs or poems in this book: *feng* (风, folksongs) which contains 160 folksongs from 15 states; *ya* (雅, standard poems), written by literati (but with some as *feng*); *song* (颂, odes composed to the kings), produced also by the literati. While nearly half of those songs are categorized as folksongs, they are clearly edited to keep consistent in style with the rest (or vice versa) which are odes to the kings. It also set the example for "editing" folksongs and ballads for the following two millennia.

The general linguistic feature of this period is that most of the ballads or folksongs have four characters as a verse/line (sometimes with an exclamation word as the fifth for rhythm). A song would begin with a metaphor (*bi* 比), and then develop into lyrical and emotional expression (*xing* 兴). This style became exemplary for the later ballads and folksongs, as seen in the following three songs in the *Book of Songs* (translations from James Legge 1898) (hereafter in this chapter, all the Chinese texts are given phonetic *pinyin* to indicate the rhyme; all translations are mine otherwise noted):

狡童 jiǎo tóng
彼狡童兮, 不与我言兮. Bǐ jiǎo tóng xī, bù yǔ wǒ yán xī.
维子之故, 使我不能餐兮. Wéi zǐ zhī gù, shǐ wǒ bùnéng cān xī.
彼狡童兮, 不与我食兮. Bǐ jiǎo tóng xī, bù yǔ wǒ shí xī.
维子之故, 使我不能息兮. Wéi zǐ zhī gù, shǐ wǒ bùnéng xī xī.
The Artful Boy
That artful boy!
He will not speak with me!
But for the sake of you, Sir,
Shall I make myself unable to eat?
That artful boy!
He will not eat with me!
But for the sake of you, Sir,
Shall I make myself unable to rest?

子衿 *zǐ jīn*
青青子衿, 悠悠我心. Qīngqīng zǐ jīn, yōuyōu wǒ xīn.
纵我不往, 子宁不嗣音. Zòng wǒ bù wǎng, zǐ níng bù sì yīn.
青青子佩, 悠悠我思. Qīngqīng zǐ pèi, yōuyōu wǒ sī.
纵我不往, 子宁不來. Zòng wǒ bù wǎng, zǐ níng bù lái.
挑兮达兮, 在城阙兮. Tiāo xī dá xī, zài chéngquē xī.
一日不见, 如三月兮. Yī rì bújiàn, rú sān yuè xī.
Your Collar
O you, with the blue collar,
Prolonged is the anxiety of my heart.
Although I do not go [to you],
Why do you not continue your messages [to me]?
O you with the blue [strings to your] girdle-gems,

Long, long do I think of you.
Although I do not go [to you],
Why do you not come [to me]?
How volatile are you and dissipated,
By the look-out tower on the wall!
One day without the sight of you,
Is like three months.

硕鼠 Shuò shǔ
硕鼠硕鼠, 无食我黍. Shuò shǔ shuò shǔ, wú shí wǒ shǔ.
三岁罐女, 莫我肯顾. Sān suì guàn nǚ, mò wǒ kěn gù.
逝将去女, 适彼乐土. Shì jiāng qù nǚ, shì bǐ lètǔ.
乐土乐土, 爰得我所. Lètǔ lètǔ, yuán dé wǒ suǒ.
Large Rat
Large rats! Large rats!
Do not eat our millet.
Three years have we had to do with you,
And you have not been willing to show any regard for us.
We will leave you,
And go to that happy land.
Happy land! Happy land!
There shall we find our place.

Stage Two (2nd c. BCE–3rd c. CE)

This was the period when the feudal system took shape and was strengthened through the united empires of the Qin and Han dynasties. As a result, two distinctive features of the ballads were developed: the emergence of a large number of ballads reflecting political or class struggles and the governmental efforts (*yuefu* 乐府, music department) for collecting, writing, and disseminating ballads. This mechanism heavily influenced the transformation of ballads as folk expressions to the regulated poetry composed by literati. As a result, the records from this period are mainly from two sources: those composed by the literati and musicians working for the courts and those collected from the folk. Even those collected from the folk can be further divided into those created by individuals and those passed down. It is the latter part that is now considered folksongs or ballads.

The purpose of collecting folksongs was "to observe the trending customs and to know how to treat the folk," as described in the *Book of the Han* (汉书). In this important book written in the second century CE, there are ballads of various types, including those by the common people about the "Red Eyebrow Rebellion" against the ruler Wang Mang (45 BCE–23 CE):

宁逢赤眉, 不逢太师! Níng féng chì méi, bù féng tài shī!
太师尚可, 更始杀我! Tài shī shàng kě, gēngshǐ shā wǒ!
Rather encountering the Red Eyebrow,
Than encountering the army from the Court.
Even survived the army from the Court,
The army led by Gengshi will kill me!

During this period, there were also many recorded folksongs about the relations between Han Chinese and the surrounding minority groups, in particular the Xiongnu from the north. The Xiongnu were the nomadic people who posed a great threat to the Han Chinese during this period, which led to the building of the Great Wall. There were also other strategies besides battles to keep peace, for example, by marrying princesses to the Xiongnu rulers. Here is one song reflecting the loneliness of the princess who was forced to be married out, as recorded in the *Book of the Han*:

吾家嫁我兮天一方, Wú jiā jià wǒ xī tiān yīfāng,
远托异国兮乌孙王. yuǎn tuō yìguó xī wū sūn wáng.
穹庐为室兮旃为墙, Qiónglú wèi shì xī zhān wèi qiáng,
以肉为食酪为浆. yǐ ròu wèi shí xī lào wèi jiāng.
居常土思兮心内伤, Jū cháng tǔ sī xī xīn nèishāng,
愿为黄鹄兮归故乡. yuàn wéi huáng gǔ xī guī gùxiāng.
My family married me out to the other side of the sky,
A remote land, to the Wusun King.
The sky is the ceiling, banner posts are the walls,
Meat as grains, milk as water.
Long time living here hurting my heart,
I wish to be a wild swan, returning to my hometown.

A ballad of resistance to the First Emperor of Qin (211 BCE–207 BCE) was passed down and recorded in the fifth century (as "A Ballad of the Qin Times" /秦世谣 by Liu Jingshu 刘敬叔 fl. 460–468), reflecting a general reaction of the common people to the crucial rulers of the times:

秦始皇, 何强梁! Qínshǐhuáng, hé qiángliáng!
开吾户, 据吾床; Kāi wú hù, jù wú chuáng;
饮吾酒, 唾吾浆; yǐn wú jiǔ, tuò wú jiāng;
餐吾饭, 以吾粮; cān wú fàn, yǐ wú liáng;
张吾弓, 射东墙, zhāngwúgōng, shè dōng qiáng,
前至沙丘当灭亡. qián zhì shāqiū dāng mièwáng.
The First Emperor of Qin, how brutally violent!
Open my door, split my bed;

Drink my wine, swallow my soup;
Eat my food, take my grains;
Pull my bows, shoot the east wall,
When [you] in battleground, should be killed!

Stage Three (3rd c.–6th c.)

This is a period when the empire was split into many states and there were constant wars. It was also in this socially tumultuous period that folk literature and, in particular, folksongs were highly developed. Folksongs were collected by the new governmental institutions with a new emphasis on the singing/chanting without music (*qingyue* 清乐). This style enforced the separation of words/texts from music or musical instrument playing, and thus emphasized the aspects of "speaking" with distinctive rhyme. The best-known style was "Mid-night Song" (*ziyege* 子夜歌), also representative of the South China style during this period. In this style, puns and homophones are frequently used. For example, in the first of the three love songs below, *furong* (for both *hibiscus* flower and for *husband's face*), *lian* (for both *lotus* flower and *sympathy*), and *ying* (for both *baby* and *ought to*) are used as homophonous puns:

高山种芙蓉, 复经黄檗坞; Gāoshān zhòng fúróng, fù jīng huángbò wù;
果得一莲时, 流离婴辛苦. guǒ dé yī lián shí, liúlí yīng xīnkǔ.
Hibiscus planted on the high mountain,
Passing by the valley of Amur cork trees;
Gaining the lotus,
Departing ought to be [baby] full of bitterness.

郎为傍人取, 负侬非一事. Láng wèi bàng rén qǔ, fù nóng fēi yīshì.
摘门不安横, 无复相关意. Chī mén bù'ān héng, wú fù xiāngguān yì.
My man, your heart is taken by someone else,
You owe me more than once.
I leave the door open without bolt,
It has nothing to do with you anymore.

夜长不得眠, 明月何灼灼. Yè cháng bùdé mián, míngyuè hé zhuózhuó.
想闻散唤声, 虚应空中诺. Xiǎng wén sàn huàn shēng, xū yìng kōngzhōng nuò.
It's hard to sleep during the long night,
The moon is simply too bright.
I seem to hear calling from somewhere,
And pretend to answer a promise in the air.

Among the nomads in North China, there were also many songs recorded as a valuable part of Chinese literature. Those songs were often accompanied with wind instruments and drums. Certainly, there was no clear distinction between those songs from the nomadic groups and those from the Han Chinese, though they could be roughly differentiated by the content or theme. Yet, even at that time, there were obvious marks of translating songs from the minority groups into the Han Chinese writing. For example, in the *Collection of the Music Department* (*Yuefu Shiji* 乐府诗集) by Guo Maoqian (郭茂倩 1041–1099), which includes the famous story of Mulan as a female warrior, there is this ballad about soldiers from different ethnic backgrounds joining the army and fighting side by side, a record of cultural integration at that time:

男儿欲作健, Nán'ér yù zuò jiàn,
结伴不须多. jiébàn bù xū duō.
鹞子经天飞, Yàozi jīng tiān fēi,
群雀两向波. qúnquè liǎng xiàng bō.
A warrior should be vigorous,
No need for many partners.
Like the eagle flying across,
Little birds shun away on both sides.

In terms of structural and style changes, the popular forms were in five or seven words/syllables, though other irregular forms were also widely used. Influenced by the nomadic groups, this style was drastically different from the delicate Southern style.

Stage Four (6th c.–10th c.)

During this period, Chinese poetry reached its peak of maturity, and the ballads or folksongs also demonstrated some new characteristics. The previously divided empire was now united, but social and political tensions were still high due to the burden laid upon the common people. Thus, a large number of ballads were about exposing and resisting social and political corruption, for example:

案后一腔冻猪肉, Àn hòu yī qiāng dòng zhūròu,
所以名为姜侍郎. suǒyǐ míng wèi jiāng shìláng.
Behind the desk a full frozen pork [to bribe],
So that can be called Minister Jiang [the briber].

生儿不用识文字, Shēng ér bùyòng shí wénzì,
斗鸡走马胜读书. dòujī zǒumǎ shèng dúshū.
No need to have a son to learn to read,
Cock-fight and horse-race are better than reading books
[as a way to win the favor from the Emperor].

The most characteristic type of the Tang Dynasty folksong was the "mountain song" (*shange* 山歌) known as "bamboo branch" songs (*zhuzhi* 竹枝). This style is believed to have emerged in the seventh century. A great number of poets used this style to compose or edit what they heard from the common people. It is also known that this style was first performed by singing and dancing while holding bamboo branches in hands to keep the musical beat, and later on it developed into pure literary/textual style and further separated from the folk singing style. By the seventeenth century, the dominance of this literary style basically drove the folk style to extinction. The content or theme of this style reflects all aspects of social and personal life, and its main structure is in four verses with seven characters/syllables in each verse, and with bamboo beating in the middle of each verse for rhythm, though there are also many variant styles. For example:

杨柳青青, 江水平, Yángliǔqīng qīng, jiāng shuǐpíng,
闻郎江上, 唱歌声. wén láng jiāngshàng, chànggē shēng.
东边日出, 西边雨, Dōngbian rì chū, xībian yǔ,
道是无晴, 却有晴. dào shì wú qíng, què yǒu qíng.
The willows are green . . . river water is smooth,
I hear my man on the river . . . singing songs.
The sun rises on the east . . . the rain is on the west,
You say there is no [clear day] qing . . . but there is [love] qing.

There is also a style known as Dunhuang Music and Song (*Dunhuang quci* 敦煌曲词; Dunhuang is in Gansu Province in Northwest China). A large number of records from the Dunhuang caves show that there is a rich treasure trove of folksongs mostly created in the seventh century. Yet, these texts were in the caves unknown to the world for over a thousand years. When they were rediscovered at the beginning of the twentieth century, they were mostly taken away by the Europeans. Most of the songs are about personal sufferings of poverty, being drafted, losing husbands, missing loved ones. For example, this *wugeng* (five *geng* 五更; one night is divided into five *geng*, and each *geng* is two-hours long) is about a wife bidding farewell to her husband going off to a battle:

一更刁斗鸣, Yī gēng diāodǒumíng
二更愁未央, èr gēng chóu wèiyāng
三更夜惊心, sān gēng yè jīng xīn
四更星汉低, sì gēng xīnghàn dī
五更催送筹. wǔ gēng cuī sòng chóu
At the first *geng*, strike the dipper

At the second *geng*, endless sorrows arise
At the third *geng* [midnight], heart-shocking,
At the four *geng*, all stars are low,
At the fifth *geng*, being urged to bid farewell

Another style of folksongs during this period is related to the interactions of the Han Chinese with the northwest and southwest minority groups. They are distinctive in both style and content. For example, one folksong recovered from the Dunhuang texts is about the life in Tubo (吐蕃; current Tibet):

啊, 小鸟呢飞枝低, Ah, xiǎo niǎo ne fēi zhī dī,
难上呢高天际. nán shàng ne gāo tiānjì.
小人呢没本领, Xiǎo rén ne méi běnlǐng,
不能呢保恩情. bùnéng ne bǎo ēnqíng.
手中呢刀不强, Shǒuzhōng ne dāo bù qiáng,
难把呢敌人降. nán bǎ ne dírén xiàng.
小驹呢跑得慢, Xiǎo jū ne pǎo dé màn,
不能呢飞速赶. bùnéng ne fēisù gǎn.
小鹿呢腿脚软, Xiǎolù ne tuǐjiǎo ruǎn,
难能呢翻大山. nán néng ne fān dàshān.
Oh, little bird, flying to the low branches,
So hard, flying up high.
Little people, without talents,
So hard, guaranteeing our feelings.
Knife in hand, not so sharp,
So hard, capturing the enemy.
Little yearling, running slow,
So hard, galloping fast.
Little fawn, with weak legs,
So hard, climbing a mountain high.

Another example related to the Southwest Bai people, containing the earliest memory of how their ancestors cultivated the land, "We use *bharal* (Chinese blue sheep) to plough":

你地我方不相同, Nǐ dì wǒ fāng bù xiāngtóng,
我们用岩羊犁地. wǒmen yòng yán yáng lí dì.
公羊用来单独梨, Gōng yáng yòng lái dāndú lí,
母的两个换着梨. mǔ de liǎng gè huànzhe lí.
新梨铧加旧梨板, Xīn lí huá jiā jiù lí bǎn,
梨得齐整整. lí dé qí zhěngzhěng.

Your place and my place are not the same,
We use *bharal* to plough.
The male ploughs alone,
The female rotates in pairs.
The old plough and the new plough,
They plough the field neat in order.

Stage Five (10th c.–14th c.)

This period was full of political turmoil while the empires were struggling between unity and disunity, with the rise of new dynasties/states, and with tension between the Han Chinese and the minority groups, especially during the Mongolian empire of the Yuan Dynasty (1271–1368). In contrast to the social and political chaos, there was a great development of cultural integration among all the cultural groups in China in everyday life, further strengthening the unity and continuity of Chinese culture.

The influence of the "nomadic music" (*huyue* 胡乐) of the northern nomads, along with those via the Silk Road, was deep and wide. The *pipa* and the *erhu* string instruments, for example, were absorbed into the Han Chinese practice, and they are today acclaimed as the traditional Chinese musical instruments. As a result, the prosperity of folk literature during this period was largely due to such cultural integration.

There are many songs recorded with clear indication that they were from the common people directly. For example, this ballad shows how the dishonest vendor tried to fool the buyers in the Song Dynasty (960–1279), when commerce was becoming more significant in Chinese history:

听得渊明, 说与刘伶, Tīng dé yuán míng, shuō yǔ liú líng,
这一瓶约迭三升. zhè yī píng yuē dié sānshēng.
君还不信, 把称来称, Jūn hái bùxìn, bǎ chēng lái chēng,
一斤酒有一斤水, 一斤瓶. yī jīn jiǔ yǒuyī jīn shuǐ, yī jīn píng.
Hearing me talk about the gods of wine, Yuanming or Liu Ling,
This bottle is about three pound heavy.
If you don't believe, just take a scale to scale,
One pound of wine, one pound of water, and one pound of the bottle.

The social upheavals due to the split of the empire led to many ballads about the peasants' uprisings:

风高放火, 月黑杀人, Fēng gāo fànghuǒ, yuè hēi shārén,
无粮同饿, 得肉均分. wú liáng tóng è, dé ròu jūn fēn.
Set fire when it's windy,

Kill [rich/bad] people when the moon's dark,
When no food, starved together,
When having meat, we share in a fair.

天高皇帝远, 民少相公多. Tiān gāo huángdì yuǎn, mín shào xiàng gōng duō.
一日三遍打, 不反待如何! Yí rì sān biàn dǎ, bù fǎn dài rúhé!
The sky is high and the emperor is far,
Fewer working people, more officials,
Still beaten thrice a day,
What to wait if not rebel!

Stage Six (14th c.–20th c.)

This period saw both the end of the feudal system in Chinese history and unprecedented ethnic integration, which resulted in social, economic, and cultural development. After the Mongolian rule, the Manchu ruled China for nearly 300 years. Yet, the Chinese culture continued on by absorbing various cultural elements while maintaining its fundamental beliefs and values.

A large number of folksongs and ballads from this period have a direct impact on contemporary oral traditions in China, whether in content or style. The best known are those "mountain songs" about love, for example, in Feng Menglong's (1574–1646) collections:

栀子花开六瓣头, Zhī zi huā kāi liù bàn tóu,
情歌郎约我黄昏头. qínggē láng yuē wǒ huánghūn tóu.
日长遥遥难得过, Rì zhǎng yáoyáo nándéguò,
双手扳窗看日头. shuāngshǒu bān chuāng kàn rì tou.
The gardenia flower has six petals,
My love-song singing lad will meet me at twilight.
What a long day, so hard to pass,
Holding the window to check the sun.

要分离除非天做了地! Yào fēnlí chúfēi tiān zuòle dì!
要分离除非东做了西! Yào fēnlí chúfēi dōng zuòle xī!
要分离除非官做了吏! Yào fēnlí chúfēi guān zuòle lì!
你要分时分不得我, Nǐ yào fēn shífēn bùdé wǒ,
我要离时离不得你. wǒ yào lí shí lì bùdé nǐ.
就死在黄泉也做不得分离鬼! Jiù sǐ zài huángquán yě zuò bùdé fēnlí guǐ!
To separate, unless the sky becomes the earth!
To separate, unless the east becomes the west!
To separate, unless a high official becomes low!
When you want to separate, don't separate me,

When I want to separate, won't separate you.
Even at death in the Yellow Spring, we are inseparable ghosts!

There are also songs about social problems such as this "Fuyang Ballad":

富阳江之鱼, 富阳山之茶, Fùyángjiāng zhī yú, fù yáng shān zhī chá,
鱼肥卖我子, 茶香破我家. yú féi mài wǒ zǐ, chá xiāng pò wǒjiā.
采茶妇, 捕渔夫, Cǎi chá fù, bǔ yúfū,
官府拷掠无完肤. guānfǔ kǎo lüè wú wán fū.
Fuyang river fish, Fuyang mountain tea,
The fish is fat, but I have to sell my son,
The tea is sweet, but my family is broken.
Tea-leaf picking wife, fish-catching husband,
The officials took all, we can't put ourselves together as a whole.

Another important component is the Cantonese folksong, which, due to its distinctive dialectical feature, has demonstrated some unique characteristics:

中间日头四边雨, Zhōng jiàn rì tou sìbiān yǔ,
记得有情人在心. jìdé yǒuqíng rén zàixīn.
In the middle is the sun, surrounded by the rain,
In the heart, remembering the loved one.

One of the best representative collections of Cantonese folksongs is *Yue Ou* (*Cantonese Folk Singing*) by Zhao Ziyong (招子庸 1793–1846). This collection also recorded the performing genre that developed from the southern music style, with seven characters/syllables per line and three lines in the long, which could be performed either by singing alone or with the accompaniment of such musical instruments as *pipa*, *xiao* (southern vertical flute), and *yangqin* (a hammered dulcimer developed from the Iranian *santūr*). *Yue Ou* included a total of 121 songs, and it was translated into English as the *Cantonese Love-Songs* (Clementi 1904). For example, Song II (The choice of a heart) runs as follows:

In the world it is heart to find a heart
Can I but win his heart, then even in death will I follow in this quest.
At a glance I would test his heart's truth, by a glance I would foil his fraud.
When I have surely tested his true love, it will indeed be good to take counsel with him.
Fraud upon fraud! Fraud has made our heart empty: one end all we beware of the truant.

So, e'en if he come true-hearted to court me, I still will test him twice and thrice over.

Me thinks that of ten thousand guest-gallants they who give true love are not even one:

True passion's flotsam and fragments are more cruel to seek, then 'twere to dredge ocean for a needle.

Moreover, if thou canst find a true heart, one and all can find it too.

Between how many maids, then, say you, can a loyal gallant share his love?

Ponder little by little on predestined fate! Each man must meet it face to face.

No need for your hastening.

Be content a while with your lot.

Each bears the doom of his former life. Do not thou envy any man! (Clementi 1904:29)

Similarly, one distinctive regional style of the Zhuang people's folksongs in the southwest is called "*fwen*" in Zhuang language (or, *fwencingz* for love song, with several variants), with "*hun*" sound, but often used "*huan*" (欢) in Chinese translation, whose characteristics can be seen in "The Zhuang Girl Yearns for Love" (壮女相思曲 Zhuàng nǚ xiāngsī qū):

妹相思, 不作风流待几时. Mèi xiāngsī, bùzuò fēngliú dài jǐshí.
只见风吹花落地, Zhǐ jiàn fēng chuī huā luòdì,
不见风吹花上枝. bùjiàn fēng chuī huā shàngzhī.
Your young sister yearns for love,
Why not now show my beauty and feelings.
There is only wind blowing flowers off branches,
But not wind blowing flowers on branches.
妹相思, 蜘蛛结网恨无丝. Mèi xiāngsī, zhīzhū jié wǎng hèn wú sī.
花不年年长在树, Huā bù nián nián zhǎng zài shù,
娘不年年伴女儿. niáng bù nián nián bàn nǚ'ér.
Your young sister yearns for love,
Spider webs that have no silk [missing].
Flowers do not grow on trees year by year,
Mother does not keep her daughter year by year.

Like many other regional and ethnic groups in China, the Zhuang people have the tradition of "talking" through "singing." Today, using the Zhuang folksongs to promote cultural tourism is widely known in China. One of the most distinctive examples is the "Impression of Liu Sanjie" (印象刘三姐), an hour-long, out-door performance on-the-water in Lijiang, Guilin, southwest China, where the singer Liu Sanjie (Third Sister Liu) is famous for (Turner 2011). The local belief is that Liu Sanjie lived in the Tang Dynasty

(618–907), and is commemorated and worshipped through many temples and statues in the region. The performance has continued every evening since 2004 and has won various awards. This performance represents the tradition, *Liu Sanjie Geyao* (刘三姐歌谣), which was listed as a National Intangible Cultural Heritage (ICH) in 2006.

Children's songs/ballads (children's songs 儿歌; children's ballads 童谣) during this period were also recorded in a number of collections. A popular *geyao* known to be from the seventeenth century, "The Ungrateful Son [Long-tailed Magpie]" (喜鹊尾巴长 Xǐquè wěibā cháng), is about how a man married a wife and forgot his mother. It has been widely disseminated as a way of teaching about the mother-in-law and daughter-in-law dilemma, and was translated into English in 1900 (Headland 1900:61):

花雀尾巴长, Huā què wěibā cháng,
娶了媳妇不要娘. qǔle xífù bùyào niáng.
妈妈要吃窝儿薄脆, Māmā yào chī wō er báocuì,
没有闲钱补笊篱. méiyǒu xiánqián bǔ zhào lí.
媳妇儿要吃梨, Xí fu er yào chī lí,
备上驴, 去赶集. bèi shàng lú, qù gǎnjí.
买了梨, 打了皮, Mǎile lí, dǎle pí,
媳妇儿, 媳妇儿你吃梨. xí fu er, xí fu er nǐ chī lí.
The tail of one magpie's as long as another,
He married a wife and he gave up his mother,
When asked by his mother to buy her some cake,
He wanted to know how much money 'twould take.
When his wife wanted pears he saddled his beast,
And started to market to buy her a feast;
He took off the peeling with every great airs,
And asked her politely to have a few pears.

Around the turn of the twentieth century, Chinese children's songs caught the attention of European missionaries, and resulted in some English translations, for example:

The Dream Junk (A Chinese Lullaby)
Sleep, my almond blossom, sleep,
The Lord of Heaven sends His command
That all the world shall close its eyes
And lie at peace beneath His hand.
Sleep, my treasure, sleep, nor fear
The Dragon who pursues the Sun,
For he must swallow up the light

Before the shadows can be born.
Sleep, wood pigeon, sleep, for now
The little golden fire-flies come
Out of the whispering bamboo-groves
To light the troops of fairies home.
Sleep, my heart, and rest thee well,
The Dream Junk sails the silver sea,
Hasten to reach the Port of Sleep
Where wait her precious freights for thee (Bredon 1922:1).

The same title, The Dream Junk, was also used to compose the following song:

Sailing, Sailing,
Down the star-shine and the moon-beam trailing,
Near now! Near now!
Comes the little fairy dream-junk's prow.
A stately lady standing there
Is shedding slumber thro' the air, thro' the air.

Home-ing, Home-ing,
Like a sleepy bird the boat is coming.
Slow oh! Slow oh!
So, the little dreams may tow'rd us blow.
The poppy nods, our eye-lids fall,
The world's asleep;
Good night for all, night for all (Terhune 1910:32–33).

Another example shows a shamanic practice (to pacify a child into good sleep). It can be compared to the "bogeyman" (as a threat to children to behave well):

天皇皇, 地皇皇, Tiānhuánghuáng, dì huáng huáng
我家有个夜哭郎. wǒjiā yǒu gè yè kū láng
过路君子念三遍, guòlù jūnzǐ niàn sān biàn
一家睡到大天亮. yījiā shuì dào dà tiānliàng
[Translation One]
The heaven is bright, the earth is bright,
I have baby who cries all night;
Let those who pass read what I write,
And they'll sleep all night, till broad daylight (Headland 1900:29).
[Translation Two]

Heavenly emperors, earthly emperors,
Our child cries all night;
Those passing-by gentleman read thrice this sign [as a prayer],
So my whole family can sleep a whole night till daylight.

One unique northern Chinese children's song with a number of variants is "Little Mouse on the Oil Lamp," which is still popular all over China for teaching little children to behave properly:

小老鼠, 上灯台, Xiǎo lǎoshǔ, shàng dēngtái,
偷油吃, 下不来. tōu yóu chī, xiàbùlái.
叫奶奶, 奶奶不在. Jiào nǎinai, nǎinai bùzài.
喵喵喵, 猫来了, Miāo miāo miāo, māo láile,
叽里咕噜滚下来. jīligūlū gǔn xiàlái.
Little mouse, up on the lamp,
Steal the oil, and can't come back.
Call grandma, grandma isn't there.
Meow, meow, meow, a cat's here,
Roll, roll, roll, quickly roll down here.

This song was put to music in the West, "Chinese Nursery Song," near the end of the nineteenth century (see figure 7.1):

The mouse ran up the candle-stick (To eat the grease from off the wick),
When he got up, he could not get down,
But squeaked to waken all the town:
Ma-ma-ma! Ma-ma-ma!

The early twentieth century saw not only the introduction of Chinese traditional *geyao* to the West but also the adaptation of the Western in Chinese practice. A distinctive example is the song "Frère Jacques" in Chinese as "Two Tigers" (*liangzhi laohu* 两只老虎). While the equivalent English version is "Are You Sleepy?," the Chinese "Two Tigers" is the best known. In fact, it has also continued in the contemporary overseas Chinese community (Butcher 2020):

两只老虎, 两只老虎, Liǎng zhǐ lǎohǔ, liǎng zhǐ lǎohǔ
跑得快, 跑得快. pǎo dé kuài, pǎo dé kuài
一只没有尾巴, 一只没有耳朵, yī zhǐ méiyǒu wěibā, yī zhǐ méiyǒu ěrduǒ
真奇怪, 真奇怪. zhēn qíguài, zhēn qíguài
Two tigers, two tigers,
Run so fast, run so fast,

Figure 7.1 A Chinese Nursery Song: A Little Mouse on the Oil Lamp. Note the figures in Chinese hair and dress styles. *Source:* Herman 1882:64.

One has no tail, one has no ears,
How very strange, how very strange.

While it is not the goal of this chapter to discuss the European translation of Chinese ballads and folksongs from the eighteenth century to the early twentieth century, it is necessary to point out that these translations have exerted a great influence on the contemporary studies and public understanding of

Chinese ballads. Besides the translations, there were also studies that have impacted Chinese scholars, for example, Marcel Granet's (1932) treatment of the *Book of Songs* as folk love songs reflecting ritual life in ancient China.

Early in the 1870s, in translating Chinese ballads and songs into English, Stent (1874, 1878) meant to bring "before the English public some of the quaint ideas, &c. to be found in Chinese ballads and songs," "and also disclose many curious customs of a country comparatively unknown to the general English reader" (Stent 1878:v–vi). His 1874 collection is now even available in a Kindle edition. A comprehensive study with a selection of 230 *geyao*, related to annual festivals based on fourteen Chinese collections from the early twentieth century, was translated into German (Eder 1945). Thereafter, unfortunately, there are very few translations of modern Chinese *geyao*.

GEYAO: THE LEADING CONCEPT OF THE NEW CULTURE MOVEMENT IN THE TWENTIETH CENTURY

The early twentieth century was the time many Western concepts were introduced to China, including "folklore" and "fairy tale" as discussed in the previous chapters. However, the most important movement that directly enabled the formation of Chinese folkloristics was the Geyao/Ballad Movement (*Geyao Yundong*) from 1918–1926. While there were efforts to introduce fairy tale (*tonghua*) as a way to promote children's education and women's education, *geyao* was the only "genre" that was native to China for thousands of years.

During the Geyao Movement, different views arose among the initiators about their theoretical basis, expectations for future direction and concrete action. These views are still reflected in the current scholarly approaches to *geyao*, especially as seen in the national project of the *Grand Collections of Chinese Ballads* (1984–2009), and the ongoing national project, *Compendium of Chinese Folk Literature* (2017–2025).

In his masterful study of the twentieth-century history of Chinese literature, Liu Xicheng (2014) scrutinizes the rise and fall of the Geyao Movement, as well as its impact on the later times. The following summary is based on his work.

The Geyao Movement began with the establishment of the Ballads Research Association (with a Geyao Collection Office) in Beijing University in February 1918. Its call for contributions resulted in a huge number of submissions. Subsequently, a weekly journal, *Geyao* (歌谣), was published beginning on December 17, 1922, and continued until June 1925. With a lapse of about seven years, the journal was resumed in 1936 for about one year. This history of eight years informed the first theoretical school in modern Chinese literary history, by collecting the ballads, proverbial expressions, and other forms of oral literature directly from the common people.

The Ballads Research Association was a loose group with scholars who could be seen as representatives of three different views: one view was more influenced by the Western anthropological/folkloristic ideas as embodied in Zhou Zuoren (1885–1967) who was also the key figure in introducing and promoting folklore and fairy tale; another view was in favor of collecting ballads, but emphasizing a literary approach; the third group, as the majority among all related individuals, promoted a folk literature approach by emphasizing the oral tradition of the local and native people. This third group included the leading folklorists in the decades just preceding the twenty-first century, including Gu Jiegang (1893–1980), Chang Hui (1894–1985), Dong Zuobin (1895–1963), and Zhong Jingwen (1903–2002), who made the greatest contribution to Chinese folk literature studies.

In modern China, the first person who proposed to collect and study *geyao/* ballads was Lu Xun (1881–1936), the elder brother of Zhou Zuoren, but he was not able to act on his idea. It was the Geyao Collection Office that first did so. The key person in this endeavor was Liu Bannong (1891–1934), who was a professor at Beijing University. In his view, *geyao* was the same as the "folk literature" that was used later.

The contributions of the Ballad Research Association can be seen from these aspects: (a) promoting folk literature that was popularly circulated among the common people which enriched Chinese literature, folklore, and culture despite being put down by literati during the past two thousand years; (b) introducing the ideas of historical evolution into Chinese literature studies, and thus making a breakthrough from the traditional philosophical view of "mandate of the heavens" (*tianming* 天命) by discussing topics like women and family in *geyao* studies; (c) integrating Western folkloristic and humanistic theories and methods into their studies of Chinese traditional culture; and (d) extending *geyao* studies to folktales, legends, and other narrative forms, and developing native methods of studying "motif" and "tale type."

Zhou Zuoren, as one of the editors of the weekly journal *Geyao*, once pointed out that there were three approaches to studying *geyao*: the first was from a folkloristic view with emphasis on national mentality; the second was through education by teaching children in this natural way of singing rhymes/lullabies; the third was artistic, with intention of providing entertainment. Certainly, there were other views as well. In fact, there was an attempt to change the name of Geyao/Ballad Research Association into Folklore Research Association, but it was not successful. When the journal was resumed in 1936, the new editor, Hu Shi (1891–1962), clearly emphasized that he wanted to create a new area of literature in China, that is, *geyao* as a basis for elite literature and arts. That also marked an opposite approach from the original intention of the journal (Liu 2004:64). These ideas are seen today, as discussed in chapter 1 and 5, regarding different approaches to folklore as a discipline and to the fairy tale as a genre.

As a result of the Geyao Movement, a total of 13,908 ballads/songs were collected during those years (Wan 2007:7). A group of *geyao* scholars also emerged from their collecting and studying. Zhong Jingwen, as one of the active participants in the movement, published one collection of 140 ballads in 1927, which was the highlight of the 500 ballads/songs that he collected from his hometown. It was the first collection where the Hakka ballads constituted the largest number of ballads. Understanding the importance of "truthfulness" in conducting fieldwork, Zhong only added punctuation to the songs he collected, and thus he set an example for collecting and publishing as well. In fact, some of the styles shown in those songs are related to the *Book of Songs* 2,000 years ago, as Zhong recognized later, and as seen in this example with puns (Wan 2007:10):

前日与妹一笼鸡, Qiánrì yǔ mèi yī lóng jī,
今日分做两路啼. jīnrì fēn zuò liǎng lù tí.
猪肝心肺落镬煮, Zhū gān xīnfèi luò huò zhǔ,
两副心肚来待我? liǎng fù xīn dù lái dài wǒ?
The day before we were chicken in one cage,
Today we are separated as two pig feet [both crying]
Pig's [your] livers, lungs and heart are cooked apart,
How come you treat me with a different heart?

Furthermore, the impact of the Geyao Movement did not only shape folkloristics within China, but also influenced the Western world because it translated the *geyao* into English. For example, in the preface to his translation, Werner mentioned (1922a:1):

Recently, the excellent idea occurred to the editor of the official gazette of the Government University at Peking to ask the scholars to send to him the popular ditties current in their respective provinces or districts. Since these scholars hail from all parts of China a large and valuable collection was thus obtained. In the belief that they may be instructing and interesting to readers of the *New China Review,* I propose to translate a portion of them, giving the Chinese text, and some notes where elucidation seems necessary.

Here is one example:

麻雀子尾巴长, Máquè zǐ wěibā cháng
讨了老婆不要娘. tǎole lǎopó bùyào niáng

娘是路边草, niáng shì lù biān cǎo
还是老婆好. háishì lǎopó hǎo
The sparrow's tail is long.
When he is married he forgets his mother.
The mother is the grass by the road-side.
The wife is best after all.
[This song is current in Nan-ch'ang, capital of Kiangsi (Jiangxi) (Werner 1922a:4)]

GEYAO: CONTEMPORARY APPROACHES

Following the *Grand Collections of Chinese Folk Literature* (1984–2009), the plan of the ongoing *Compendium of Chinese Folk Literature* (2017–2025) is to publish 1,000 volumes. In the former project, *geyao* was one of the three categories of folk literature, and in the current project, *geyao* is one of the twelve categories. Both projects have strengthened the theoretical orientation toward folk literature, and the participants represent the current scholarship in both theory and method.

At the beginning of the 1984–2009 project, there was a national survey of folk literature in 1985, which found in a total of 3,020,000 *geyao*, among other genres/forms (Jia 1997:6), including folksongs and repetitions. In a recent report, as of 2015, in the Chinese Oral Literature Heritage Database (中国口头文学遗产数据库), there are more than 877,000 *geyao* collected with a narrow definition that excludes some long songs and those about "current political situation."

The current project is carried out by following the *Handbook of Compendium of Chinese Folk Literature Publication Project* (*Handbook* hereafter, 2020), which deserves a closer look. According to the *Handbook*, this project set the priority as editing what was already published, while collecting new *geyao* through fieldwork was secondary. Furthermore, the scope of collection is limited to the period from the early twentieth century to the early twenty-first century because earlier *geyao* were treated as part of classic literature and were already included in the previous publications.

The guiding principles and standards for collection and selection are: scientific, extensive, regional, and representative. "Regional" (*difangxing* 地方性), highlighting regional/local uses, is the new principle that was not mentioned in the previous *Grand Collections* (1984–2009). Also, in the current project, there is an emphasis on the folk literature of the minority groups either in Chinese language or in their own languages.

Geyao is also called folk ballads (*minjian geyao* 民间歌谣) and is one of the twelve categories of the current categorization. The other eleven categories are: myths, epics, folk legends, folk tales, folk long poems, folk chante fables, folk dramas, proverbs, riddles, customary expressions/sayings, and folk literature theory.

The definition in the *Handbook* states that *geyao* refers to the short songs in prose style that are distributed orally. Its characteristics of rhyme, shortness, and tune differentiate *geyao* from other prosaic styles like epics, narrative songs, or folk chante fables. In particular, the *Handbook* notes that folksongs are for singing with or without music, but through its long history, musical notes have been lost, and thus the text has become the prose with rhyme for chanting. As a result, "folksong" is used to mean the folksongs both with or without musical tunes.

The specific categorization of *geyao* includes six types: work songs, ritual songs, current political songs, everyday life songs, love songs, and children's songs, which are the same as those defined forty years ago (Zhong 1980:240–276). Children's songs are divided into three types based on function: for games, for teaching morals, and for training language skills. A caution is also emphasized in the *Handbook* that the "current political songs," in particular, must be truthful to their original context, although they must also be in accordance with "our country's basic socialist principles."

Regarding folksongs, there is also an emphasis in the *Handbook* that "If there are exceptional folksongs, they can be included into other categories," meaning that such a folksong can be listed across the six types. Thus, the standard of collection is set to include ballads/songs without music and songs with music in the ratio of 4 to 1. Long folk songs are put into a different category called "folk long poems" (*changshi* 长诗). This is very much in line with the Western "narrative folksongs" defined as

A concept that assumes two things: first, that the item or complex in question is linked to the repertoire of a particular group (that is, it must have entered tradition at some level), and second, that its textual material is rooted in a sequence of past actions of dynamically involved characters, normally progressing through stages of stasis, disequilibrium, and resolution. (Moreira 1997b:348)

In close relation to *geyao*/ballad, it is necessary to point out that the direct motivation of publishing the *Grand Collections of Chinese Folk Literature* (1984–2009), by including volumes of Geyao/Ballad, was the fact that the project of the *Grand Collection of Chinese Folksongs* was launched in 1979 (the entire project was completed in 2009) (Jia 1997:1). Whereas the *Grand Collection of Chinese Folksongs* emphasized music, that is, recording and transcribing music notes, although words were also given relevant attention, the *Grand Collection of Chinese Geyao* paid more attention to words than music.

Similarly, the current project (2017–2025) also gives priority to words/ texts. This separation of text and music may have made the collection and publication "easier" from disciplinary perspectives (music versus folk literature), but has created a big problem in studying *geyao* as a whole (e.g., separating music/song, word/prose, and context), leading to the reality that Chinese *geyao* is understudied from any disciplinary approach.

As a result, while *folk music* (*minjian yinyue* 民间音乐) is the official term used by the International Folk Music Council (IFMC) and in university departments, *folk ballad* (*minjian geyao* 民间歌谣) and *folklore music* (*minsu yinyue* 民俗音乐), and *folk song* (*minge* 民歌) are used as *informal* equivalents in the music circle with closer connection to theatre and dance studies than to (folk) literature.

This problem is obviously shown in the current textbooks of Chinese folk literature, in terms of definition and categorization of *geyao* (Zhong 1980; Huang 2013; Wan 2016; Duan 2018). In terms of examples of current *geyao*, interestingly, most of them are about the folksongs from the minority groups, and the "current political situation" (*shizheng* 时政) is always about the ancient times. As a matter of fact, *shizheng* may be the most direct expression of the common people's feeling about their socioeconomic conditions and attitudes toward the governments, as seen in the previous examples in ancient times.

In terms of approaches to *geyao*, most current studies in China are oriented toward linguistic and literary structural studies and social implications. To a great extent, they are similar to what is seen in the Western world, where contemporary studies of ballads tend to be "more synchronically oriented," seeking "the role of formulas and other repetitive patterns within the larger framework of ballad poetics," and focus on the poetic processes of composition and interpretation "with particular emphasis on the role of formulas and other verbal and structural patterns" (Moreira 1997a:83). This tendency is clearly influenced by Milman Parry and Albert B. Lord's oral-formulaic theory (Foley1988; Moreira 1997a).

However, the separation of music and words in treating *geyao* in China may be more problematic than elsewhere. One of the major reasons is that disciplinary training may be hard to change; students of literature have little chance to engage in musical aspects of the ballads or songs, and students of music have limited training in textual analysis.

GEYAO IN CONTEMPORARY EVERYDAY PRACTICE

Today, all of the six types of *geyao* are widely practiced among different ethnic, cultural, and regional/dialectic groups in China, though at various degrees. For example, the folksong/ballads of Danzhou (儋州调声) in Hainan Province, listed as a National ICH (Folk Music) item in 2006, has a rich repertoire. Its typical musical pattern is illustrated in the song, "I still want to be friends with you" (哥照合侬义仁和) sung by the Han Chinese in their local dialect (see figure 7.2):

The meaning of this song is as such:
Waters of a thousand miles miss the fish,
Oh, fish also misses the water.
I have feelings to you, feelings deep,
Want to be friends with you, will you?
Even if you wait, I still want to be friends with you.
Waters of a thousand miles are for fish to have fun,
Oh, water also for fish to have fun.
I have feelings to you, feelings deep,
Want to be friends with you, will you?
Even if you wait, I still want to be friends with you.

It is particularly significant to note that new technologies like the internet and cell-phone have greatly increased the "space" of folksong-singing. With the socioeconomic development in the recent decades (e.g., the mode of production and lifestyle), there has been a decline in the traditional folksong-singing in the mountains and among young people (Gibbs 2018). However, folksong/mountain song singing (*duige* 对歌, singing folksongs to each other in two or more groups, either individually or in small groups, or *chang shangge* 唱山歌, singing mountain songs) in most regions in China has been

Figure 7.2   A Danzhou Folksong: I Still Want to be Friends with You. This music notation is transcribed from the number notation. *Source*: Hainan Volume, 1997:586 by Teddy E. Zhang in Oct. 2020.

in an unprecedented widespread and popular state, whether in Northwest (in the form of *huaer* 花儿), Northeast (in the form of *errenzhuan* 二人转), or Southwest (e.g., Hainan; Yunnan; Guangxi; and Hunan), as seen in many regional Song King (*gewang* 歌王) competitions among amateurs and numerous "folksong fairs" (*gexu* 歌圩).

For example, in many public parks in Guangxi, *duige* or *chang shangge*, known as part of the Liu Sanjie Folksong tradition, are so popular and attractive to both singers and audiences of different age, gender, occupation, that it functions in the same way as the square dance (*guangchang wu*) or morning exercises in other places of China, showing its irresistible vitality. *Duige* is no longer limited to specific place and time, but it transmits the tradition in such a way as the breath of life that people practice while entertaining themselves without questioning why they do so—it simply makes sense in their everyday life to sing, watch, or listen to it in crowds, which becomes part of their persona, group, and regional identity.

Furthermore, with the new technology, folksong-singing has become so "handy" that it moves from the fixed and limited physical space to the flexible and unlimited internet space, and expands to broader age and gender groups. It also extends the temporal space that people can sing to each other, through "screen-to-screen" interaction instead of "face-to-face." A study that followed nineteen groups on QQ and three "folksong fairs" on WeChat (two popular social media platforms in China) among the Zhuang people in Guangxi from 2013–2019 has shown that through the internet space, the scope of transmission among the Zhuang people, and the impact to broad society has expanded. The number of singers has increased due to the convenience of teaching and learning through various associations and individual teachers, which, on the one hand, challenges the traditional transmission of folksong-singing, and on the other hand, provides new space for developing this tradition (Cen and Cen 2020). Similar situations are also seen in other regions among other styles of folksong singing in China.

Since the 1980s, with the increasing popularity of TV and radio entertainment programs, one particular genre of storytelling performance has become widespread, that is, *xiaopin* (小品 short [comic] skits). It has been playing an increasingly important role even on the national stages through the *Chunwan* (春晚, the six-hour-long Spring Festival Gala Evening via China's national TV, CCTV, since 1983). The success of this form of performance, integrating various features of local folk performances, is essentially based on its use of one form of *geyao* style, that is, *shunkouliu* (顺口溜, literally, what slips out of the mouth), and sometimes called *duanzi* (段子, a short passage) in the current fashion.

Shunkouliu is very similar to doggerel (or jingle rhyme) in English, which is irregular in rhythm, rhyme, verse, and syllable in its style. This is because a *shunkouliu* may have two lines or more lines, and may rhyme every two lines or throughout the whole piece, as seen in the following three examples. Also, because Chinese is a tonal language with more homophonous puns, it provides more opportunities to create *shunkouliu*. Another reason may be due to the fact that, in Confucian ethics of rite-and-music (*li-yue* 礼乐), folksongs or ballads that are not in line with the ethical teaching are suppressed in the society. As a result, the Han Chinese, as compared with the ethnic minority groups, are often seen as a group without songs and dances in everyday life, but perhaps with more *shunkouliu*.

In everyday life, *shunkouliu* is the most direct and prevalent form for the common people to express their reactions to social, economic, and political situations. Yet, in the academic world, this is the least recorded and published topic, as "cautioned" by the *Handbook* for the current national project, mentioned earlier, in order to keep in accordance with China's basic socialist principles.

Shunkouliu is also called "new *geyao*/ballads," or "urban ballads" (*cheng-shi minyao* 城市民谣). The popularity of *shunkouliu* is also due to the Chinese linguistic feature of "easy" composition of syllables (rhythm) and rhyme. In the digital world, *shunkouliu* has shown an even stronger vitality and validity.

For example, in a satire of various corrupt government officials, the verb "eat" (*chi* 吃) is metaphorically used while the ending *zi* is used as a rhyme in modern colloquial usage:

工商吃摊子, Gōngshāng chī tānzi,
税务吃厂子, shuìwù chī chǎngzi,
交通吃车子, jiāotōng chī chēzi,
公安吃婊子, gōng'ān chī biǎo zi,
学校吃孩子, xuéxiào chī háizi,
组织部门吃章子. zǔzhī bùmén chī zhāngzi.
The Industrial and Commercial [officials] eat vendor stands,
The Tax [officials] eat factories,
The Transportation [officials] eat vehicles,
The Public Security [officials] eat prostitutes,
The School and Education [officials] eat children,
The Personnel [officials] eat rubber stamps.

In another *geyao* about corrupt officials, the rhythm (in four syllables) and rhyme (in every two verses like aa; bb; cc . . .) play a distinctive role:

酒杯一端, 政策放宽. Jiǔbēi yīduān, zhèngcè fàngkuān;
酒足饭停, 不行也行. jiǔ zú fàn tíng, bùxíng yě xíng;

饭饱酒醉, 不对也对. fàn bǎo jiǔ zuì, bùduì yě duì.
When liquor cups are raised, policies are loosened;
When a feast is ended, all the impossible become possible;
When the stomach is filled and the head is intoxicated, all the wrongs are also
  alright.

The following sharp satire reflects the reality of contemporary life in which "a sheet of paper" (*yī zhāng zhǐ* 一张纸) is often used as the proof of one's education, social status, or quality of "one's whole life" (*yíbèizi* 一辈子), rhyming with *zhǐ* and *zi* (ab, ab . . .) for each verse:

出生一张纸, 开始一辈子. Chūshēng yī zhāng zhǐ, kāishǐ yíbèizi.
毕业一张纸, 奋斗一辈子. bìyè yī zhāng zhǐ, fèndòu yíbèizi.
婚姻一张纸, 幸福一辈子. hūnyīn yī zhāng zhǐ, xìngfú yíbèizi.
金钱一张纸, 辛苦一辈子. jīnqián yī zhāng zhǐ, xīnkǔ yíbèizi.
看病一张纸, 痛苦一辈子. kànbìng yī zhāng zhǐ, tòngkǔ yíbèizi.
悼词一张纸, 了结一辈子. dàocí yī zhāng zhǐ, liǎojié yíbèizi.
淡化这些纸, 明白一辈子. dànhuà zhèxiē zhǐ, míngbái yíbèizi.
忘了这些纸, 快乐一辈子! wàngle zhèxiē zhǐ, kuàilè yíbèizi!
A sheet of paper at birth, the beginning for a whole life;
A sheet of paper for graduation, striving for a whole life;
A sheet of paper for marriage, happiness for a whole life;
A sheet of paper as money, hard and bitter work for a whole life;
A sheet of paper as diagnosis, suffering for a whole life;
A sheet of paper for eulogy, ending a whole life;
Diluting these sheets of paper, being clear-minded for a whole life;
Forgetting these sheets of paper, joyful for a whole life!

Such *geyao* are most commonly sung in a competitive game at various gatherings, in particular, when there are toasts with alcohol. This further illustrates how *geyao* functions, just like any other form of folklore practices, to release tension through entertainment and to provide a world of hope in making sense of daily life.

In conclusion, while *geyao* has a rich and long history in China, as both a literary form studied by literati and a handy expression of the common people's attitudes toward social life, there has also been a reluctance to treat *geyao* as a whole. The separation of the text/words, music/tunes, the playing of musical instruments, and context of "performance" has led to the current situation: few published collections based on contemporary fieldwork versus huge collections in print from historical literature; scarcity in contemporary recording versus abundance in everyday uses (especially in current digital age); musical studies of the musical characteristics of folksongs versus literary studies of the words of the folksongs or ballads, among others. These should also be challenges for future studies of Chinese *geyao* or ballad.

Yet, the handiness of *geyao* without music or instrument-playing has embodied many fundamental aspects in Chinese culture. It may be the only form of verbal expression that is not limited by gender, age, occupation, social status, or religious belief, although the content or theme varies. *Geyao* can be directly created and circulated among the common people, by following certain structures, without being re-created or mediated by the intellectuals, as seen in the use of *shunkouliu*. Indeed, the vitality of *geyao* lies in its wide use by the common people, who are the living bearers of Chinese traditions.

In fact, during the COVID-19 pandemic in 2020, many regional folksong singers used their improvised songs to help spread knowledge about preventing contagion of the virus. As a result, their singing in various public spaces, including social media on the internet, not only transmits the tradition and entertains the public, but also serves public health and social stability in a more effective way than official rules and propaganda. Such folksongs and ballads, along with other forms of oral traditions discussed (and those forms that are not included) in this book, have demonstrated their vitality by sticking to their "roots," and their validity by adapting to new environments. As proven throughout human history, it is during such social crises as the COVID-19 pandemic that attests whether a tradition, a culture, or a nation can be self-healed and revitalized through its own cultural self-healing mechanism, while the practitioners of those traditions make sense of their everyday life and gain a stronger sense of personal, group, and national identity.

Chapter 8

Stories without Words

The Traditionalization of a Musical Instrument

Musical instruments are essential in many forms or genres of traditional oral/storytelling performances (*quyi* 曲艺). For certain oral performances, without musical instruments, or if the oral telling and music-playing are separated, there would not be such performances at all. This is in contrast to folksong-singing and folktale-telling, in which musical instruments are often not needed.

In Kunqu Opera (昆曲, an oral storytelling/performance), the horizontal bamboo *di*-flute (*dizi* 笛子) is the "soul" of this oral tradition. Among the storytelling forms in South China, Suzhou chantefable (*Suzhou pingtan* 苏州评弹; *Suzhou tanci* 苏州弹词) (Blader 1999; Bender 2003) would not be possible without the *pipa* (four-string) and/or *sanxian* (three-string) instruments. This form of storytelling was listed on China's First List of National Intangible Cultural Heritage (ICH) in 2006. In North China, among many popular storytelling forms, Shandong chantefable (*Shandong kuaiban* 山东快板, a single-person stand-up performance) would not be possible without bamboo clappers (or *paiban*, a procession instrument similar to the castanet). This form was also listed on China's First List of National ICH in 2006. In the Southwest, Dong people's *pipa* (three-string 侗族琵琶) is the most common instrument to accompany storytelling or singing. In fact, in the Dong villages, most people can craft and play the Dong *pipa*, which is a true sense of a folk instrument.

Furthermore, there are also traditional storytelling performances in which music-playing itself constitutes part of the "telling," independent of singing, telling, or chanting. This can be seen as storytelling without words. For example, among the Kazakh and Kyrgyz people in the Xinjiang Uyghur Autonomous Region in Northwest China, Dombra (two-string instrument, *dongbula* 冬不拉 in Chinese) is used not only to accompany singing but also to "tell" stories or have conversations between two players/singers (Aitysh/Aitys, in Kazakhstan and Kyrgyzstan; *A'ken* 阿肯 in Chinese) who can improve with each other. This form of oral tradition was inscribed on UNESCO's Representative List of the ICH of Humanity in 2015. Similarly, *kouxian* (口弦, literally *mouth-string*, often called Jew's harp; usually made of bamboo with variations) is commonly used by the young people to express love, as a way of "talking" to each other without speaking or singing, among the Yi, Naxi, Dong, Qiang, Mongolian, and many other minority groups in China. This instrument is truly replacing "mouth" for talking or singing.

In this sense, this chapter emphasizes that some oral traditions should not only be understood from a (print or verbal) text-centered view, but also from a musical perspective, or essentially, a holistic view. The clay vessel *xun*-flute discussed here is a story in itself that has been told for several thousand years in China by the elite and by the common people. It is being made, played, displayed, and consumed by the common people, with a number of variants in shape, color, and key. It has become a national cultural identity marker embodying the *fundamental beliefs and values* in Chinese culture, particularly through the movement of heritagization and traditionalization in this new century. It is also a storyteller that has even crossed the barriers of language and territory, telling stories without words across cultures in and outside China. For example, besides the *CHINOPERL: Chinese Oral and Performing Literature* based in the United States (https://chinoperl.osu.edu/), there is the *CHIME*, an organization with its journal (http://chimemusic .net) based in Germany and the Netherlands, as the worldwide platform for scholars and students interested in Chinese music. (Another example may be a comparative study of the clay flutes of the Shang Dynasty in China and of the Chavín Cultures in Peru over 3,000 years ago, which illustrates the nature of cultural integration in humanities and the role of instruments in oral traditions, but it has to be treated as a separate topic.)

No doubt, the making, playing, gazing, and consuming of traditional musical instruments are certainly part of the process of continuing oral traditions. By examining these aspects of the recently revitalized clay vessel *xun*-flute in relation to the ICH movement in China, this chapter suggests that the vitality of the *xun* lies in its symbolism of traditional Chinese ethics and cosmology which are the basis of the fundamental beliefs and values in Chinese culture, and argues that the *xun* has transformed itself from a musical instrument into a core identity marker of the Chinese culture. To further illustrate the ideas of cultural hybridity (or a *third culture*; see also, chapter 2) and the concept of practice as a holistic embodiment of transmitting traditions (Bronner 2019), I discuss my own experience in the processes of learning, making, playing, and promoting this instrument.

In this chapter, the *xun*-flute is scrutinized for the purpose of exploring the root of its revitalization. By probing the *xun*'s history as a musical instrument and as an ethical symbol, and by evaluating its role in the "root-seeking" movement of the 1980s and the current ICH movement, this chapter argues that it is the transformation of the *xun*'s symbolic role in Chinese fundamental beliefs and cultural values that has enabled the *xun*'s revitalization as a core cultural identity marker in contemporary China. Furthermore, while the vitality of this instrument helps reconstruct individual, regional, and national identities within Chinese cultural domain, its validity serves to connect it to cultural industry and cross-cultural communication as a musical instrument, an art form, as well as a cultural identity marker.

After all, studying the causes and processes of the invention, transmission, and transformation of traditions is of central interest for folklorists. When practitioners choose to continue or discontinue a tradition, are they conscious of the reasons for doing so? Do they have conscious awareness of the vitality and validity of a tradition? Or, what enables a tradition to become a core identity marker so that it can survive social upheavals? The Chinese example of revitalizing traditions at the turn of the twenty-first century by taking advantage of the concept of ICH has provided a case where these questions can be examined through the lens of the interpretive framework of *cultural self-healing mechanism* discussed throughout this book.

THE CLAY VESSEL *XUN*-FLUTE AS A MUSICAL INSTRUMENT

The *xun* (埙, 塤, or 壎) is one of the oldest musical instruments in human history. It is often mistakenly called "ocarina," but it should be known as a "clay vessel flute" (Chuang 1972). Semantically, the word *xun* 塤 (埙 as the simplified version) was defined two thousand years ago in *Shuowen Jiezi* (说文解字) (Xu 1963:287) to be the same as *xun* 壎 (which has an origin in the Oracle Bone Inscriptions, related to *xun* 熏, meaning "to smoke" through a stove/chimney, but now with an earth (土) radical on the left). There is no clear evidence for the origin of the word *xun* 塤/壎 in the Oracle Bone Inscriptions, as I learned through a number of discussions on this topic during 2012–2013 with Professor Sarah Allan at Dartmouth College and a few experts of the Shang Dynasty in China, although there are reasonable guesses (e.g., Song 2005:519; Bao 2010; Dai 1986).

The *xun* is listed in "Olsen's Category 5": "globular or vessel flute with ductless, single-hole, cross-blown mouthpiece (ocarina type I)" (Olsen 2013:7). The Korean equivalent is the *hun* (Hangul: 훈; Hanja: 塤), and the

Japanese version is called *tsuchibue* (hiragana: つちぶえ; kanji: 土笛, literally, *earthen flute*).

The oldest *xun*, excavated from the Hemudu Cultural Relics in Zhejiang Province, China, is believed to be nearly 7,000 years old (*Gems of the Hemudu Culture* 2002:154; Liu and Yuan 2008:14–16). Other excavations have revealed that around 6,500 years ago there were *xun* with more than one hole. Other examples include a one-hole *xun* from the Banpo, Jiangzhai, and Erlitou Cultural Relics (Song 2005:526; Wu 1988:549–554), and a *xun* with multiple holes from Henan (*Zhongguo Yinyue Wenwu Daxi* 2001:26; Fang 2008; Zhou 2009).

The next 4,000 years saw the *xun* appear throughout China. "Clay *xun* are also widely distributed in Neolithic sites of the Zhongyuan [Central China] region and occasionally in the Yangzi River Delta and Middle Yangzi region (Hubei)" (Li 1996:387; English quoted from Furniss 2008:30). A number of other *xun*, excavated from the large region spanning the east coast (e.g., Zhejiang and Shandong Provinces) to the upper valley of the Yellow River (e.g., Qinghai and Gansu Provinces) and mid-valley of the Yangtze River (e.g., Hubei Province), also span a long time period from 5,000 BCE to 200 BCE in China (Leng 2011; Fang 1988, 2009; Li 1964; Xue 2007; Zhang 2012; Zhang 1998).

Glazed stoneware *xun* were created by the Han Dynasty, around 2,000 years ago. While there were examples of *xun* made of other materials (e.g., wood and bamboo) throughout its history, the use of earth-clay as a standard material was particularly enforced in the Song Dynasty (960–1279). By the Song Dynasty, the *bayin* (八音, Eight Sounds) system, which began by the eleventh century BCE with the *xun* as one of the Eight Sounds (i.e., the earth, *tu* 土), was reinforced by linking Confucian ethical virtues to those musical instruments. This effort was part of the Neo-Confucianist movement around the eleventh to thirteenth century.

Regarding the origin of the *xun*, its widespread use during the Neolithic period may well suggest that the *xun* functioned first in hunting, and then in ritual celebrations, though there is a lack of documentation of the extent to which the *xun* was used in these activities prior to the Shang Dynasty around the fifteenth century BCE. For example, one view is that the *xun* was used as a hunting tool because it was once known as *shiliuxing* (石流星 shooting star stone) (Lü 1978:56; Li 2005). During the Shang it became a court instrument, and was institutionalized through the *bayin* system in the late Zhou (11th c. BCE–256 BCE).

The sound chamber of the *xun* has generally been egg-shaped, though it has also appeared in other shape such as various animals. The development of the number of sound holes (*yinkong* 音孔) on the *xun* has been a long process, and even the way of counting sound holes has not been consistent (Lu 2008).

For example, the mouthpiece is also a sound hole, determining the base key of the *xun* (Zhao 1993; Guo 2011). After all, it has taken 7,000 years to develop from the one-hole *xun* of the Hemudu period to the 8 (or even 9 or 10)-hole *xun* invented at the turn of the twenty-first century.

It is impossible to understand the *xun* in Chinese history of music and culture without knowing its partner, the *chi*, even though this chapter focuses on the *xun*. The *chi* (籂) is a bamboo flute with two ends closed. Unfortunately, there is little record of any kind about the making and playing of the *chi*. The earliest record of the *chi*, in companionship with the *xun*, is from the *Book of Songs* (*Shi Jing*, around the fifth century BCE; the poem *Herensi* 何人斯; see English translation, Karlgren 1950).

One theory is that the blowhole on the *chi* is in the middle, and the player places his hands on both sides of the flute while playing. Another describes it as similar to playing the *di*-flute (with an off-center blowhole and both hands on one side). There was no mention of the *chi* in the musical instruments excavated from the Xia and Shang sites prior to the fifteenth century BCE (Song 2005; Mao 2012; Wu 1981), and the *chi* was also rarely mentioned in non-court music, especially after the Song Dynasty. This made it hard to revive or reinvent the *chi*, unlike the *xun*. Although the *chi* from the tomb of Marquis Yi can play a full pentatonic scale, there is no definite knowledge as to how to make the "correct" *chi* and play it. But, there are efforts to reinvent the *chi*. In the summer of 2012, I visited Zhang Jingzheng in Beijing, who showed me a *chi* made by her father, Zhang Ronghua, a dedicated *xun* maker. That *chi* was an imitation of the one from the tomb of Marquis Yi (曾侯乙 ca. 475 BCE–433 BCE; currently on display in the Hubei Museum, Wuhan, China) (Huang 1979).

The *Book of Zhou Rites* mentions the *xun* and the *chi* in the *bayin* system, with the *chi* having seven holes, which is echoed by the *Er Ya* (尔雅, the earliest dictionary) annotated by Guo Pu (郭璞 276–324). According to Guo Pu, one annotation to the *Book of Zhou Rites* mentions that the *chi* has seven holes, and the *Guang Ya* (广雅) says that there are eight holes, but Guo Pu comments that the difference is whether or not counting the blowhole, and that it should be seven holes. (All references to the *Er Ya* in this book are from the *Shisanjing Zhushu* 十三经注疏, 1980:2601–2602; Ruan 1980). These two descriptions are confirmed by the two excavated *chi* in Hubei known as the extant earliest objects, which show that there are five tone holes and one blowhole in addition to one key hole, as seen in the Hubei Museum.

Musically, the *chi* plays the same tonal scale as the *xun* so that the *xun* and *chi* are in harmony and mutual companionship. It seems reasonable to infer that by the time when the *xun* and the *chi* were used together, both instruments had five tone holes and one blowhole, that they were played in similar positions with one hand on each side and fingertips pointing inward (for the *xun*, palms facing each other; for the *chi*, both palms facing inward to the body)—maintaining an upright body position. Furthermore, it was the time when the *bayin* system was integrated and enforced with the *wusheng* (Five Notes) system and *wude* (Five Virtues) system.

Regarding the sizes of the *xun* and the *chi*, according to *Er Ya*, the big *xun* is called *jiao* (䴏), and is the size of a goose egg, and the small one is called *xun* (埙) and is the size of a chicken egg. In contrast, the big *chi* is called *yi* (沂), one foot and four inches long, and the small one is called *chi* (篪), one foot and two inches long (*Annotated Er Ya* 1980:173). Accordingly, all *xun* have six holes (one blowhole and five tone holes). The *chi*, however, is said to have seven holes, we now know from the object from Hubei, the *chi* has one blowhole, one key hole, and five finger tone. As for their timbres, the *xun*'s deep and thick, as if it were shouting. Later, according to the chapter on the Records of Music in the *Book of the Former Tang* (旧唐书), it was described as the sound of "the beginning of the autumn." The big *chi* is described as "sad, as if a baby crying" (*Annotated Er Ya* 1980:173).

Although the *xun* has been "reinvented," the relatively small importance placed on it today in official education (e.g., music conservatories) is attributable to its low volume and its only having one octave range. Similarly, the *chi* from the Zeng Hou Yi Tomb can produce six notes, a full pentatonic scale from c#2 to a#2. However, since such instruments as *xun* and *chi* were not to be played soloistically, their volume and scale limitations were not important because several instruments in different keys could be used to produce more octaves. Yet, this limitation of the *xun* led to the development of more tone holes that allow more than one octave to be played. For example, the eight-hole Liangshan *Xun* plays one and a half diatonic octaves.

Since many popular folk instruments also do not have a range of more than one octave (although some modern reconstructed *xun* can play more diversely), we may reason that the "lost and found" stories of the *xun* and *chi* may not pertain solely to their musicality but might also relate to cultural views toward them, as seen in the popularity of the *xun* as a tourist souvenir and as an ICH in China today.

THE RECONSTRUCTION OF THE *XUN* AT THE TURN OF THE TWENTY-FIRST CENTURY

It took several thousand years for the *xun* to transform from a practical artifact (i.e., possibly a hunting or a ritual tool) to a musical instrument in the Shang court. By the Zhou Dynasty, the *xun* became a unique representative of the *bayin* (Eight Sounds) system which was connected to the fundamental cosmology and ethics in Chinese culture, and continued to be indispensable in the court until the late nineteenth century when the wars with the West discontinued many traditions in China. In Chinese history, the rise of the *xun* was largely due to the attachment of Confucian ethical meaning to its naturalistic nature; the fall of the *xun* was essentially due to the wars caused by external force which eventually discontinued social and political order.

The Eight Sounds (*bayin* 八音) represent eight types of materials, with exemplary instruments as such:

- Metal 金: The bell, *zhong*, 钟
- Stone 石: The chime, *qing*, 磬
- Silk 丝: The string instruments like the *qin*, 琴
- Bamboo 竹: The *chi*, 篪; horizontal *di*-flute, 笛; vertical *xiao*-flute, 箫
- Gourd 匏: The *sheng*-flute; 笙; the *yu*-flute, 竽
- Earth 土: The *xun*, 埙
- Leather 革: The drum, *gu*, 鼓
- Wood 木: The percussion instruments like the *zhu*, 柷

This correlation was first illustrated by Chen Yang of the Song Dynasty, in the chapters of "The Eight Sounds Following the Eight Winds (八音从八风)" and "Eight Sounds" in his *Music Book*, now collected in *Si Ku Quan Shu* (四库全书). Chen Yang used the after-birth Eight-Diagram (后天八卦) as a tradition in explaining the orthodox ritual-music relationship.

The earliest text that mentioned the Eight Sounds is the *Book of Documents*, and the system later was quoted by the *Book of the Zhou Rites*. According to Yi Bo of the Song Dynasty in his *Complete Duties of the Zhou Officials*, the Five Notes are embodied in the Eight Sounds, and the Eight Sounds are in fact directly from the Eight Diagrams. According to *Lü Shi Chun Qiu*, Zhuan Xu "ordered the Flying Dragon to imitate the Eight Wind Sounds." Gao You's annotation says, "The Eight Winds are the winds of the Eight Diagrams." According to Ban Gu (32–92) in his the *Book of the Han*, the wind is generated from the combination of the *qi* from the sky and the *qi* from the earth, and when the *qi* and wind from the sky and earth are in accordance they determine the twelve-tone-modes (Lynn 1994).

Like any tradition that has demonstrated its vitality and validity, the *xun*'s falls in certain situation or period of time does not mean it discontinues as a tradition, or it loses its vitality. The revitalization of the *xun* in the late twentieth century shows that, because of its root in the fundamental beliefs and values in Chinese culture, its vitality is able to be restored when the social conditions allow.

As seen from the continuity of the *xun*, the division between high and low culture, or between official and folk culture, is but a methodology for understanding certain traditions. The fact is that a specific tradition is an expression of culture as a whole, whether as a core marker or an arbitrary marker, and thus is impossible to be understood only from one view. Along with the tradition of the *xun* being a cosmological and ethical symbol, as well as a musical instrument, the prototype *xun* has always been an entertaining or ritualistic instrument in everyday life across China, for example, *ninigou* (泥泥狗) in the Northwest and *sanyanxiao* (三眼箫) in Yunnan. Furthermore, when the thread along the imperial court was broken in the nineteenth century, it was the folk tradition along with some elite effort that sustained the *xun*. Today, with the elite effort since the 1980s, the *xun* is now made by both the elite and the folk, and widely spread among the folk through cultural tourism.

The *xun* was sustained among the folk like a thin thread by the late twentieth century. Then in the process of revitalizing the *xun*, there is clear influence among different makers as well as from other instruments. In 1983, Zhao Liangshan (赵良山 1939–2011) presented the first public national performance on the *xun*, as a result of many years' experiments entrusted by his teacher Chen Zhong (陈重 1919–2001), on his own reinvented *xun* with eight finger/tone holes plus the blow hole (Zhao 1991). Along with this elite line, there are also others who played important roles in the revival of the *xun*. For example, professional musicians Cao Zheng (曹正 1982), Lu Jinshan (陆金山 2008), Du Ciwen (杜次文), Wang Tiechui (王铁锤 2010), and Liu Sen (刘森).

Meanwhile, there appeared several other styles of *xun* with different numbers of tone holes and fingerings, and some of them are now widespread regionally or even through the internet. For example, there are Fengshi (冯氏) and Yinshi (阴氏) *xun* for sale through internet. Yu Xuejun (于学军) in Hebei and Zhang Ronghua (张荣华) in Beijing are also making their own styles. There are still many makers selling their own at various tourist sites or stores. So far, there is no standard fingering system on the *xun* (Zhao 1991; Zhou 2011), which is a rare situation in contrast to other musical instruments. The publication of writings on the *xun* also shows a continuity of the interaction between the elite and folk practices (Liu 1996; Chen 2001; Wang 2002; Liu 2004; Wang 2011; Guo 2011; Qin 2006; Duan 2011, Chen and Li 2000).

The unique *xun* concert in Beijing National Theatre in 2011 presented by Liu Kuanren (刘宽忍), who mostly used a ten-finger-hole *xun*, marked a pinnacle of the history of the *xun* as a musical instrument as well as a national identity marker. Liu is known to have often used the *xun* made by Zhang Ronghua. Liu is the president of China *Xun* Culture Society (中国埙文化学会), a leading figure in revitalizing the *xun* and a government official in Shaanxi Province (Jia and Liu 2012).

Outside China, the *xun* is also becoming known as both a musical instrument and a cultural identity marker, as seen through the works by the composer Tan Dun of New York (Tan 1993, 2005). In his 1993 work "Death and Fire," he used the ceramic *xun* made by Barry Hall (2006). My own experience of making, playing, and teaching the *xun* may represent another everyday practice in the United States, as discussed in the last section of this chapter.

For people today, perhaps there is one more layer of meaning to the *xun*, that is, it is a sound of nostalgia, as described by the famous writer Jia Pingwa (贾平凹) who is partly accountable for the popularity of the *xun* in the 1990s in China. In his essay "Blowing Earth as Voice" (吹土为声, 2011), Jia Pingwa recalled his hearing a person playing the *xun* in the suburbs of Xi'an, which inspired him to write the novel, *Feidu (Abandoned Capital*, 废都, first published in 1993 in Beijing, then banned until 2009). That person was Liu Kuanren mentioned earlier. Both of them have worked together to promote *xun* instrument and music. Today, the *xun* is claimed to be one of the regional identity marker of the city of Xi'an, or Shaaxi Province. Similarly, it is also a way to call back the lost soul of Chinese culture in reconstructing a national identity at the crucial turn in Chinese history in the 1980s, a decade of root-seeking (*xungen*) through literature and arts, such as the films: *Burning Yuanmingyuan* (火烧圆明园, dir. Li Hanxiang, 1983) and *Judou* (菊豆, dir. Zhang Yimou, 1990) (Zhang 2013).

The emergence of the ICH movement since 2003 has irreversibly influenced the scope and methods in folkloristics, and has had a great impact on the questions in discussion. At the world level, as "folklore" is becoming "cultural heritage," or even being replaced by "ICH" (Kuutma 2012:24), folklorists must reflect upon the relationship between, and the nature of folklore and heritage. China has been a very active participant in this worldwide movement of recognizing, diversifying, and preserving human cultures. Within its domestic strategies, China has set the national Cultural Heritage Day (the second Saturday in June since 2006; renamed Cultural and Natural Heritage Day since 2017) and promulgated the national ICH Law (taking effect on June 1, 2011). Thus far, thousands of items have been listed as ICH at different levels. As a result, ICH in China and Chinese folkloristics have become an increasingly meaningful reference for folklorists everywhere to reflect upon the very history and nature of folkloristics (Zhang and Zhou 2017).

Currently, the *xun* is recognized as an ICH item at the Provincial Level in Shandong and Hebei Provinces, and at the City Level in cities like Dezhou, Baoding, and Xiamen. This trend demonstrates the reconstruction of regional and national cultural identities after the 1980s when the efforts were made in "seeking roots" and searching for "self-awareness" after a century's worth of disruption of everyday life in China. The 1980s were a turning point for Chinese intellectuals to gain self-awareness of their cultural roots through various efforts: the debate of the Chinese yellow-earth culture versus the

Western blue-ocean culture; the use of the *qin* and *xun* music in films when Western music was prevalent across the country; and the reflection and comparison of the 1919 New Culture Movement and the 1980s "root-seeking" movement. As a result, Chinese elites began to promote self-confidence in Chinese traditions as a way to reconstruct China as an equal nation in the world to face the twenty-first century. In the recent two decades, with the socioeconomic development, Chinese people have gestured to get rid of the "inferior mentality" resulted from previous semi-colonized century (Zhang 2017a). It is within these contexts, the *xun* has transformed itself from a musical instrument to a symbol of identity, and its revitalization shows its vitality in Chinese traditions and its validity in cross-cultural communication, as further discussed below.

THE ROOT OF THE REVITALIZATION

The *xun* and *chi* are more than musical instruments. They are the embodiment of central philosophical and ethical principles, and thus are core identity markers of Chinese culture. The association of important traditional Chinese ethical terms with the *xun*, beginning in the Han Dynasty (202 BCE–220 CE), enabled it to become a transcendental symbol for individuals through music, and for the culture as a whole through the *bayin* (Eight Sounds) system, as well as the systematized correlation of the *wusheng* (Five Notes) with the *wude* (Fiver Virtues) systems (see figure 8.1). It was during the Han Dynasty that the dominance of Confucian ethics took root in Chinese ruling ideology. Confucian ethics were reaffirmed through the Neo-Confucian movement during the Song Dynasty (960–1127), and they have played a major role in shaping Chinese culture from the twelfth century until today.

In the process of correlating the Five Virtues system to the other five-or eight-concepts, the role of the earth (*tu* 土) made the *xun* particularly important. This same reason may lie behind the revival of the *xun* today simply because it is the only playable instrument made of *tu*. In addition, the sense of "root" and "earth" or "soil" (both of which translate as *tu* in Chinese) for a culture whose primary method of production was agriculture helped lend both a cosmic and ethical significance to the *xun*. In the Chinese cosmology embodied in the Five Elements, *tu* is at the center of the universe. Consequently, the base note in the Five Notes system in music corresponds to *tu* as *gong* (宫, the first note in any tone mode or scale). In Confucian ethics, the constant Five Virtues are co-related to the Five Elements, in which earth represents the virtue of trust (*xin* 信) and thus becomes the foundation of other constant virtues, including the sub-virtues of *xin*, namely filial piety (*xiao* 孝) and loyalty (*zhong* 忠).

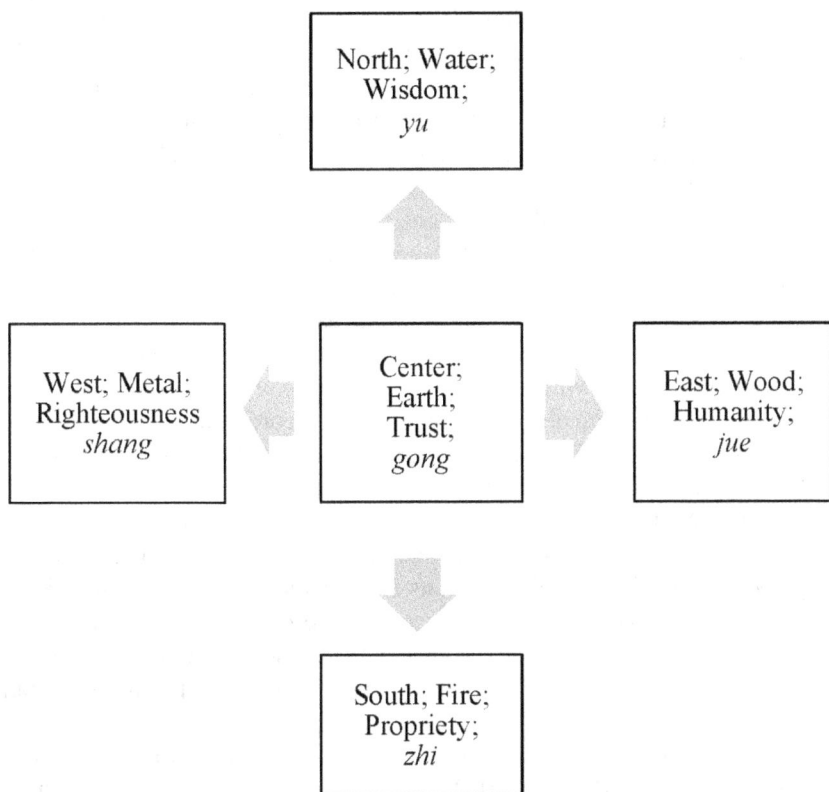

Figure 8.1   The Correlations among the Five Elements, Five Virtues, Five Notes, and Five Directions. The generative correlation (in contrast to the suppressive correlation) of the Five Elements is: Wood (Mu 木) –> Fire (Huo 火) –> Mental (Jin 金) –> Earth (Tu 土) –> Water (Shui 水). The progressive or accumulative relationship of the Five Virtues is: Trust (Xin 信) –> Wisdom (Zhi 智) –> Propriety (Li 礼) –> Righteousness (Yi 义) –> Humanity (or Benevolence Ren 仁). The correlation among the Five Notes is: E (Gong 宫) – G (Shang 商) – C (Jue 角) – D (Zhi 徵) – A (Yu 羽). The concept of Five Directions is also essential to the ancient Chinese cosmic view about the shape of the universe (Allan 1991; Zhang 2017b).

The concept of six was also significant in Chinese cosmology and music. For example, according to the *Book of Rites*, "The sages created *tao* (鼗), *gu* (鼓), *kong* (箜), *jie* (楬), *xun* (埙), and *chi* (篪). These six instruments make the sounds of the tone of virtue (德音之音)," and the concept is translated into "tones of De" or "virtue and tones" (Brindley 2012:92; Major 1979:66–80). In the *Book of the Zhou Rites*, there was the concept of "the music of the six dynasties," and the terms of "six-tone-modes" (六律), "six-samenesses" (六同), "six-notes" (六声), and "six-dances" (六舞), which were similar to the records from the Oracle Bone Inscriptions (Song 2005:521). One reason why five somewhat overshadow six was that the Five Virtues system was attached to the previous belief systems by the late Zhou, which resulted in overemphasis of Five in correlation to the cosmological and ethical values, making six relatively less important (this idea was agreed with by Sarah Allan in personal conversations in April and May 2013 at Dartmouth College; see also, Lau 1979a; Ames and Hall 2001).

Furthermore, the *xun* and *chi* became the symbols of brotherhood, a concept first explored in the *Book of Songs*, where they were connected with practice of the virtue of *xin* among brothers (as *di* 悌, which correlates with *xin* toward parents as *xiao* 孝). For example, early in the Han Dynasty there was a *Fu on Parrots* by Mi Heng, in which the "companionship of the *xun* and *chi*" (塤篪之相须) was used as a metaphor of inseparable companionship or love. Similar uses are also common in many records such as *Anthology of Literature* (*Wen Xuan*) by Xiao Tong (501–531) and *Collection of Arts and Literature* (*Yiwen Leiju*) by Ouyang Xun (557–641).

This symbolism remains in use in Chinese literature, though not common in everyday life. Although the *chi* belonged to the category of bamboo in the *bayin* system, it was well-known as a companion of the *xun* to help keep the yin-yang balance for both sound quality and ethical symbolism. People still use the idiom, *xunchi zhijiao* (塤篪之交) to mean pure and fast friendship, a virtue required of a "person of virtue" (*junzi* 君子) in Confucian culture.

It is reasonable to understand "music" as a "master metaphor" in the natural-spiritual cosmos (Brindley 2012:5). Likewise, music stood as the foundation of Chinese cosmology by the Shang Dynasty and further informed the fundamental beliefs and values like "the harmony of nature and man" and the essence of Confucian ethics by the late Zhou Dynasty. Confucius (551–479 BCE) said that to become a *junzi*, "one should be aroused with poetry (songs), established through ritual propriety, and accomplished in music." This important passage in *The Analects* (8.8) is also translated differently (Lau 1979a); for example, "Confucius said, Let a man be stimulated by poetry, established by the rules of propriety, and perfected by music" (Wing-tsit Chan 1963:33), or "The Master said, I find inspiration by intoning the songs, I learn where to stand from observing ritual propriety (*li* 礼), and I find fulfillment in playing music" (Ames and Rosement 1998:122).

The entirety of Confucian ethics emphasizes the daily practice of ritual propriety (*li*) and music (*yue*). In this sense, playing the *xun* both embodies this Confucian advice and specifically exhibits one of the fundamental virtues, *xin*. Thus, in the modern restoration of the Confucian idea of harmony and as an expression of the Chinese ICH, the *xun* plays a unique symbolic role.

It is particularly important to understand that the system of Five Notes does not mean that the ancient Chinese music system was based only on these five notes, generating the pentatonic scale. In fact, in that system, the note Gong was/is the movable "1" ("do," or C), and there are also F# (changed-*zhi*) and B (changed-*gong*) used. As proved by the documents and objects (e.g., the Tomb of Marquis Yi of Zeng in Hubei Province) from the late Zhou Dynasty, the twelve tone-mode system was already widely used to produce nearly all the majors and minors as we use nowadays. Related to this system is the historical fact that Zhu Zaiyu (Chu Tsai-yü 朱载堉) discovered the twelve equal temperaments in the sixteenth century (before the Europeans), while there was a discussion among the early Jesuit missionaries on the chord in Chinese music system (Zhu 1997; Pan 1980; Moule 1989; Li 2005; Kuttner 1975; Dai and Meng 1985; Lee and Shen 1999; Amiot 1997; Huang 1979).

The limited discussion earlier on the philosophical and ethical elements of the *xun* in relation to its role in the official and folk music histories in China shows that the *xun* has embodied these *fundamental beliefs and values* in Chinese culture: (1) The immortality of the soul; (2) The unity of man and nature; (3) The Confucian "Great Unity"; (4) The importance of following local customs; (5) The emphasis of harmony with differences; (6) The search for auspiciousness and avoidance of inauspiciousness through the practice of *zhanbu* (fortunetelling or divination) (see more detailed discussion on these aspects in chapter 2).

In addition, the *xun*'s symbolism of earth (or soil) is essential to Chinese culture which is based on agriculture. For this reason, the calendric correlation between the Twelve-Tone-Modes and the Twelve-Months (in Chinese lunar calendar) is built into Chinese conception of music-nature-humanity, as seen here (based on *The Book of Rites*):

- 1st spring month 孟春: *taicu* 太簇 (D)
- 2nd spring month 仲春: *jia zhong* 夹钟 (#D)
- 3rd spring month 季春: *guxian* 姑洗(E)
- 1st summer month 孟夏: *zhong lü* 仲吕 (F)
- 2nd summer month 仲夏: *ruibin* 蕤宾 (#F)
- 3rd summer month 季夏: *lin zhong* 林钟 (G)
- 1st autumn month 孟秋: *yice* 夷侧 (#G)
- 2nd autumn month 仲秋: *nanlü* 南吕 (A)
- 3rd autumn month 季秋: *wuyi* 无射 (#A)
- 1st winter month 孟冬: *ying zhong* 应钟 (B)
- 2nd winter month 仲冬: *huang zhong* 黄钟 (C)
- 3rd winter month 季冬: *dalü* 大吕 (#C)

The *xun* embodied the virtue of friendship, particularly, between brothers and friends. This ethical aspect is different from the Western virtue of friendship in which (in the secular sense) the love between man and woman is often more important than the friendship between friends of the same gender. This aspect is well illustrated through Chinese literature and music in the past two thousand years and through everyday speech such as *xunchi zhijiao* (the relationship between the *xun* and the *chi*), referring to the relationships between brothers or of brotherhood. In everyday life, the concept of yin-yang and five elements is basic to the Chinese people of all social backgrounds. From food to toy, from names to gifts, trying to balance the relationship through a symbolic object is a common practice. In this sense, the *xun*'s popularity through cultural tourism (e.g., ICH tourism) becomes natural.

TRADITIONALIZATION AND HERITAGIZATION IN THE RECONSTRUCTION OF IDENTITY

The primary concern in folkloristics is about the continuity and discontinuity of tradition with two related goals: the process of traditionalization and the purpose of doing so. The concept of "traditionalization" (Hymes 1975) puts an end to the previously dominant idea of folklore as "survival" or "product," shedding light on the studies of tradition within its mechanism of transmission and transformation, and enhancing "the science of tradition" (Hartland 1968 [1899]:11). Taking a step further, it gets clear that folklore tradition is all about self-awareness and reconstruction of the concept of identity at different levels (Zhang 2020b). It is at least since Herder (1744–1803) that "the concept of identity has always been central in folklore studies" (Oring 1994:226). In this sense, folklore studies are indeed at "the center of humanities" (Wilson 1988:158).

The ups and downs of the *xun* in Chinese history may be an example to support this argument: What determines the continuity and discontinuity of a tradition is, in addition to the choice of the practitioners largely determined by the social context, the vitality and validity inherent to the tradition itself, which contain the fundamental beliefs and values as well as the expressions of the cultural identity. This point can also be examined in the context of folkloristic studies of traditionalization.

Folklorists seem to have recognized that, in the changing process of transmitting and transforming traditions, it is the choice of practitioners to determine what to keep and what to discard (Brunvand [1968] 1978:1; Toelken 1979:32; Glassie 1989:31). Certainly, "there is no such thing as tradition without individuals who enact it," as "tradition and the individual are inseparable" (Cashman, Mould, Shukla 2011:2, 5). Some further questions, however, should be asked: What makes the practitioners absorb or abandon a tradition or a cultural element? Is it the self-conscious choice of the practitioners, or is it simply situational or pragmatic? Do the practitioners make choices on the basis of the temporary validity or the vitality of the tradition to their group identity? Or, are they even aware of these differences? (Zhang 2015b:467).

The studies of tradition can be considered from two perspectives: within the field of folkloristics, and beyond the field. For folklorists, there has been a journey of defining and redefining "tradition" and "folklore" (e.g., Dundes 1965, 1983; Hymes 1975; Ben-Amos 1971, 1984; Handler and Linnekin 1984; Glassie 1995, 2007; Jones 2000; Bronner 2000; Noyes 2009; Honko 2013): from conducting studies at the microlevel of what they are to developing perspectives that view folklore as "the center of humanities" (Wilson 1988:158) through the reconstruction of the notion of "identity." Two concepts are particularly meaningful to this discussion: Hyme's (1975) "traditionalization" and Honko's (2013) "second life" of tradition. These ideas show that tradition is a process of constant revitalization by means of integrating the new, adding personal creativity, absorbing "outside" cultural elements, and reaching the goal of reconstructing new identities for the practitioners and their groups.

Beyond folkloristics, there have been different theories regarding how human tradition or history has been maintained. In philosophy, there is teleology, as known in Aristotle's works in ancient times and Herder's in early modern times, which essentially holds that there is a purpose for everything extant. There is also determinism that is ramified in different fields. But perhaps the most direct influence to folkloristics is the historians' idea of "invention of tradition" (Hobsbawm and Ranger 1983), which has become a "mainstream" theory in interpreting the reconstruction of modern nations and led to serious folkloristic discourses (Briggs 1996; Noyes and Abrahams 1999). In fact, this idea is a modern reinforcement of Johann Gottfried von Herder's notion of "identity" at the level of gaining "nation" status and, consequently, defining "race" and "ethnicity" in order to maintain a "nation."

Regarding the central idea of "identity" in folkloristics, the dominant paradigm has been based on "race/ethnicity-based" hierarchy that has its history rooted in on colonization, which was, to a certain extent, theorized by such minds as Immanuel Kant and Herder. Folklorist Elliott Oring (1994) has traced the idea of identity in folklore studies to Herder and pointed out that folklore is centrally about identity. However, studies of identity have fundamentally been based on the *status quo* "race" and "ethnicity" in many fields of cultural studies. Folklorist Alan Dundes (1983) made a visionary point that "folklore identity" could be a better concept than "ethnic identity" in looking at the folklore tradition. It is based on Dundes's idea that the notion of "folkloric identity"—emphasizing the formation of identity based on shared practices and traditions rather than common "race"—was recently proposed to call for a paradigm shift in folkloristic studies of identity (Zhang 2020b).

The idea of folkloric identity can also be attested by the example of the *xun* in China. The continuity of the *xun* was carried on by individual practitioners, and these individuals were people of various backgrounds: different social status, different geographical locations, different languages or dialects, different religions, and different lifestyles. Clearly, it is never a particular "race/ blood" that unites people of different cultures. Therefore, it is the folkloric identity of the *xun* that enables its continuity, as it is being practiced today in China and abroad. It is the vitality embodied in the *xun*, not the "racial/ ethnic" categorization imposed upon the practitioners, that determines the moment when the *xun* is to be "reinvented" for personal, local, or national identity.

Indeed, various efforts in revitalizing traditions and reconstructing identities at all levels have proven that folklore practices and folklore studies are all about identity. The revitalization of tradition in modern societies begins with the awareness of the crisis in maintaining identity at national, group, and personal levels against the background of globalization in the post-colonial period. Clearly, this process of reconstructing identity is an integration of multiple cultural elements, while the practitioners make choices about keeping or discarding certain traditional practices so as to reconstruct and retell/ rewrite their cultural memories. Also in this process, identity markers are created to convey new meanings, but some of these markers are core identity markers and some are arbitrary identity markers. The *xun* discussed here, as I argue, has become a marker that embodies core beliefs and values in Chinese traditions.

Regarding the specific situation in China since the early 1980s, revitalization of tradition has experienced the struggle of two ideologies: One is that the modernization of China, which had been the goal for the Chinese through several major cultural revolutions (e.g., the May Fourth Movement in 1919, the Great Proletarian Cultural Revolution from 1966–1976) since the mid-nineteenth century, should be a thorough Westernization by abandoning all the traditional (labeled as feudal or superstitious) ideas and lifestyle; the other is that the advancement of China should be based on its distinctive history and culture which contain national essence and national spirit of the Chinese culture. These two ideas are still in tense conflict, but it seems clear that China has learned that modernization does not necessarily mean to totally deny and abandon its traditions, and that the traditional and the modern can exit side by side. As a result, we see great efforts in China today to revitalize traditions, particularly since the introduction of ICH to China in 2003, which can be seen as a new effort of "seeking roots," and at the same time to modernize with latest science and technology.

Folkloristic studies of the ICH movement in China have largely dwelled in a political perspective: efforts in China are largely to reinvent traditions for the sake of nation-construction or nationalistic goal (Yan 2016; Bodolec 2012; Wu 2015). China is also seen as an example in strengthening or challenging "the simplistic East/West binary" (Logan and Aygen 2016:411). But there are other studies that look deeper into the dynamic mechanism of tradition in its transmission and transformation. It is this mechanism of constantly "reinventing" a "second life of folklore" that is also characteristic of the inclusive Chinese culture, different from the exclusive Western system that upholds one ideology or religion.

The history of the *xun* being "reinvented" again and again shows the process of "traditionalization" and the "second life of folklore." It is through this process that one can also understand the basis of such traditionalization: if a tradition is rooted in its fundamental beliefs and values, it not only gains its vitality to survive social upheavals, but also transmits and transforms those beliefs and values.

In relation to the concept of vitality, the concept of validity may better explain the modern notion of nation-construction through commercializing or industrializing traditions. On this issue, some recent studies have further approved it. For example, the folk cultural revival in a remote underdeveloped area in North China (Wu 2015) shows that such changes are typical throughout Chinese history. And the sonic dimension of nationalism (Tuohy 2001) and the lives of musicians (Rees 2009) in modern China are also examined through the representation and transformation of music. This is consistent with the transmission mechanism of Chinese culture in operation and is "the means for deriving the future from the past" (Glassie 2003:192).

The *xun* example also shows that its revitalization is about *cultural self-awareness*, a concept that entered the public domain at the turn of the twenty-first century as a result of seeking roots in Chinese culture (Fei 1997, 2003). This concept also shows that in Chinese culture multiple traditions can exist side by side, and that its revitalization demonstrates its inherent self-healing mechanism. This reality is crucial in understanding the revitalization or "traditionalization" in China: theories developed from the dualistic Western mindset may not correctly explain the reality in a different cosmic and ethical system. In this sense, the concept of "heritagization," a topic also tackled by folklorists (Kirshenblatt-Gimblett 1995, Noyes 2014), is essentially the practice of "traditionalization" (Zhang 2017a).

The *xun* as a musical instrument has a long history in both imperial court and folk performances. Like many instruments or traditions, the *xun* at times was discontinued due to various social upheavals. Yet, unlike some other instruments or traditions, the *xun* now has not only been reconstructed today but also gained greater popularity among the elite and the folk. Since the 1980s, it has been used in film music, taught in music conservatories, for sale as a tourist souvenir across the country, made by various individuals with diverse fingerings, materials, and shapes or designs, and discussed in the academic arena. Taking advantage of the concept of ICH, the *xun* has gained a symbolic role as an intangible cultural heritage in many regions in China.

In examining the root of revitalizing the *xun*, one may find that these factors have played essential roles in transforming the *xun* to be a cultural identity marker beyond a musical instrument: the center (*zhong* for the virtue of loyalty) role in Chinese cosmic view; the first note in a scale (as the *gong* note); the virtue to be first obtained in Confucian ethics (*xin* for the virtual of trust/fidelity); the brotherly friendship as the base for any interpersonal relationship (*yi* for righteousness); the integration of Confucian, Daoist, and other thoughts about the Dao as the base of all Chinese philosophies; and the unique role in the Eight Sounds system (*tu*-earth). It is reasonable to expect that the *xun* will continue to be used not only as a musical instrument but also a core marker in the reconstruction of China's national identity. Obviously, the revitalization of the *xun* reminds us of a different way of "thinking through tradition" (Oring 2013).

LOCALIZATION OF TRADITIONS IN THE MAKING OF A THIRD CULTURE AND NEW IDENTITY: A PERSONAL REFLECTION

As discussed in chapter 2, the vitality of a tradition lies in its capability to incorporate new cultural elements in a new environment. Through such a mechanism of multicultural interaction, a new culture is developed. This new culture is, as I call it, a *third culture*. This concept can explain the development of diasporic cultures as seen in the making of a Chinese American culture, a culture not simply mix of the two, but rather of many, cultures in the United States (Zhang 2015a; 2015b).

Through this process, such musical instruments as the *pipa* and the *erhu*, which were absorbed into Chinese culture from Central Asia more than a thousand years ago, are cherished today as traditional Chinese musical instruments, that is, national cultural identity markers in contemporary global communication. The *pipa* (known in Japan as the *biwa*), for example, has gained its own vitality by adapting to different cultures from Central Asia to East Asia, and then all the way to the fusion of Blues and Jazz music in the United States.

It is for this reason that I have argued that folklore traditions are sustained, endured, and are handed down through practitioners who share the same interests and lifestyles, thus forming new folk groups with their *folkloric identity* (Zhang 2020b). The result of this is the creation of an ideological paradigm shift against the racist notion of "racial identity" or race-based "ethnic identity." As seen throughout Chinese history, the Chinese and their culture have endured because of their cultural self-healing mechanism, which enables them to absorb different peoples and cultures. Indeed, the process is no different than the one that has shaped "American culture."

Here I would like to discuss how the *xun* has developed and spread in the US context. Using my personal experience, I will illustrate the point that people are drawn together as a cultural or folk group because of their shared practice. This example will demonstrate that traditions are continued by both the members of such groups who directly practice them and by those outsiders who also practice or identify with them.

As noted earlier, the *xun* tradition virtually disappeared during the twentieth century, except for a few intellectuals who preserved the skills of making and playing it. Born in the early 1960s in China, I had never heard or seen a *xun* in the first thirty years of my life. In 2005, ten years after I had emigrated to the United States, I returned to China for the first time. During that trip, I noticed that *xun* were sold as souvenirs in many tourist sites across the country. Out of curiosity, I bought a few. Like many who first heard the sound of the *xun*, I was drawn into the deep, weeping, chanting, and "earthy" sound made from only one or two notes. Since *xun* were sold as tourist souvenirs, they were not tuned. As I tried to tune them by adjusting their tone holes, I wondered why there were no good ones available for serious playing. Suddenly, as I began to explore the cultural significance and symbolism of the object, the idea of making *xun* myself emerged. As a child in the early 1970s, I had learned to play revolutionary songs on the *di*-flute (horizontal bamboo flute), so it was clear to me that, to play the *xun* properly, I needed some of better quality. I was able to travel to China during summer vacations and bought a few *xun* of different sizes and hole-counts each time. As a result, I had a collection of a number of *xun* made by different craftsmen and with different fingerings. It was in 2009, during a trip to Xiamen University, Xiamen city, that I had the good luck to meet the famous *xun* maker, Professor Zhao Liangshan, who generously gifted me a beautiful white ceramic *xun* that he and his son made.

As mentioned earlier, the Liangshan *Xun* (良山埙) has a unique fingering system for eight tone holes. Through my comparison of this fingering with others (e.g., different tone holes and different fingerings for eight tone holes), I was convinced that Prof. Zhao's fingering for the eight-hole *xun* were indeed the most efficient and physiologically convenient among all I had encountered. For example, his system allows half-notes to be played easily and allows for a range of one and a half octaves (e.g., from C4 to F5, or from "Do" to "Fa" an octave and a fourth above). For this reason, I have been following this fingering system in my own making and playing, hoping to promote Liangshan *Xun* to the marketplace, which is dominated by other styles.

Having done further research on its history and meaning, my desire to make *xun* myself deepened and eventually led me to a ceramic studio in the fall of 2011. It was through a colleague's support and help that I made my first attempt. After the success of my first attempt, my ambition grew bigger. Since my initial goal was to create a good sound—in tune and "earthy" as a *xun* supposed to be—I did not pay much attention to the aesthetics of the shape and color. Of course, I shaped each *xun* by hand, without a wheel or a mold, a "style" I have maintained so far.

As I was learning to make the *xun* in different keys with different timbres, I began eagerly to share my joy by playing with my other musician friends and teaching my students through a regular cocurricular "Chinese Culture Hour." Those students who were drawn to this practice had the same reaction as I first had when hearing the sound and learning the stories behind its long history.

As I learned to make the *xun* in different keys with different timbres, I eagerly began to share my joy by playing with my musician friends and teaching my students through a regular, cocurricular "Chinese Culture Hour." Those students who were drawn to this practice had the same reaction as I had had when I first heard the mesmerizing sound of the *xun*.

In March 2012, I gave a presentation at the ASIANetwork Conference about Chinese *xun* and Japanese *tsujibue* to illustrate the one of many cultural connections between China and Japan in the past two thousand years. I compared two poems/songs, which I played on the *xun*, entitled *Yangguan sandie* (Three Variations at the Yangguan Pass 阳关三叠), by Wang Wei (701–761) of China and *Kojo no tsuki* (The Moon over the Ruined Castle 荒城の月) by Bansui Doi (1871–1952). At the annual meeting of the Western States Folklore Society in April 2012, I presented a paper titled, "Reinventing a Tradition: A Folklorist's Self-Reflection upon Making the Chinese Musical Instrument *Xun*," after which I played a few traditional Chinese tunes.

During my year of teaching at Dartmouth College in 2012–2013, I also tried to interest students in making and playing the *xun*, and gave a talk on the transformation of the *xun* in Chinese history, along with a performance with some students (see figure 8.2).

In March 2013, I took a trip from Dartmouth College back to Willamette University to present a talk and a performance. With *xun* in the shape of clouds, rocks, and coyotes, I named my presentation, "The Sound of Earth, Sky, and Spirit." It was an improvisation in which *xun* of different shapes created a conversation among the symbolic "creatures," that is, the clouds blowing in the sky, the rocks echoing the wind, and the coyotes talking to each other between the earth and sky.

In September 2015, I gave a presentation "From Mud to Music: A History of 7000 Years" at the University of Oregon, and played two songs. The first

Figure 8.2 Some Xun in Traditional Form. Made out of the local clay in Hanover, New Hampshire, fired at different temperatures, Spring 2013. *Source:* Made and photographed by Juwen Zhang.

was *Ai Ying* (哀郢, Lamenting the Lost Capital City of Ying) (composed by Gong Guofu and Zhao Liangshan; first played by Zhao Liangshan in 1984), which was based on a poem by *Qu Yuan* (340 BCE–278 BCE). The second was *Meihua sannong* (Three Variations on the Plum Blossom 梅花三弄), a song legendarily known to have first been played by Huan Yi (317–420) on the bamboo *di*-flute.

My research on the history and cultural meaning of the *xun* eventually led to a publication with translations of two prose-poems or rhapsodies (*fu* 赋) on the *xun* from the Tang Dynasty (618–960), which are the only two pieces of literature specifically on this instrument in the history of Chinese literature (Zhang 2017b). This also encouraged me to make, play, teach, and demonstrate the *xun* on an even broader scale.

In the past, I have invited local musicians in the Willamette Valley area and organized several concerts of traditional Chinese music during the Spring and Mid-Autumn Festivals. I was able to join the local musicians on my *xun*. Each time, members of audience asked me what instrument I was playing since they had never heard that kind of sound or seen such a musical instrument before and how they could obtain one.

During the fall semester of 2016 and the spring semester of 2019, I offered a course on the "making and playing of traditional musical instruments" at Willamette University. Each student in the course made a PVC *di*-flute, a bamboo *di*-flute, and a clay vessel *xun* flute, with their own hands, and learned a few traditional songs from different cultures. Of course, they did research about the music they played and the instruments they made. Their performances were broadcast on the local radio station (KMUZ.com). Some students also created their own musical instruments. Nearly every student gained a new understanding of what "music" meant, how they could "do" what they had never thought they could, and, most importantly, how they had broadened and enhanced their identities by absorbing different cultural elements in everyday life.

During the Qingming Festival (April 5) 2019, the city of Salem, Oregon organized a commemorative gathering at the Pioneer Cemetery where several hundred Chinese men were buried more than a century ago. It was in recognition of the contribution of the early Chinese immigrants made to the city, the state, and the country. At the ceremony, I played the song of *Shepherd Su Wu* (苏武牧羊) on the *xun*. The story is about Su Wu who, over two thousand years ago, traveled from the Central Plain to the Northwest of China to make peace. But he was kept there in custody for nineteen years before he was able to return home. The story tells about the patriotic loyalty and the longing for family and friends that are carried by all those who have lived a diasporic life.

In addition, I have also kept up email correspondence with people in other states of the United States who, without "Chinese" background, simply loved the *xun* and even made their own *xun* to perform for their friends and for themselves. Clearly, it is the *xun* itself, with its sound and image, that attracts these "non-Chinese" individuals. It is the artistic or cultural aspect of the *xun* that helps build a folk group that continues the tradition of the *xun* even outside China.

For me, and for those who accept and absorb the *xun* into their personal identity, it is self-evident that it is the *folkloric identity* based on shared practices or traditions (from any cultures), that sustains the meaning of life with such a group identity. It is in this process that traditions are continued beyond social/political boundaries, that the *third culture*, or new culture, is created, and that human cultures are diversified and enriched. It is in this process that practitioners of traditional music like me fulfill their nostalgic longing and sense of having bicultural (or multicultural) identity. As the *xun* becomes better and better known beyond China, it continues telling its own long history of connecting peoples and cultures without words!

The increasingly popular performances of traditional Chinese music, both in the United States and elsewhere outside China, serve to connect people of different cultural backgrounds. Furthermore, the names/titles of traditional Chinese musical compositions, the tales on which the pieces are based, as well as idioms and proverbs related to the tales, and the Chinese musical instruments all serve to enrich and broaden the cultural identity of the individuals in the local audiences. After all, the vitality of the Chinese oral tradition originates in the inclusiveness centered on its core values. By the same token, while Chinese traditions get energized through interactions with other cultures, many other inclusive cultures and individuals find themselves also energized to reconstruct their personal identities as well.

In fact, the call for collaborative research on music, folklore, global health, and other subject matters has reached a critical moment in history. An influential multidisciplinary conference on "Music and Global Health: Seeking New Paradigms," held in 2013, resulted in a special issue of the *Journal of Folklore Research* (2017); the conference emphasized "ethnomusicology's unique place in the study of music and global health," the new subdiscipline of "medical ethnomusicology," and warned that "If we, as ethnomusicologists and folklorists, fail to engage seriously with health researchers and the health sciences literature, then we risk trapping ourselves in a disciplinary echo chamber" (Allison, Reed, and Cohen 2017:5). Prior to this collective effort, there were already individual or disciplinary studies that highlighted the role of folklore and music in health; there was even a call to initiate a multidisciplinary research area of "new folkloristics of health" (Briggs 2012).

Most of such efforts, however, focused on "health" in a medical sense, and even pointed out that "music and dance performance . . . [were] not just a vehicle for the delivery of . . . educational messages, but [were themselves] a form of medical treatment" and for "healing and prevention" (Allison, Reed, and Cohen 2017:6). I would expand the ideas of self-healing and prevention to argue that the issue of folklore/music versus health should not only be considered from medical point of view in regards to health issues but also from the view that folklore/music is to elevate, improve or nurture mental, spiritual, and intellectual health for everyone.

Indeed, the role that folklore/music plays in cultivating body-mind-heart (or the Chinese notion of body/*shen* and mind-heart/*xin*) for all humans should be emphasized in dealing with both physical and mental health. Those who play music alone or with close friends, as the ancient Chinese literati did, may well agree with this point. My story about making and playing the *xun* is but one example. As mentioned in the previous discussion on folksong-singing during the COVID-19 pandemic in China, or similar examples around the world, folk music, as part of oral traditions, has multiple dimensions and functions. As I have shown earlier, one of its most important functions is its *cultural self-healing mechanism* that is essential to maintain personal, regional, group, and national identities.

Glossary

- baihua (wen) 白话(文): vernacular speech (writing)
- bentu gainian 本土概念: local concept
- bentuhua 本土化: localizing
- chengshi minyao 城市民谣: urban ballads/folksongs
- chengyu 成语: fixed idiom/phrase
- chuanshuo 传说: legend
- chuantonghua 传统化: traditionalizing; traditionalization
- chushi 出世: exiting the world
- dayitong 大一统: great unity
- disan wenhua 第三文化: third culture
- duanzi 段子: joke/riddle (urban legend; tall tale)
- duoyuan yiti geju 多元一体格局: the Pattern of Diversity within Unity (in China)
- dushi 渡世: passaging the world
- fanyong yanyu 反用谚语: counter-proverb
- Feiwuzh wenhua yichan (feiyi) 非物质文化遗产(非遗): Intangible Culture Heritage (ICH)
- fengsu 风俗: Customs; current-lore
- gexu 歌圩: folksong fairs
- geyan 格言: maxim/aphorism
- geyao 歌谣: ballad/folksong
- gushi 故事: stories/tales
- guocui 国粹: national essence
- guojia rentong 国家认同: national identity
- heerbutong 和而不同: harmonizing with differences
- hexin rentong fuhao 核心认同符号: core identity marker
- kongxincun 空心村: hollow-hearted village

- koutou chuantong 口头传统: oral tradition
- koutou wenxue 口头文学: oral/verbal literature
- laishi 来世: the next world
- linghui bumie 灵魂不灭: the immortality of the soul
- meiren 媒人: matchmaker
- minjian gushi leixing 民间故事类型: folk tale types
- minjian tonghua 民间童话: folk fairy tale
- minjian wenxue 民间文学 (suwenxue 俗文学): folk/vernacular literature
- minsu leixing 民俗类型: folklore genre
- minsu rentong 民俗认同: folkloric identity
- minsu (xue) 民俗(学): folklore (studies)/folkloristics
- minsuzhi 民俗志: folkloregraphy
- minzu chuantong 民族传统: national tradition
- minzu zhuyi 民族主义: nationalism
- minzuzhi 民族志: ethnography
- muti 母题: motif
- nuwü 女巫: female *wu*-shaman
- quyi 曲艺: folk storytelling performance
- quji bixiong 趋吉避凶: search for auspiciousness and avoid inauspiciousness
- rensheng guan 人生观: life-view
- rushi 入世: entering the world
- rutu weian 入土为安: entering the earth as peace (in burial)
- ruxiang suisu 入乡随俗: following local customs
- sanjiao heyi 三教合一: three-teaching-in-one
- shange 山歌: mountain song
- shaoshu minzu 少数民族: ethnic minority (minority nationality)
- shengmingli 生命力: vitality
- shenhua 神话: myth
- shunkouliu 顺口溜: folk rhyme/ballad
- su 俗: folk; vernacular; vulgar; customs
- suiji rentong fuhao 随机认同符号: arbitrary identity marker
- suyu 俗语: customary/proverbial saying
- tianren heyi 天人合一: unity of man and nature
- tonghua 童话: fairy tale
- tongyao 童谣: children's ballad/rhyme
- wenhua chanye 文化产业: cultural industry
- Wenhua Zhongguo 文化中国: Cultural China
- Wenhua ziyu jizhi 文化自愈机制: cultural self-healing mechanism
- xian 仙: fairy; immortal (Daoist)
- xiannü 仙女: fairy
- xianren 仙人: Immortal (Daoist)
- xianzhi 县志 (difangzhi 地方志): county annals (local annals)

- xiehouyu 歇后语: two-part proverb
- xiyong yanyu 戏用谚语: anti-proverb
- xun 埙: clay-vessel flute
- xungen 寻根: root-seeking
- yanyu 谚语: proverb
- yaoyan 谣谚: balladic proverb/rhyme
- yichanhua 遗产化: heritagizing; heritagization
- youxiaoxing 有效性: validity
- zhiguai 志怪: strange/wonder/ghost tales
- Zhongguo tese 中国特色: Chinese characteristics

Bibliography

Aarne, Antti, and Stith Thompson. 1961. *The Types of the Folktale: A Classification and Bibliography*. (2nd revision). FF Communications No. 184. Helsinki: Suomalainen Tiedeakatemia, Academia Scientiarum Fennica.

Allan, Sarah. 1991. *The Shape of the Turtle: Myth, Art and Cosmos in Early China*. Albany: State University of New York Press.

Allison, Theresa A., Daniel B. Reed, Judah M. Cohen. 2017. Toward Common Cause: Music, Team Science, and Global Health. *Journal of Folklore Research*. 54 (1–2): 1–13.

Ames, Roger T. and Henry Rosement. 1998. *The Analects of Confucius: A Philosophical Translation*. New York: Ballantine Books.

Ames, Roger T. and David L. Hall. trans. 2001. *Focusing the Familiar: A Translation and Philosophical Interpretation of the Zhongyong*. University of Hawaii Press.

Amiot, J. J. Marie (钱德明). 1997. 中国古今音乐考. Trans. Ye Deng. *Yiyuan* (艺苑). Vol. 3–4. (Original as *La Musique des Chinois: tant Anciens que Modernes*. 1779.)

An Deming (安德明). 2004. 家乡: 中国现代民俗学的一个起点和支点 (Hometown: A Pivot in Contemporary Chinese Folkloristics). *National Art (Minzu Yishu)* 2: 25–31.

———. 2008. 非物质文化遗产保护: 民俗学的两难选择 (The Protection of ICH: A Dilemma for Folkloristics). *Henan shehui kexue (Henan Social Sciences)* 1: 14–20.

———. 2008. 谚语编 (Proverbs). In 中国民间文学史 (*History of Chinese Folk Literature*). Pp. 581–608. Shijiazhuang: Hebei jiaoyu chubanshe.

An, Deming, and Lihui Yang. 2015. Chinese Folklore since the Late 1970s: Achievements, Difficulties, and Challenges. *Asian Ethnology*. 74: 273–290.

Apel, Willi. 1972 [1944]. *Harvard Dictionary of Music*. Boston: Harvard University Press.

Arizpe, Lourdes and Cristina Amescua, eds. 2013. *Anthropological Perspectives on Intangible Cultural Heritage*. New York: Springer.

Bacchilega, Cristina. 1997. *Postmodern Fairy Tales: Gender and Narrative Strategies*. Philadelphia: University of Pennsylvania Press.

———. 2013. *Fairy Tales Transformed? Twenty-First-Century Adaptations and the Politics of Wonder.* Wayne State University Press.

Bai Shouyi (白寿彝). 1980. 中国通史 (*A Complete History of China*). 22 vols. Shanghai: Shanghai renmin chubanshe.

Balázs, Béla and Jack D. Zipes. 2010. *The Cloak of Dreams: Chinese Fairy Tales.* Mariette Lydis (Illustrator). Princeton University Press.

Bao Shubo (鲍树柏). 2010. 古代汉语乐器名源研究 (A Study of the Origin of Names for Ancient Musical Instruments). Diss., Shanghai Normal University.

Baron, Robert. 2017. First Impressions, Enduring Memories. In *Metafolklore: Stories of Sino-US Folkloristic Communication,* eds. Juwen Zhang and Junhua Song. Guangzhou: Sun Yat-sen University Press.

Bascom, William. 1954. Four Functions of Folklore. *Journal of American Folklore.* 67: 333–349.

Baughman, Ernest W. 1960. *Type and Motif-Index of the Folktales of England and North American.* Indiana University Folklore Series No. 20. The Hague: Mouton & Co.

Bauman, Richard and B. Babcock, eds. 1977. *Verbal Art as Performance.* Prospect Heights: Waveland Press.

Beauchamp, Fay. 2010. Asian Origins of Cinderella: The Zhuang Storyteller of Guangxi. *Oral Tradition.* 25 (2): 447–496.

Ben-Amos, Dan, Dov Noy, and Ellen Frankel, eds. 2006. *Folktales of the Jews.* Philadelphia, PA: Jewish Publication Society.

Ben-Amos, Dan. 1969. Analytical Categories and Ethnic Genres. *Genre.* 2 (3): 275–301.

———. 1971. Toward a Definition of Folklore in Context. *Journal of American Folklore.* 84 (331): 3–15.

———. 1984. The Seven Strands of Tradition: Varieties in Its Meaning in American Folklore Studies. *Journal of Folklore Research.* 21 (2/3): 97–131.

———. 1993. "Context" in Context. *Western Folklore.* 52 (2/4): 209–226.

———. 1995. Are There Any Motifs in Folklore? In *Thematics Reconsidered: Essays in Honor of Horst S. Daemmrich*, ed. Frank Trommler. Amsterdam: Rodopi. Pp. 71–85.

———. 1995. Meditation on a Russian Proverb in Israel. *Proverbium.* 12: 13–26.

———. 1999. Rella Kushelevsky, *Moses and the Angel of Death.* (Book review) *Jewish Quarterly Review.* 89: 396–399.

———. 2010. Straparola: The Revolution That Was Not. *Journal of American Folklore.* 123 (490): 426–446.

———. 2014. A Definition of Folklore: A Personal Narrative. *Estudis de Literatura Oral Popular/Studies in Oral Folk Literature.* 3: 9–28.

———. 2017. The Brothers Grimm: Then and Now. In *The Tale from the Brothers Grimm to Our Times: Diffusion and Study*, eds. M. G. Meraklis, G. Papantonakis, Ch. Zafiropoulos, M. Kaplanoglou, and G. Katsadoros. Athens: Gutenberg. Pp. 83–121.

———. 2018. 民俗学概念与方法: 丹·本-阿默思文集 (*Concepts and Methods in Folkloristics: Essays by Dan Ben-Amos*). Trans. by Juwen Zhang, et al. Beijing: Zhongguo shehui kexue chubanshe.

Bender, Mark. 2003. *Plum and Bamboo: China's Suzhou Chantefable Tradition.* Urbana: University of Illinois Press.

———. 2006a. Chinese Folklore. In *The Greenwood Encyclopedia of World Folklore and Folklife,* ed. William Clements. 4 vols. Westport: Greenwood Press, vol. 2, Pp. 211–233.

———. 2006b. *Butterfly Mother: Miao (Hmong) Creation Epics from Guizhou Province, China.* Indianapolis: Hackett Publishing.

———. 2016. Landscapes and Life-Forms in Cosmographic Epics from Southwest China. *Chinese Literature Today.* 5 (2): 88–97.

Bender, Mark, Aku Wuwu, and Jjivot Zopqu. 2019. *The Nuosu Book of Origins: A Creation Epic from Southwest China.* Seattle: University of Washington Press.

Birch, Cyril. 1961. *Chinese Myths and Fantasies.* New York: Henry Z. Walck.

Birrell, Anne. 1999. *The Classic of Mountains and Seas.* London: Penguin.

Blader, Susan. 1999. Oral Narrative and Its Transformation into Print: The Case of *Bai Yutang.* In *The Eternal Storyteller: Oral Literature in Modern China,* ed. Vibeke, Børdahl. London and New York: RoutledgeCurzon. Pp. 161–180.

Bodolec, Caroline. 2012. The Chinese Paper-Cut: From Local Inventories to the UNESCO Representative List of the Intangible Cultural Heritage of Humanity. In *Heritage Regimes and State,* eds. Regina Bendix, et al. Universitätsverlag Göttingen. Pp. 249–264.

Bottigheimer, Ruth. 2002. *Fairy Godfather: Straparola, Venice, and the Fairy Tale Tradition.* Philadelphia, PA: University of Pennsylvania Press.

———. 2012. *Fairy Tales Framed: Early Forewords, Afterwords, and Critical Words.* Albany, NY: State University of New York Press.

Bouvet, Joachim. 1697. *Etat présent de la Chine, en figures gravées par P. Giffart sur les dessins apportés au roi par le P. J. Bouvet.* Paris.

Brace, Captain A. J. 1916. *Five Hundred Proverbs Commonly Used in West China.* Chengtu.

Brednich, Rolf Wilhelm. 1986. Frau: Die vorbestimmte. *Enzyklopädie des Märchens.* Vol. 5: 207–211. Berlin: de Gruyter.

Bredon, Juliet. 1922. *Chinese Shadows.* Peking: The Pei Kuan Press.

Briggs, Charles L. 1993. Metadiscursive Practices and Scholarly Authority in Folkloristics. *Journal of American Folklore.* 106 (422): 387–434.

———. 1996. The Politics of Discursive Authority in Research on the 'Invention of Tradition.' *Cultural Anthropology.* 11 (4): 435–469.

———. 2012. Toward a New Folkloristics of Health. *Journal of Folklore Research.* 49 (3): 319–345.

Brindley, Erica Fox. 2012. *Music, Cosmology, and the Politics of Harmony in Early China.* State University of New York Press.

Bronner, Simon J. ed. 2007. *The Meaning of Folklore: The Analytical Essays of Alan Dundes.* Logan: Utah State University Press.

Bronner, Simon and Cindy D. Clark. eds. 2016. *Youth Cultures in America.* 2 Vols. Greenwood.

Bronner, Simon J. 2019a. *The Practice of Folklore: Essays toward a Theory of Tradition.* Jackson: University Press of Mississippi.

———— (西蒙·布朗纳). 2019b. 民俗和民间生活研究中的实践理论 (Practice Theory in Folklore and Folklife Studies). Trans. Xiaotian Long. Folk Cultural Forum. 4: 50–68.

————. 2000. The Meanings of Tradition: An Introduction. Special Issue: The Meaning of Tradition. *Western Folklore*. 59 (2): 87–104.

————. 2021a. 迈向实践中的民俗定义 (Toward a Definition of Folklore in Practice). Trans. by Lei Cai. *Folklore Studies*. 1: 5–17, 2021.

————. 2021b. 在实践中界定民俗的"实践民俗理论"——西蒙·布朗纳教授访谈录 (The Practice Theory and the Definition of Folklore in Practice: An Interview of Simon Bronner by Juwen Zhang). *Folklore Studies*. 1: 18–22.

————. 2021c. 传统之便利 ("Handiness" of Tradition). Trans. by Fang Yun and Juwen Zhang. *Cultural Heritage*. 1: 18–28, 2021.

————. 2021d. The (Re)Cognition of Folklore: A History and Philosophy. *Western Folklore*. 80 (3/4). Special Issue on Mind, Folklore, and Structures. Forthcoming.

Brown, Brian. 1922. *Chinese Nights Entertainment: Stories of Old China*. Westphalia Press. Reprint in 2015.

Brown, C. Campbell. 1907. *China: In Legend and Story*. New York: Fleming H. Revell, Co.

Brunvand, Jan Harold (布鲁范德). 2016. 都市传说类型索引 (Urban Legend Type Index). tr. Zhang Jianjun and Li Yang. *Folk Culture Forum* (3): 53–70.

————. [1968] 1978. *The Study of American Folklore: An Introduction* (2nd edition). New York: W. W. Norton.

Buccitelli, Anthony Bak. 2014. The Reluctant Folklorist: Jon Y. Lee, Paul Radin, and the Fieldwork Process. *Journal of American Folklore*. 127 (506): 400–424.

————. 2016. Telling Chinatown, Writing America: Jon Y. Lee's WPA Manuscripts. Special issue, *Folklore Historian*: 32–33.

Buccitelli, Anthony (布切泰利). 2021. 表演 2.0: 对迈向数字民俗表演理论的思考 (Performance 2.0: Theorizing Performance in Digital Folklore). Trans. by Jia Zhijie and Juwen Zhang. *Northwestern Journal of Ethnology*. 1: 82–101, 2021.

Buccitelli, Anthony and Wenhong, Buccitelli. 2021. 传统的"重"与"轻": 解读民俗实践中的重复性行为 (The Weight and Lightness of Tradition: Interpreting Repetitive Behaviors in Folklore Practice). *Folklore Studies*. 1: 44–52.

Butcher, Beverly J. 2020. "Two Little Tigers" in the Lives of One Family: History and Politics through Folksong. *Western Folklore*. 79 (1): 45–58.

Cai Shuliu. 1985. 关于林兰 (About Lin Lan). 鲁迅研究月刊 (*Lu Xun Studies Monthly*). 5: 45.

Cai, Jingquan (蔡靖泉). 2014. 文化遗产学 (*Cultural Heritage Studies*). Wuhan: Central China Normal University Press.

Cao Xueqin (曹雪芹). 2010. *Dream of the Red Chamber* (*Hong Lou Meng* 红楼梦). Beijing: Renmin Wenxue Chubanshe.

Cao Zheng (曹正). 1982. 埙和埙的制作工艺 (*Xun* and its Craftsmanship). *Musical Instruments* (乐器). 4: 5–7.

Cashman, Ray, Tom Mould and Pravuba Shukla, eds. 2011. *Individual and Tradition: Folkloristic Perspectives*. Bloomington: Indiana University Press.

Cen Xuegui and Cen Qi (岑学贵, 岑琪). 2020. 网络歌圩: 当代山歌文化传承与传播的新空间——基于 2013–2019 年网络山歌的跟踪调查 (Internet Folksong Fairs: The New Space for Transmission and Diffusion of Contemporary Mountain Song Culture: An Investigation from 2013–2019). Journal of Nanning Normal University (南宁师范大学学报). 5: 34–46.

Chan, Wing-tsit. 1963. *A Source Book in Chinese Philosophy*. Princeton, NJ: Princeton University Press.

Chang, Carsun, Tang Chun-I, Mou Tsung-san and Hsu Fo-kwan (张君劢, 唐君毅, 牟宗三, 徐复观). 1958. A Manifesto on the Reappraisal of Chinese Culture: Our Joint Understanding of the Sinological Study Relating to World Cultural Outlook (为中国文化敬告世界人士宣言: 我们对中国学术研究及中国文化与世界文化前途之共同认识). *Democracy Critique* (民主评论) and *National Renaissance* (再生). New Year Issue. Also, in De Bary, Wm. Theodore; Lufrano, Richard (2000). *Sources of Chinese Tradition*. Vol 2. Columbia University Press. Pp. 550–558.

Chang, Fu-Liang. 1957. Cultural Patterns as Revealed in Chinese Proverbs. *Kentucky Foreign Language Quarterly*. 4: 171–176.

Chang, Kwang-Chih. 1980. *Shang Civilization*. New Haven: Yale University Press.

Chao, Wei-Pang. 1942. Modern Chinese Folklore Investigation. *[Asian] Folklore Studies*. 1: 55–76, 79–88.

Che Xilun (车锡伦). 2002. "林兰"与赵景深 (Lin Lan and Zhao Jingshen). *New Literature History*. 1: 36–37.

Chen Bingyi (陈秉义). 2001. *The Art of Guxun* (古埙艺术). Shenyang: Liaoning Huabao Chubanshe.

Chen Duanquan and Li Yong (陈瑞泉, 李永). 2000. "埙"的传统与革新: 谈传统埙及其制作工艺 (The Tradition and Renovation of the *Xun*: The Making of the Traditional *Xun*). *Journal of Zaozhuang Teachers' College*. 17 (3): 40–43.

Chen Jianxian. 2000. 论比较神话学的"母题"概念 (The Concept of Motif in Comparative Mythological Studies). *Journal of Central China Normal University*. 1: 44–48.

———. 2016. 故事类型的不变母题与可变母题: 以中国洪水再殖型故事为例 (The Variant Motif and the Constant Motif in Tales: A Study of the Chinse Flood Myths). *Journal of Guangxi Minzu University*. 3: 2–6.

———. 2017. Alan Dundes's Visit to China. In *Metafolklore: Stories of Sino-US Folkloristic Communication*, eds. Juwen Zhang and Junhua Song. Guangzhou: Sun Yat-sen University Press.

Chen Jiang (陈江). 1984. 中国童话的开山祖师孙毓修先生 (The Founder of the Chinese Fairy Tale: Sun Yuxiu). *Bianji ziyou (Friends of Editors)*. 3: 136–142.

Chen Juanjuan (陈娟娟). 2019. 中国谚语研究70年 (Chinese Proverb Studies in 70 Years). *Folk Culture Forum*. 4: 27–37.

Chen Lina. 2010. 中国民间故事类型研究 (The Research of Chinese Folktale Types). PhD diss., National East China University.

Chen Ping (陈平). ed. 2015. 非物质文化遗产蓝皮书:中国非物质文化遗产发展报告 (2015) (*Annual Report on the Development of China's Intangible Cultural Heritage, 2015*). Beijing: Shehui kexue wenxue chubanshe.

Chen Shuping. 2006. 北新书局: 新文化运动的推动者 (The North New Books: The Promoter of the New Culture Movement). *New Literature History* (新文学史料). 1: 164–170.

Chen Yiyuan and Fan Jiang (陈益源, 江帆), eds. 2010. 谭振山及其讲述作品 (*Tan Zhenshan and the Tales He Told*). Taibei: Lexue shuju.

Chen Zhong (陈重). 1981. 九孔陶埙的研制 (The Making of the Nine-hole *Xun*). *Musical Instruments*. 2: 11–12, 36.

Cheng Feng (成风). 2012. 宁波民间故事类型索引 (*Ningbo Folk Tale Type Index*). Beijing: Zhongguo wenshi chubanshe.

Chin, Yin-Lien C, ed. 2015. *Chinese Folktales: An Anthology*. Hoboken, NJ: Taylor and Francis.

China Folk Literature Collections Committee. 1984–2009. *The Three Grand Collections of Folk Literature in China (Zhongguo minjian wenxue sanda jicheng)*. Editor-in-Chief Zhou Yang. 298 vols. Beijing: Zhongguo ISBN Zhongxin. Including, *The Grand Collection of Folktales in China*; *The Grand Collection of Folk Songs in China*; and *The Grand Collection of Proverbs in China*.

Chuang Pen-Li (莊本立). 1972. 埙的歷史與比較之研究 (A Historical and Comparative Study of Hsun, The Chinese Ocarina). *Bulletin of the Institute of Ethnology*. 33: 177–293.

Clarke, Kenneth W. 1958. A Motif-Index of the Folktales of Cultural-Area V: West Africa. PhD diss., Indiana University.

Clementi, Cecil. 1904. *Cantonese Love-Songs*. Oxford: The Clarendon Press.

Clements, Jonathan. 2001. *The Little Book of Chinese Proverbs*. New York: Paragon. (Reprint, New York: Barnes & Noble Books.)

Clements, William. 2006. *The Greenwood Encyclopedia of World Folklore and Folklife*. 4 vols. Westport: Greenwood Press.

Cox, Marian. 1892. *Cinderella; Three Hundred and Forty-Five Variants of Cinderella, Catskin, and Cap O'Rushes*. London: Folk-Lore Society.

Cross, Tom Peete. 1952. *Motif-Index of Early Irish Literature*. Folklore Series No. 7. Bloomington: Indiana University Press.

Cui Huayun (崔花云). 2008. 中华武术谚语文化特征管窥 (The Cultural Characteristics of Chinese Martial Arts Proverbs). *Journal of Shanghai Physical Education College*. 6: 67–69.

Dai Jiaxiang (戴家祥). 1986. "社""杜""土"古本一字考 (The investigation of the same ancient word: she, du, tu). *Shanghai bowuguan jikan*. Vol. 3. Shanghai guji chubanshe.

Dai Nianzu and Meng Xianfu (戴念祖, 孟宪福). 1985. 李约瑟和库特纳论朱载堉 (Joseph Needham and Kuttner on Zhu Zaiyu). *Kexueshi yicong* (科学史译丛). 4: 1–7.

Davis, John Francis. 1822. *Chinese Novels: Proverbs and Moral Maxims*. London: John Murray.

Dawkins, Richard. 2006. *The Selfish Gene*. (30th Anniversary Edition). Oxford: Oxford University Press.

Dawson-Gröne, H. 1911. *Ming Hsien Chi: Being a Collection of Proverbs and Maxims in the Chinese Language*. Shanghai: Kelly & Walsh Ltd.

De Bary, W. T. and I. Bloom. 1999. *Sources of Chinese Tradition*. Vol. 1. 2nd ed. Columbia University Press.

De Bary, W. T. and R. J. Lufrano. 1999. *Sources of Chinese Tradition*. Vol. 2. Columbia University Press.

De Groot, J. J. M. 1892–1910. *The Religious System of China, Its Ancient Forms, Evolution, History and Present Aspect, Manners, Customs and Social Institutions Connected Therewith*. 6 vols. Brill: The Dutch Colonial Government.

Denecke, Ludwig, ed. 1968. *Jacob Grimm Circular wegen Aufsammlung der Volkspoesie* (Jacob Grimm's Circular-Letter Concerned with Collecting of Folk Poetry). Kassel: Brüder-Grimm Museum.

Denny, N. B. 1876. *The Folk-Lore of China: And Its Affinities with that of the Aryan and Semitic Races*. London: Trübner.

DeWoskin, Kenneth J., and J. I. Crump. 1996. *In Search of the Supernatural: The Written Record*. Stanford, CA: Stanford University Press.

Dong Xiaoyu (董小玉). 2005. 俗语小词典 (*Pocket Dictionary of Folk Sayings*). 3rd ed. Chengdu: Sichuan cishu chubanshe.

Dorson, Richard. M. 1965. Foreword to *Folktales of China*, ed. Wolfram Eberhard. Chicago: University of Chicago Press. Pp. v–xxxi.

Du Wenlan (杜文澜). 1958. 古谣谚 (*Ancient Ballads*). Beijing: Zhonghua shuju.

Duan Baolin (段宝林). 2018. 中国民间文学概要 (*An Outline of Chinese Folk Literature*). 5th ed. Beijing: Beijing University Press.

Duan Chengshi. 1981. 酉阳杂俎 (*Miscellaneous Morsels from Youyang*). Beijing: Zhonghua shuju.

Duan Wen (段文). 2011. The Rise and Fall of the *Xun* and its Development in New China (陶埙兴衰原因及建国后的新发展). *Musical Instruments*. 8: 45–47.

Duara, Prasenjit. 1995. *Rescuing History from the Nation: Questioning Narratives of Modern China*. Chicago: University of Chicago Press.

Duggan, Anne E. 2013. *Queer Enchantments: Gender, Sexuality, and Class in the Fairy-Tale Cinema of Jacques Demy*. Detroit: Wayne State University Press.

Dundes, Alan, ed. 1988. *Cinderella: A Casebook*. Second edition. New York: Wildman Press.

Dundes, Alan. 1962. "From Etic to Emic Unit in the Structural Study of Folktales." *Journal of American Folklore*. 75 (296): 95–105.

———. 1965. *The Study of Folklore*. Englewood Cliffs, NJ: Prentice Hall College Division.

———. 1971. Folk Ideas as Units of Worldview. *Journal of American Folklore*. 84 (331): 93–103.

———. 1983. Defining Identity through Folklore. In *Identity: Personal and Socio-Cultural: A Symposium*, ed. Anita Jacobson-Widding. Uppsala: Academiae Upsaliensis. Pp. 235–261.

———. 1984. On Whether Weather 'Proverbs' Are Proverbs. *Proverbium: Yearbook of International Proverb Scholarship*. 1: 39–46.

———. 1997. "The Motif-Index and the Tale Type Index: A Critique." *Journal of Folklore Research*. 34 (3): 195–202.

————. 2007 [1982]. "The Symbolic Equivalence of Allomotifs: Towards a Method of Analyzing Folktales." In *The Meaning of Folklore: The Analytical Essays of Alan Dundes*, ed. Simon J. Bronner. Logan: Utah State University Press. Pp. 319–328.

Eberhard, Wolfram (艾伯华). 1999. 中国民间故事类型 (*Typen Chinesischer volksmarchen*). Tr. Wang Yanshen and Zhou Zushen. Beijing: Shangwu yinshuguan. [Rev. ed. 2017.]

————. 1937a. *Typen Chinesischer volksmarchen* (Chinese Folktale Types). FF Communications No. 120. Helsinki: Academia Scientiarum Fennica.

————. 1937b. *Chinese Fairy Tales and Folk Tales*. Trans. Desmond Parsons. London: K. Paul, Trench, Trubner.

————. 1941. *Volksmärchen aus Südostchina*. FFC, CXXVIII.

————. 1965. *Folktales of China*. Chicago: Chicago University Press.

————. 1967. Some Notes on the Use of Proverbs in Chinese Novels. *Proverbium*. 9: 201–209.

————. 1970. The Use of Folklore in China. In *Studies in Chinese Folklore and Related Essays*. Bloomington: Indiana University Research Center for the Language Sciences. Pp. 1–16.

————. 1985. Proverbs in Selected Chinese Novels. *Proverbium*. 2: 21–57.

Ebrey, Patricia, Anne Walthall, and James Palais. 2009. *East Asia: A Cultural, Social, and Political History* (2nd edition). Boston: Cengage Learning.

Ebrey, Patricia. 1991. *Chu Hsi's Family Rituals: A Twelfth-Century Chinese Manual for the Performance of Cappings, Weddings, Funerals, and Ancestral Rites*. Princeton, NJ: Princeton University Press.

————. 2010. *The Cambridge Illustrated History of China* (2nd edition). Cambridge: Cambridge University Press.

Edouard Chavannes. 1910–1934. Cinq cent contes et apologues extraits du Tripitaka chinois. 4 vols. Paris: Société Asiatique.

Eder, Matthias. 1945. Das Jahr im chinesischen Volkslied (The Year in Chinese Folk-Songs)/中國歲時歌謠. *Folklore Studies*. 4: 1–160.

Edwards, Evangeline D. 1926. *Collection of Chinese Proverbs* (in Mandarin) *for Students*. Shanghai: Kwang Hsueh Pub. House.

El-Shamy, Hasan M. 1995. *Folk Traditions of the Arab World: A Guide to Motif Classification*. Bloomington: Indiana University Press.

————. 2006. *A Motif Index of the Thousand and One Nights*. Bloomington: Indiana University Press.

————. 2017. *Motific Constituents of Arab-Islamic Folk Traditions: A Cognitive Systemic Approach*. IU ScholarWorks Repository.

Eminov, Sandra. 1975. Folklore and Nationalism in Modern China. *Journal of the Folklore Institute*. 12: 257–277.

Fang Jianjun (方建军). 1988. 先商和商代埙的类型与音列 (The Types and Scales of the *Xun* before and during the Shang Dynasty). *Musicology in China*. 4: 120–130.

————. 2008. 洛阳北窑周埙研究 (Research of Zou-*Xun* in Beiyao, Luoyang). *Musicology in China*. 3: 68–72.

———. 2009. 太室埙、韶埙新探 (A New Exploration of the Taishi *Xun* and Shao *Xun*). *Journal of China Central Music Conservatory* (中央音乐学院学报). 116 (3): 90–92.

Fang Xuanling (房玄龄). 2008. 晋书 (*The Book of the Jin*). Beijing: Zhonghua Shuju.

Fang, H. Thomé. 1956. *The Chinese View of Life: The Philosophy of Comprehensive Harmony*. Taipei: Linking Publishing Co., Ltd. (Chinese version in 1980.)

Fei Xiaotong (费孝通). 1997. 反思·对话·文化自觉 (Reflection, Dialogue, and Cultural Self-Awareness). *Journal of Beijing University*. 3: 15–22.

———. 1999. 中华民族多元一体格局 (*The Pattern of Diversity in Unity of Chinese Nation*). Rev. ed. Beijing: Minzu University of China Press.

———. 2003. 文化自觉的思想来源与现实意义 (The Intellectual Origin and Practical Meaning of Cultural Self-Awareness). *Wenshizhe* (*Literature, History, Philosophy*). 3: 15–16.

Fei Zonghui (费宗惠) and Zhang Ronghua (张荣华). eds. 2009. 费孝通论文化自觉 (*Fei Xiaotong on Cultural Self-Awareness*). Huhehaote: Neimenggu renmin chubanshe.

Feng Fenglin (冯凤麟). 2001. 试以<邓小平文选>的谚语选用谈谚语的修辞作用 (The Rhetoric of Proverbs in Deng Xiaoping's Selected Works). *Journal of Haihai Institute of Industry*. 10: 63–65.

Feng Menglong (冯梦龙). 1956. 醒世恒言 (*Xing Shi Heng Yan*). Beijing: Renmin wenxue chubanshe.

———. 1959. *Stories from a Ming collection: Translations of Chinese Short Stories Published in the Seventeenth Century*, trans. C. Birch. Bloomington: Indiana University Press.

———. 2004. 情史 (*History of Love, Qing Shi*). Changchun: Changchun Chubanshe.

Fielde, Adele M. 1912. *Chinese Fairy Tales: Forty Stories Told by Almond-Eyed Folk* (2nd edition). New York: G. P. Putnam's Sons.

Flowers, Helen L. 1952. A Classification of the Folktale of the West Indies by Types and Motifs. PhD diss., Indiana University.

Foley, John Miles. 1988. *The Theory of Oral Composition: History and Methodology*. Bloomington: Indiana University Press.

Fu Dongming and Chen Dejun (付东明、陈得军). 2014. 维吾尔谚语研究趋势与反思 (Uygur Proverb Research Trends and Reflection). *Language and Translation*. 1: 29–33.

Fu Jianrong (付建荣). 2018. 论"多元一体"民族观视域下的中华谚语史构建 (Constructing the History of Chinese Proverbs in the Perspective of Multiple Unit in One Unit). *Social Sciences of Inner Mongolia*. 4: 117–122.

Furniss, Ingrid. 2008. *Music in Ancient China*. Amherst, NY: Cambria Press.

Gan, Bao. 1996. *In Search of the Supernatural: The Written Record*. Translated into English by Kenneth J. DeWoskin and James Irving Crump. Palo Alto: Stanford University Press.

Gao Youpeng. 2013. 中国现代民间文学史上的"林兰女士"与《民间故事》 ("Miss Lin Lan" and *Folktale* in Modern Folk Literature History in China). *Wenhua yichan* (*Cultural Heritage*). 3: 79–87.

Gao Bingzhong (高丙中). 2006. 一座博物馆－庙宇建筑的民族志: 论成为政治艺术的双名制 (An Ethnography of a Museum-Temple: On the Political Art of Becoming Double-Named). *Sociological Studies* (社会学研究). 1: 154–168.

———. 2007. The Use and Current Meaning of Folkloregraphy and Ethnography. *Folk Culture Forum (Minjian Wenhua Luntan).* 1: 29–32.

———. 2008. The 30-Year Development of Chinese Folklore Studies. *Folklore Studies (Minsu Yanjiu).* 3: 5–19.

———. 2015a. 中国民俗学的新时代: 开创公民日常生活的文化科学 (The New Ear of Chinese Folkloristics: Establishing a Discipline of Cultural Studies through Citizens' Everyday Life). *Folklore Studies.* 1: 5–15.

———. 2015b. 民俗学的中国机遇: 根基与前景 (The Opportunity of Folkloristics in China: Foundation and Prospective). *Journal of Guangxi University of Nationalities.* 5: 81–84.

Garry, Jane, and Hasan El-Shamy, eds. 2005. *Archetypes and Motifs in Folklore and Literature: A Handbook.* Armonk, NY: M. E. Sharpe.

Ge Hong. 1986. 抱朴子 (*Baopuzi; Book of the Master who Embraces Simplicity*). Annoated by Wang Ming. 2nd ed. Beijing: Zhonghua shuju.

Geertz, Clifford. 1973. *The Interpretation of Cultures: Selected Essays.* New York: Basic Books.

Gems of the Hemudu Culture (河姆渡文化精粹). 2002. Ed. The Museum of the Hemudu Site. Beijing: Cultural Relics Publishing House.

Geng Jingjing (耿静静). 2005. 谚语中的中国古代女性文化透视 (The Female Culture in Ancient Chinese Proverbs). Diss., Hebei University.

Georges, Robert A. 1983. The Universality of the Tale-Type as Concept and Construct. *Western Folklore.* 42 (1): 21–28.

Gibbs, Levi S. 2018. *Song King: Connecting People, Places, and Past in Contemporary China.* University of Hawaii Press.

———. ed. 2020. *Faces of Tradition in Chinese Performing Arts.* Bloomington: Indiana University Press. Giskin, Herbert. 1997. *Chinese Folktales.* Lincolnwood, IL.: NTC Pub.

Glassie, Henry. 1989. *The Spirit of Folk Art.* New York: Abrams.

———. 1995. Tradition. Common Ground: Keywords for the Study of Expressive Culture. *Journal of American Folklore.* 108 (430): 395–412.

———. 2007. Traditional Art: A Theory for Practice. In *Living Traditions,* eds. Henry Glassie and Firoz Mahmud. Dhaka: Asiatic Society of Bangladesh. Pp. 25–70.

Goldberg, Christine. 1984. The Historic-Geographic Method: Past and Future. *Journal of Folklore Research.* 21(1): 1–18.

———. 2006. Motif. In *The Greenwood Encyclopedia of World Folklore and Folklife,* ed. William M. Clements. Westport: Greenwood Press. Pp. 54–57.

Graham, David Grockett. 1954. *Song and Stories of the Ch'uan Miao.* Washington: Smithsonian Institution, XI.

Granet, Marcel. 1932. *Festivals and Songs of Ancient China.* Translated from the French by E. D. Edwards. London: George Routledge & Sons. (Original French published in 1919)

Greiner, Leo. 1913. *Chinesische Abende: Novellen und Geschichten (Chinese Evenings: Novellas and Stories)*. Berlin, Erich Reiß.

Gu Xijia (顾希佳). 2014. 中国古代民间故事类型 (*Chinese Ancient Folk Tale Types*). Hangzhou: Zhejiang University Press.

Guo Pu (郭璞). 2010. 尔雅注疏 (*Er Ya Zhu Shu*). Shanghai: Shanghai Guji Chubanshe.

Guo Shaoyu (郭绍虞). 1925. 谚语的研究 (*The Studies of Proverbs*). Shanghai: Shanghai shangwu yinshuguan (Original in 小说月报 *Monthly Stories* (2–4) 1921).

Guo Wei (过伟). 1997. 民间谚语学家朱介凡与《中华谚语志》(Paremiologist Zhu Jiefan and his *Ethnography of Chinese Proverbs*). *Journal of Guangxi Normal University*. 3: 102–107.

Guo Wenmo (郭文茉). 2011. 埙的传承与发展研究 (A Study of the Continuity and Development of the *Xun*). Diss., Xi'an University of Architecture and Technology.

Guo Zongling (郭宗岭). 2011. 新郑馆藏的七音孔陶埙 (The *Xun* with Seven Sound Holes in the Xinzheng Museum). *Zhongyuan Wenwu* (中原文物). Vol. 3.

Haase, Donald, ed. 2008. *The Greenwood Encyclopedia of Folktales and Fairy Tales*. Westport, CT: Greenwood Press.

Hall, Barry. 2006. *From Mud to Music*. Westerville: American Ceramic Society.

Han Zhongzhi (韩忠治). 2015. 农政全书与齐民要术农谚异文考辩 (Investigations of Agriculture Proverbs and their Variants in *Nongzheng quanshu* and *Qinmin yaoshu*). *Journal of Hebei Normal University*. 1: 129–131.

Handbook of Compendium of Chinese Folk Literature Publication Project (中国民间文学大系出版工程工作手册). 2020. Organizing Office and Editorial Committee of Compendium of Chinese Folk Literature Publication Project. (Unofficial publication)

Handler, Richard and Jocelyn Linnekin. 1984. Tradition, Genuine or Spurious. *Journal of American Folklore*. 97 (385): 273–290.

Hanks, D.T. 2003. The Rhetoric of the Folk Fairy Tale in Sir Thomas Malory's 'Tale of the Sir Gareth'. *Arthuriana*. 13 (3): 52–67.

Haring, Lee. 1982. *Malagasy Tale Index*. FF Communications No. 231. Helsinki: Suomalainen Tiedeakatemia.

Hart, Henry H. 1937. *Seven Hundred Chinese Proverbs*. Translated. Forewarded by Patrick Pichi Sun. Stanford: Stanford University Press.

Hartland, Edwin Sidney. 1968 [1899]. Folklore: What Is It and What Is the Good of It? In *Peasant Customs and Savage Myths*, ed. Richard Dorson. I. Chicago: University of Chicago Press. Pp. 230–251.

Headland, Issac T. 1900. *Chinese Mother Goose Rhymes*. New York: Fleming H. Revell Company.

———. 1901. *The Chinese Boy and Girl*. New York: Fleming H. Revell.

Hearn, Lafcadio. 1887. *Some Chinese Ghosts*. Boston: Roberts Brothers.

Heng Xiaojun and Zheng Xuezhi. 1998. *A Chinese-English Dictionary of Idioms and Proverbs*. Tubengin: Niemeyer.

Herman, Reinhold L. 1882. *Cradle Songs of Many Nations*. New York: Dodd, Mead & Company.

Herrmann, Konrad. 1984. *Chinesische Sprichwörter. Reiskörner fallen nicht vom Himmel.* Leipzig: Gustav Kiepenheuer.

Herzberg, Qin Xue and Larry Herzberg. 2012. *Chinese Proverbs and Popular Sayings: With Observations on Culture and Language.* Stone Bridge Press.

Hobsbawm, Eric and Terence Ranger, eds. 1983. *The Invention of Tradition.* London: Cambridge University Press.

Hodgen, Margret. 1942. Geographical Diffusion as a Criterion of Age. *American Anthropologist.* 44 (3): 345–368.

Honey, David B. 2001. *Incense at the Altar: Pioneering Sinologists and the Development of Classical Chinese Philology.* New Haven: American Oriental Society.

Hong Fulai (洪福来). 1989. 月下老人配夫妻 (The Moon Man Arranges Marriages). In *Stories Collected by Xu Kui Sheng* (徐奎生采录故事集). Beijing: Zhongguo minjian wenyi chubanshe. Pp. 17–19.

Hong Mai. 1981. 夷坚志 (*Records by the Listener*). Beijing: Zhonghua shuju.

Hong, Chang-Tai. 1985. *Going to the People: Chinese Intellectuals and Folk Literature, 1918–1937.* Cambridge: Harvard University Press.

Honko, Lauri. 2013. "The Folklore Process." In *Theoretical Milestones: Selected Writings of Lauri Honko*, eds. Pekka Hakamies and Anneli Honko. Folklore Fellows Communications no. 304, Helsinki: Academia Scientiarum Fennica. Pp. 29–54.

Hou Jie (侯杰) and Fan Lizhu (范丽珠). 2001. 世俗与神圣: 中国民众宗教意识 (*Secular and Sacred: The Religious Consciousness of the Chinese Public*). Rev. ed. Tianjin: Tianjin renmin chubanshe.

Hrdličková, Věnceslava. 1965. The Professional Training of Chinese Storytellers and the Storytellers' Guilds. *Archiv Orientalni.* 33: 225–248.

Hsu, Francis L. K. 1973. Prejudice and Its Intellectual Effect in American Anthropology: An Ethnographic Report. *American Anthropologist.* 75: 1–19.

Hu Jiaxi and Fu Yufang (胡家喜、傅玉芳). 2006. 谚语小词典 (*Pocket Dictionary of Proverbs*). Shanghai: Fudan University Press.

Hu Wan-Chaun (胡万川). 2008. 台湾民间故事类型 (*Types and Motifs of Taiwanese Folktales*). Taipei: Liren shuju.

Hu Xiaoyan (胡晓研). 2015. 近百年来东北官话俗语研究回顾与前瞻 (Review and Prospect of the Official Speech in Northwest in the Past Century). *Journal of Tonghua Teachers College.* 11: 29–32.

Hu Pu'an (胡扑安). 1923. 中华全国风俗志 (*All Customs over China*). 4 vols. Shanghai: Guangyi Shuju.

Hu, Xiaohui (户晓辉). 2017. What a Pity: Alan Dundes Did Not Receive This Book. In *Metafolklore: Stories of Sino-US Folkloristic Communication*, eds. Juwen Zhang and Junhua Song. Guangzhou: Sun Yat-sen University Press.

Hua Xia (华夏). 2010. 广州话谚语与歇后语使用状况调查: 兼论詈语 (The Survey of the Use Status of Cantonese Idioms: In Combination with Cursing Words). Thesis. Sun Yat-sen University.

Huang, Huanyou. 1998. *Chinese Proverbs, Quotations, and Fables.* Fellinfach/ Wales: Llanerch.

Huang Jinshi (黄锦石). 2015. 先秦两汉的谶谣研究 (Studies of Divination Proverbs in the Qin and Han Dynasties). Diss., Southwest University for Nationalities.

Huang Tao (黄涛). 2013. 中国民间文学概论 (*An Introduction to Chinese Folk Literature*). 3rd ed. Beijing: Renmin University Press.

Huang Tao. 2014. 论非物质文化遗产的保护主体 (On the Subject of ICH Protection). *Henan Social Sciences*. 1: 109–117.

Huang Xiangpeng (黄翔鹏). 1979. 先秦音乐文化的光辉创造——曾侯乙墓的古乐器 (The Glorious Creation of Music Culture in Pre-Qin Era: The Ancient Musical Instruments in the Tomb of Marquit Yi). *Wenwu* (文物). 7: 32–39.

Hymes, Dell. 1975. "Folklore's Nature and the Sun's Myth." *Journal of American Folklore*. 88 (350): 345–369.

Jameson, Raymon D. 1932. *Three Lectures on Chinese Folklore*. Peking: North China Union Language School Cooperating with California College in China.

———. 1949. Chinese Folklore. In *Funk & Wagnalls Standard Dictionary of Folklore, Mythology and Legend,* eds. Maria Leach. New York: Funk & Wagnalls. Pp. 220–227.

Ji Xiaojian (纪晓建). 2004. 《史记》中道家思想占主导 (The Dominant Daoist Ideas in the *Grand Histories*). *Journal of Hunan Industrial University*. 3: 20–23.

Jia Ying (贾英) and Liu Zhao (刘昭). 2012. 记刘宽忍埙乐专场学术研讨会 (A Report of the Seminar on the *Xun* Music by Liu Kuanren). *Renmin Yinyue*. 8: 28–30.

Jia Zhi (贾芝). 1997. General Preface. In *Grand Collection of Chinese Ballads: Hainan Volume*. Beijing: China ISBN Center Press.

Jiang Fan (江帆). 2003. *Eco-Folklore (Shengtai Minsuxue)*. Harbin: Heilongjiang Renmin Chubanshe.

———. 2004. 民间叙事的即时性与创造性 (The Spontaneity and Creativity of Folk Narrative). *Folk Culture Forum*. 4: 21–26.

———. 2007. 谭震山故事精选 (*A Highlight of the Stories Told by Tan Zhen Shan*). Shenyang: Liaoning jiaoyu chubanshe.

Jiang Shaoyuan. 1928. *Hair, Beard, and Nail: Superstitions about Them (Faxuzhao: Guanyu tamen de mixin)*. Shanghai: Kaiming Shudian.

Jiang Shuzhen (姜淑珍). 1988. 姜淑珍故事选 (*Selected Stories Told by Jiang Shuzhen*). Shenyang: Shenyang volume committee of the Grand Collections of Chinese Folk Literature.

Jiao, Liwei, and Benjamin N. Stone. 2014. *500 Common Chinese Proverbs and Colloquial Expressions*. New York: Routledge.

Jin Ronghua (金榮華). 2000. 中國民間故事集成類型索引 (*Comprehensive Chinese Folk Tale Type Index*). Taipei: 中國口傳文學學會.

Jin, Yanyu (金燕玉). 1992. 中国童话史 (*History of Chinese Fairy Tales*). Nanjing: Jiangsu shaonian ertong chubanshe.

Jones, A. F. 2011. *Developmental Fairy Tales: Evolutionary Thinking and Modern Chinese Culture*. Cambridge, MA: Harvard University Press.

Jones, Michael Owen. 2000. "Tradition" in Identity Discourses and an Individual's Symbolic Construction of Self. *Western Folklore*. 59 (2): 115–141.

Kang Baocheng (康保成). ed. 2013. 中国非物质文化遗产保护发展报告 (*2013*) (*Annual Development Report on Chinese Intangible Cultural Heritage Safeguarding 2013*). Beijing: Shehui kexue wenxian chubanshe.

Karlgren, Bernhard. 1950. *The Book of Odes* (*Shi Jing*). Stockholm: The Museum of Far Eastern Antiquities.

Kirshenblatt-Gimblett, Barbara. 1995. Theorizing Heritage. *Ethnomusicology*. 39 (3): 367–380.

Kirtley, Bacil F. 1971. *A Motif-Index of Traditional Polynesian Narratives*. Honolulu: University of Hawaii Press.

Kordas, Bronislawa. 1987. *Le proverbe en chinois moderne*. Taipei, Taiwan: Editions Ouyu.

Kordas, Bronislawa. 1990. The Poetic Function and the Oral Transmission of Chinese Proverbs. *Chnoperl Papers*. 15: 85–94.

Kühnel, Paul. *Chinesische Novellen* (*Chinese Novellas*). Munich: Müller, 1914.

Kuttner, Fritz A. 1975. Prince Chu Tsai-Yü's Life and Work: A Re-Evaluation of His Contribution to Equal Temperament Theory. *Ethnomusicology*. 19 (2): 163–206.

Kuutma, Kristin. 2012. Between Arbitration and Engineering: Concepts and Contingencies in the Shaping of Heritage Regimes. In *Heritage Regimes and the State*, eds. Regina F. Bendix, Aditya Eggert, Arnika Peselmann. Universitätsverlag Göttingen. Pp. 21–36.

Labadi, Sophia. 2013. *UNESCO, Cultural heritage, and outstanding universal value: value-based analyses of the World Heritage and Intangible Cultural Heritage Conventions*. Lanham: Rowman & Littlefield Publishers.

Lambrecht, Winifred. 1963. A Tale Type Index for Central Africa. PhD. diss., University of California, Berkeley.

Lau, D. C. trans. 1979a. *Confucius: The Analects (Lun yü* 论语*)*. Hong Kong: The Chinese University Press.

Lau, D. C., trans. 1979b. *Mencius*. 2 vols. Hong Kong: Chinese University Press.

Lau, Theodora. 1995. *Best-Loved Chinese Proverbs*. New York: Harper Collins.

Laufer, Berthold. 1915. *The Diamond: A Study in Chinese and Hellenistic Folk-Lore*. Chicago.

Lee, Davis Lin-Chuan. 1979. Chinese Proverbs: A Pragmatic and Sociolinguistic Approach. Diss. Georgetown University.

Lee, Jon. 1971. *The Golden Mountain: Chinese Tales Told in California*, ed. Paul Radin, with notes by Wolfram Eberhard. Taipei: Orient Cultural Service.

Lee, Yuan-Yuan and Sin-yan Shen. 1999. *Chinese Musical Instruments*. Chicago: Chinese Musical Society of North America.

Legge, James. 1861. *Confucian Analects*. In *The Chinese Classics*, Vol. 1. London: Trubner.

———. [1885] 1967. *Li Chi: Book of Rites: An Encyclopedia of Ancient Ceremonial Usages, Religious Creeds, and Social Institutions*. New Hyde Park, NY: University Books.

———. 1898. *The She King or the Book of Poetry*. In *Sacred Books of the East, The Chinese Classics*. Vol. 4. London: The Clarendon Press. https://ctext.org/book-of

-poetry. (Reprint, 1971. *The She King or the Book of Poetry*. Taipei: Wen Shi Zhe Chubanshe.)

Lei Yan (雷艳). 2006. 土家族谚语研究 (Studies of Tujia Proverbs). Diss., Central South University for Nationalities.

Leng, Xuemei (冷雪梅). 2011. 昆明城郊子君村彝族土埙的调查和研究: 兼谈古埙的发现及有关问题 (The Investigation and Study of the *Xun* from the Yi Village of Zijun Near Kunming: A Discussion of the Discovery of the *Xun*). *Journal of Shenzhen University*. 28 (6): 151–159.

Li Chunyi (李纯一). 1964. 原始时代和商代的陶埙 (The Earthenware *Xun* in the Primitive Times and the Shang Dynasty). *Kaogu Xuebao* (考古学报). 1: 51–55.

———. 1996. 中国上古出土乐器综论 (*A Comprehensive Introduction to the Excavated Musical Instruments in Early China*). Beijing: Wenwu Chubanshe.

———. 2005. 先秦音乐史 (*A History of Music before the Qin Dynasty*). Beijing: Renmin Chubanshe.

Li Fang (李昉). 1960. 太平御览 (*Imperial Readings of the Taiping Era*). Beijing: Zhonghua shuju.

———. 2008. 太平广记 (*Extensive Records of the Taiping Era*). Beijing: Zhaonghua shuju.

Li Fu-yan (李复言). 1973. 订婚店 (Engagement Shop, *Ding hun dian*). In *Xu You Guai Lu*, ed. Li Fuang, Vol. 82, sec. 4: 78–79. Taibei: Xinwenfeng Chuban Gongsi.

Li Kang (李亢). 1983. 独异志 (*Records of Unique Strange Stories, Du Yi Zhi*). Beijing: Zhonghua Shuju.

Li Huawei (李华伟). 2014. 非物质文化遗产对妙峰山庙会之影响——以妙峰山庙会申报非遗前后的活动为中心 (The ICH Impact on the Mt Miaofeng Temple Fair). *Folk Culture Forum*. 6: 74–81.

Li Liang (黎亮). 2018. 中国人的幻想与心灵: 林兰童话的结构与意义 (*The Chinese Fantasy and Heart-Mind: The Structure and Meaning of Lin Lan Fairy Tales*). Beijing: Shangwu yinshuguan.

Li Lifang (李丽芳). 2005. 谚语格言中的儒家思想精髓 (Confucian Ideas in Proverbs). *Studies of National Arts*. 2: 21–27.

Li Linqing (李林青). 2016. 20世纪以来中国农谚研究概评 (Review of Studies of Agriculture Proverbs since the 20th Century). *Shanxi Agriculture and Economy*. 5: 5–10.

Li She (李社). 2015. 习近平讲话中的古语名言 (Classical Sayings in Xi Jinping's Speeches). *Theory and Contemporary*. 3: 105–112.

Li Yang (李扬). 1996. 中国民间故事形态学研究 (*A Morphological Study of Chinese Folktales*). Shantou: Shantou University Press.

Li Yaozong (李耀宗). 1995. 少数民族谚语汉译三题: 中国谚语集成译编手记 (Three Issues in Translating Proverbs from the Ethnic Minority Groups). *Journal of Minzu University of China*. 5: 79–81.

Li Yaozong. 2001. 中国谚学若干问题谭要 (Some Issues in Chinese Proverb Studies). *Journal of Hainan University*. 1: 28–33.

Li, Dechao. 2014. The Influence of the Grimms' Fairy Tales on the Folk Literature Movement in China (1918–1943). In *Grimms' Tales around the Globe*, eds.

Vanessa Joosen and Gillian Lathey. Detroit, MI: Wayne State University Press. Pp. 119–133.

Li, Jing. 2015. Chinese Folklore Studies toward Disciplinary Maturity. *Asian Ethnology*. 74: 259–272.

———. 2016. Chinese Tales. In *Folktales and Fairy Tales: Traditions and Texts from around the World: Volume 1*, eds. A. E. Duggan and D. Haase, with H. J. Callow, 2nd edition, Santa Barbara, CA: ABC-CLIO. Pp. 199–203.

Li, Yih-yuan. 1995. Notions of Time, Space and Harmony in Chinese Popular Culture. In *Time and Space in Chinese Culture,* eds. Chun-Chieh Huang and Erik Zurcher. Leiden: E. J. Brill. Pp. 383–398.

Liang, Mingyue. 1985. 中國音樂通論 (*Music of the Billion: An Introduction to Chinese Musical Culture*). New York: Heinrichshofen Edition.

Lin Lan. 1930. 对金钗 (Matching the Golden Hair Pin). In *Huan Xi Hou* (After Replacing the Heart), ed. Lin Lan. Shanghai: Xibei shuju. Pp. 83–91.

———. 1938. 农夫之妻 (The Peasant's Wife). In *Hui Da Wang* (The King of Ashes), ed. Lin Lan. Shanghai: Xibei shuju. Pp. 42–46.

Lin, Marjorie and Leonard Schalk. 1998. *Dictionary of 1000 Chinese Proverbs*. NY: Hippocrene Books.

Lister, Alfred. 1874–1875. Chinese Proverbs and Their Lessons. *The China Review*. 3: 129–138. (Reprinted in The Wisdom of Many: Essays on the Proverb. New York: Garland Publishing. Eds. Mieder and Dundes, 1981. Pp. 242–256.)

Liu Dongsheng and Yuan Quanqiu (刘东升, 袁荃猷). 2008. 中国音乐史图鉴 (*A Pictorial Guide to the History of Chinese Music*). Rev. ed. Beijing: Remin Yinyue Chubanshe.

Liu Fengshan (刘凤山). 1996. 埙的演奏技巧与练习 (*The Techniques of the Xun Performance*). Beijing: Renmin Chubanshe.

Liu Kuanren (刘宽忍). 2004. 埙演奏法 (*Performing Methods of the Xun*). Beijing: Renmin yinyue chubanshe.

Liu Jiexiu (刘洁修). 2000. 汉语成语考释词典 (*A Dictionary of Chinese Idioms with Origins)*. Beijing: Shangwu yinshuguan.

Liu Kuili (刘魁立). 2010. 民间叙事的生命树 (*The Life Tree of Folk Narrative*), Beijing: Zhongguo shehui chubanshe.

Liu Mingyi (刘明怡). 2009. 风俗通义的文体特点及其文学意义 (The Stylistic and Literature Meanings of *Feng Su Tong Yi*). *Literature Heritage*. 2: 20–29.

Liu Shouhua (刘守华). 1985. 中国民间童话概论 (*Introduction to Chinese Folk Fairy Tales*). Chengdu: Sichuan minzu chubanshe.

———. 2002. 中国民间故事类型研究 (*The Studies of Chinese Folktale Types*). Wuhan: Central China Normal University.

———. 2009. 民间故事的艺术世界 (*The Artistic World of the Folktale*). Wuhan: Central China Normal University.

———. 2016. 一个蕴含史诗魅力的中国民间故事 (*A Chinese Folktale with the Epic Charm*). Beijing: Beijing University Press.

———. 2017. 中国民间故事史 (*A History of Chinese Folktales*). Beijing: Shangwu yinshuguan.

Liu Xiaochun (刘晓春). 2009. 从民俗到语境中的民俗: 中国民俗学研究的范式转换 (From "folklore" to "contextual folklore": Shifting Paradigms of Chinese Folklore Studies). *Folklore Studies*. 2: 5–35.

Liu Xicheng (刘锡诚). 2004. 北大歌谣研究会与启蒙运动 (The Ballads Research Association of Beijing University and the Enlightenment Movement). *Folk Culture Forum*. 3: 59–64.

———. 2014. 二十世纪中国民间文学学术史 (*The History of Chinese Folk Literature Scholarship*). 2 vols. Enlarged ed. Beijing: Zhongguo wenlian chubanche.

Liu, Lydia H. 1995. *Translingual Practice: Literature, National Culture, and Translated Modernity – China, 1900–1937*. Stanford University Press.

Lord, Albert B. 1960. *The Singer of Tales*. Cambridge: Harvard University Press.

Lou Tsu-kuang, ed. 1971. 东方故事 (*Tales from the Orient*). Taibei: Chinese Association for Folklore.

———. 2004. *Folklore and Folk Literature Series. Diancang Minsuxue Congshu*. Ed., Ye Chunsheng. 3 vols. Harbin: Heilongjiang renmin chubanshe. First published 1970.

Lu Jinshan (陆金山). 2008. 关于埙孔称谓和埙孔孔数计算方法的思考 (A Thought on the Names and Hole-Counting about the *Xun*). *Musical Instruments* (乐器). 7: 42–43.

Lü Ji (吕骥). 1978. 从原始氏族社会到殷代的几种陶埙探索我国五声音阶的形成年代 (In Search of the Formation of Pentatonic Scale through the *Xun* from Tribal Societies). *Wenwu*. 10: 54–61.

Lü Shuxiang (吕叔湘). 1987. 《中国俗语大词典》序 (Preface to the Grand Dictionary of Chinese Sayings). *Chinese Language Studies*. 8: 1–2.

Lü Wei and An, Deming. (吕微　安德明), eds. 2006. 民间叙事的多样性 (*The Diversity of Folk Narrative*). Beijing: Xueyuan chubanshe.

Lü Wei. 2015. *Folkloristics as a Great Discipline: Studies on the History and Logic of Paradigm Shift from Theoretical Reflections to Practical Science*. Beijing: Zhongguo Shehui Kexue Chubanshe.

Luo Baozhen and Lin Ruiyi (罗宝珍、林端宜). 2008. 福建谚语的医药文化内 (Medical Culture in Fujian Proverbs). Proceedings of the Conference of Chinese Medicine Association.

Luobusangquedan. 1918. *Annals of the Mongolian Customs*. Translated into Chinese by Zhao Jingyang. 1988. Shenyang: Liaoning minzu chubanshe. (Original in Mongolian)

Lynn, Richard John. 1994. *The Classic of Changes: A New Translation of the I Ching as Interpreted by Wang Bi*. New York: Columbia University Press.

Ma Xueliang (马学良), ed. 1984–2009. 中国谚语集成 (*Grand Collections of Chinese Proverbs*). 30 Vols. Various Publishers.

Ma Yangyang and Zhao Yaodan (马洋洋、赵瑶丹). 2019. 近十年来中国古代谣谚研究, 2008–2018 (Studies of Ancient Chinese Proverbs in the Recent Ten Years, 2008–2018). *Journal of Haiyin Teachers College*. 1: 64–68.

Mah, Adeline Yen. 2002. *A Thousand Pieces of Gold: My Discovery of China's Character in Its Proverbs*. San Francisco, California: Harper.

Mair, Victor and Mark Bender, eds. 2011. *Columbia Anthology of Chinese Folk and Popular Literature*. New York: Columbia University Press.

Major, John. 1979. Notes on the Nomenclature of the Winds and Directions in the Early Han. *T'oung Pao*. 65 (1/3): 66–80.

Mao Junyu (毛俊玉). 2011.寻访最后的歌者：谭振山的"一千零一夜" (In Search of the Last Singer: Tan Zhenshan's "One Thousand and One Night"). *Wenhua yuekan* (*Culture Monthly*), April 9.

Mao Zhenlei (毛贞磊). 2012. 簴之疑说 (Doubtful Points on Chi). *The Yellow Bell* (黄钟). 4: 51–56.

Mateo, Fernado. 1971–72. Linguistic and Literary Structure of the Chinese Proverbs. *Tamkang Review*. 2/3: 453–466.

Mei Li (美丽). 2018. 蒙古族谚语研究综述 (Review of Mongolian Proverb Studies). *Chinese Mongolian Studies*. 3: 20–24.

Mieder, Wolfgang. 1989. *American Proverbs: A Study of Texts and Contexts*. Bern: Peter Lang.

———. 1992. Paremiological Minimum and Cultural Literacy. In *Creativity and Tradition in Folklore,* ed. Simon J. Bronner. Logan: Utah State University Press. Pp. 185–203.

———. 1996. "No Tickee, No washee": Subtleties of a Proverbial Slur. *Western Folklore*. 55 (1): 1–40.

———. 2006. "The Proof of the Proverb Is in the Probing": Alan Dundes as Pioneering Paremiologist. *Western Folklore*. 65 (3): 217–262.

———. 2008. Anti-Fairy Tale. *In The Greenwood Encyclopedia of Folktales and Fairy Tales*. Ed. D. Haase. Westport, CT: Greenwood Press.

———. 2014. Origin of Proverbs. In *Introduction to Paremiology,* eds. H. Hrisztova-Gotthardt and M. A. Varga. Warsaw/Berlin: De Gruyter Open Ltd. Pp. 28–48.

———. 2020. "Age Is Just a Number": American Proverbial Wisdom about Age and Aging. Unpublished paper for the Western States Folklore Society annual meeting, Willamette University, Oregon, April 16–18, 2020.

Min, Eun Kyung. 2010. Thomas Percy's Chinese Miscellanies and the Reliques of Ancient English Poetry (1765). *Eighteenth-Century Studies*. 43 (3): 307–324.

Moreira, James. 1997a. Ballad. In *Folklore: An Encyclopedia of Beliefs, Customs, Tales, Music, and Art,* ed. Thomas A. Green. ABC-CLIO, Inc. Pp. 81–83.

———. 1997b. Narrative Folksong. In *Folklore: An Encyclopedia of Beliefs, Customs, Tales, Music, and Art,* ed. Thomas A. Green. ABC-CLIO, Inc. Pp. 348–354.

Moule, A. E. 1874. Chinese Proverbial Philosophy. *Chinese Recorder*. 5: 72–77.

Moule, Arthur C. 1989. *A List of the Musical and other Sound-Producing Instruments of the Chinese*. Buren: Frits Knuf Publishers.

Moy, Clarence. 1952. Communist China's Use of the Yang-ko (Rice Sprout Dramas). *Papers on China*. VI: 112–148.

Needham, Joseph. 1956. *Science and Civilisation in China*. Vol. 2. Cambridge: Cambridge University Press.

Noyes, Dorothy and Roger Abrahams. 1999. From Calendar Custom to National Memory. In *Cultural Memory and the Construction of Identity*, eds. Dan Ben-Amos and Lilliane Weissberg. Detroit: Wayne State University Press.

Noyes, Dorothy. 2009. Tradition: Three Traditions. *Journal of Folklore Research.* 46(3): 233–268.

———. 2014. Heritage, Legacy, Zombie: How to Bury the Undead Past. In *Cultural Heritage in Transit: Intangible Rights as Human Rights,* ed. Deborah Kapchan. Philadelphia: University of Pennsylvania Press. Pp. 58–86.

Olsen, Dale A. 2013. *World Flutelore: Folktales, Myths and Other Stories of Magical Flute Power.* University of Illinois Press.

Oring, Elliott. 1976. Three Functions of Folklore: Traditional Functionalism as Explanation in Folkloristics. *Journal of American Folklore.* 89: 67–80.

———. 1994. The Arts, Artifacts, and Artifices of Identity. *Journal of American Folklore.* 107: 211–233.

———. 1996. Functionalism. In *American Folklore: An Encyclopedia,* ed. Jan H. Brunvand. New York and London: Garland Publishing, Inc. Pp. 654–656.

———. 2013. Thinking through Tradition. In *Tradition in the Twenty-First Century: Locating the Role of the Past in the Present,* eds. Blank Trevor J. and Howard Robert Glenn. University Press of Colorado. Pp. 22–48.

———. 2014a. Memetics and Folkloristics: The Theory. *Western Folklore.* 73 (4): 432–454.

———. 2014b. Memetics and Folkloristics: The Applications. *Western Folklore.* 73 (4): 455–492.

Osterbrauck, Cornelia. 1996. *Fernöstliche Weisheiten.* Illustrations by Sabine Wittmann. München: Compact/Minipräsent Verlag.

Paczolay, Gyula. 1997. *European proverbs in 55 languages with equivalents in Arabic, Persian, Sanskrit, Chinese and Japanese.* Veszprem: Veszpreni Nyomda.

Pan Jianming (潘建明). 1980. 关于原始社会陶埙探索我国五声音阶形成年代的商榷 (A Discourse on the Study of the Pentatonic Scale through the *Xun* in the Tribal Societies). *Yinyue yishu* (音乐艺术). 1: 53–59.

Pang Juan (庞娟). 2017. 汉语传统工匠类谚语研究 (Studies of Proverbs about Handcrafts). Diss., Inner Mongolia University.

Park, Nancy. 1998. Power in Imperial Chinese Proverbs. *Proverbium.* 15: 243–263.

Parry, Milman. 1928. *L'epithèt traditionnelle dans Homère.* Paris.

Peng Weiguo (彭卫国). 1988. 中华武术谚语 (*Proverbs about Chinese Martial Arts*). Beijing: Dianzi gongye chubanshe.

Peng Zhaorong (彭兆荣). 2012. 文化遗产学十讲 (*Ten Lectures on the Studies of Cultural Heritage*). Kunming: Yunnan jiaoyu chubanshe.

Perny, Paul. 1869. *Proverbes Chinois, Recueillis et mis en ordre.* Paris: Firmin Didot Fraeres, Fils et C^le.

Pitman, Norman H. 1910. *Chinese Fairy Stories.* New York: Thomas Y. Crowell.

———. 1919. *A Chinese Wonder Book.* New York: E. P. Dutton.

Plopper, Clifford Henry. 1926. *Chinese Religion Seen Through the Proverb.* Shanghai: China Press. (Reprint, New York: Paragon Book Reprint Corporation, 1969.)

Propp, Vladimir. 1968[1928]. *The Morphology of the Folktale.* 2nd ed. Trans. Laurence Scott. Revised by Louis A. Wagner. Austin: University of Texas Press.

———. 1984. The Wondertale. In *Theory and History of Folklore.* tr. A. Y. Martin and R. P. Martin. Ed. A. Liberman. University of Minnesota Press. Pp. 65–146.

Pu Songling (蒲松龄). 1989. 聊斋志异 (*Liao Zhai Zhi Yi Strange; Stories from a Chinese Studio*). Beijing: Renmin Wenxue Chubanshe.

Qi Lianxiu and Lü Wei (祁连休、吕微), eds. 2019. 中国民间文学史 (*A History of Chinese Folk Literature*). 8 Vols. Baoding: Hebei Jiaoyu chubanshe. (Enlarged edition from the 2008 edition.)

Qi Lianxiu. 2007. 中国古代民间故事类型研究 (*Chinese Ancient Folktale Type Studies*). 3 vols. Shijiazhuang: Hebei Jiaoyu Chubanshe.

Qi Lingyun and Wan Jianzhong (漆凌云，万建中). 2019. "母题"概念再反思：兼论故事学的术语体系 (Re-refection of the Concept of Motif: A Discourse on the Construction of Chinese Tale Studies). *Folklore Studies*. 4: 89–98.

Qin Taiming (秦太明). 2006. A Simple Analysis of the *Xun* Culture (简论古埙的历史与创新). *Journal of Quanzhou Normal University (Social Science)*. 24 (5): 107–110.

Racėnaitė, Radvilė. 2007. Structural-Semantic Analysis and Some Peculiarities of Lithuanian Novelle Tales. *Folklore*. 36: 101–112.

Ranke, Kurt. 1966. *Folktales of Germany*. Trans. Lotte Baumann, with a foreword by Richard Dorson. Chicago: University of Chicago Press.

Rees, Helen. ed. 2009. *Lives in Chinese Music: The Unique Lives of Careers of Contemporary Musicians*. Champaign: University of Illinois Press.

Roberts, Moss. 1979. *Chinese Fairy Tales and Fantasies*. NY: Pantheon.

Rohsenow, John S. 2001. *Proverbs*. The Columbia History of Chinese Literature. NY: Columbia University Press. Pp. 149–159.

———. 2002. *ABC Dictionary of Chinese Proverbs*. Honolulu: University of Hawai'i Press.

Rosenberg, Neil V. 1997. Folk Music. In *Folklore: An Encyclopedia of Beliefs, Customs, Tales, Music, and Art,* ed. Thomas A. Green. ABC-CLIO, Inc. Pp. 340–342.

Roth, Klaus, and Gabriele Wolf, eds. 1994. *South Slavic Folk Culture: A Bibliography of Literature in English, German, and French on Bosnian-Hercegovinian, Bulgarian, Macedonian, Montenegrin and Serbian Folk Culture*. Columbus, OH: Slavica Publishers.

Rooth, Anna. 1951. *The Cinderella Cycle*. New York: Arno Press.

Ruan Yuan (阮元), ed. 1980. *Er Ya Annotated* (尔雅注疏). In *Shisanjing Zhushu* (十三经注疏·尔雅注疏). 2 Vols. Beijing: Zhonghua Shuju.

Rudelsberger, Hans. 1914. *Chinesische Novellen (Chinese Novellas)*. Leipzig: Inselverlag.

Russell, Bertrand. 1922. *The Problem of China*. London: George Allen & Unwin.

Russell, Nellie N. 1915. *Gleanings from Chinese Folklore*, comp. Mary H. Porter. Detroit, MI: Singing Tree Press.

Scarborough, William. 1875. *A Collection of Chinese Proverbs*. Shanghai: American Presbyterian Mission Press. (Reprint by HardPress Publishing, 2013)

Schwarzbaum, Haim. 1968. *Studies in Jewish and World Folklore*. Berlin: De Gruyter.

Shen Fu (沈复). 2002. 浮生六记 (*Six Chapters of a Floating Life, Fu Sheng Liu Ji*). Nanjing: Jiangsu Guji Chubanshe.

Shen Liran (沈立冉). 2011. 近二十年对外汉语俗语教学研究综述 (A Review of Teaching Proverbs in Chinese for Foreigners in the Past Twenty Years). *Journal of Liaocheng University.* 2: 159–160.

Shenhar, Aliza. 1983. The Jewish Oicotype of the *Predestined Marriage* Folktale: AaTh 930*E (IFA). *Fabula.* 24 (1–2): 43–55.

Sima Qian (司马迁). 1982. 史记 (*The Records of the Grand Historian, Shi Ji*). Beijing: Zhonghua Shuju (trans. Burton Watson, New York: Columbia University Press, 3rd edition, 1995).

Smith, Arthur H. 1902. *Chinese Proverbs.* Shanghai: American Presbyterian Mission Press.

Song Yongpei and Duanmu Liming (宋永培、端木黎明). 2001. 汉语成语词典（修订本）(*Dictionary of Chinese Idioms*). Rev. ed. Chengdu: Sichuan cishu chubanshe.

Song Zhenhao (宋镇豪). 2005. 夏商社会生活史 (*The Social Life History of the Xia and Shang Dynasties*). Beijing: Zhongguo Shehui Kexue Chubanshe. (Reprint of 1994 edition.)

Song Junhua (宋俊华), ed. 2014. 中国非物质文化遗产保护发展报告 (*2014*)(*Annual Development Report on Chinese Intangible Cultural Heritage Safeguarding 2014*). Beijing: Shehui kexue wenxian chubanshe.

Staden, Hermann Von. 1914. *Chinesische Novellen (Chinese Novellas).* Munich: Müller.

Stent, George Carter. 1874. *The Jade Chaplet in Twenty-Four Beads: A Collection of Songs, Ballads, &C. (from the Chinese).* Sixth edition. London: Trubner & Co. 57 & 59 Ludgate Hill.

Stent, George Carter. 1878. *Entombed Alive and Other Songs, Ballads, & C. (from the Chinese).* Sixth edition. London: William H. Allen and Co.

Stevenson, Burton. 1949. *Stevenson's Book of Proverbs, Maxims and Familiar Phrases.* London: Routledge and Kegan Paul.

Sun Litao (孙立涛). 2013. 汉代谣谚文化研究综述 (A Review of the Proverb Culture in the Han Dynasty). *Lanzhou Studies.* 8: 76–82+91.

Sun, C.C. 1981. *As the Saying Goes: An Annotated Anthology of Chinese and Equivalent English Sayings and Expressions, and an Introduction to Xiēhòuyǔ (Chinese Wit).* St. Lucia, Queensland: University of Queensland Press.

Tan, Dun. 1993. *On Taoism -- Death and Fire: Dialogue with Paul Klee.* (Orchestral Theatre I). Music CD.

———. 2005. *Tea: A Mirror of Soul.* Opera. Directed by Pierre Audi. DVD. 120 min.

Tao Lifan. 2003–2004. 中国民俗大系 (*Grand Series of Chinese Folklore*). 31 vols. Lanzhou: Gansu Renmin Chubanshe.

Taylor, Archer. 1959. The Predestined Wife (Mt. 930*). *Fabula.* 2 (1): 45–82.

Terhune, Anice. 1910. *A Chinese Child's Day.* Picture by Albertine R. Wheelan. New York: G. Schirmer.

The Book of Rites (礼记). 2009. In *Shisanjing Zhushu*, ed. Sun Yirang. Beijing: Zhonghua Shujua. 5 vols.

The Book of the Zhou Rites (周礼). 2009. In *Shisanjing Zhushu.* 5 vols. Ed. Sun Yirang. Beijing: Zhonghua Shujua.

The Grand Collections of Folktales in China: Liaoning (中国民间故事集成: 辽宁卷). 1994. Editorial Committee of The Grand Collection of Folktales in China, Liaoning (中国民间文学集成辽宁卷编辑委员会). Beijing: Zhongguo ISBN Zhongxin.

The Three Grand Collections of Folk Literature in China (中国民间文学三大集成). 1984–2009. China Folk Literature Collections Committee. Editor-in-Chief, Zhou Yang (周扬). Beijing: Zhongguo ISBN Zhongxin. Including *The Grand Collection of Folktales in China* (中国民间故事集成); *The Grand Collection of Folk Songs in China* (中国歌谣集成); and *The Grand Collection of Proverbs in China* (中国谚语集成). 298 vols.

Thompson, Stith. 1946. *The Folktale*. New York: Holt, Rinehart and Winston.

———. 1955–1958. *Motif-Index of Folk-Literature*. 6 vol. Revised and enlarged edition. Bloomington: Indiana University Press.

———. 1961. *The Types of the Folktale*. Helsinki: Suomalainen Tiedeakatemia, Academia Scientiarum Fennica.

Tian Chong (田冲). 2009. 齐民要术中的谚语研究 (A Study of the Proverbs in Qi Min Yao Shu). *Journal of Weifang Education College*. 2: 10–12.

Tian Ying (天鹰). 1957. 中国古代歌谣散论 (*Smattered Discussion of the Ancient Ballads in China*). Shanghai: Gudian wenxue chubanshe.

Ting Nai-tung (丁乃通). 1983. 中国民间故事类型索引(*A Type Index of Chinese Folktales*). Tr. Meng Huiying et al. Shenyang: Chunfeng wenyi chubanshe.

———. 1986. 中国民间故事类型索引 (*A Type Index of Chinese Folktales*). Tr. Zheng Jiancheng et al. Beijing: Zhongguo minjian wenyi chubanshe.

———. 2008. 中国民间故事类型索引 (*A Type Index of Chinese Folktales*). Rev. ed. Tr. Zheng Jiancheng et al. Wuhan: Huazhong shifan daxue chubanshe.

Ting, Nai-Tung. 1972. Chinese Weather Proverbs. *Proverbium*. 18: 649–655.

———. 1974. *The Cinderella Cycle in China and Indo-China*. Helsinki: Suomalainen Tiedeakatemia.

———. 1978. *A Type Index of Chinese Folktales*. FF Communications No. 223. Helsinki: Suomalainen Tiedeakatemia.

Toelken, Barre. 1979. *The Dynamics of Folklore*. Boston: Houghton Mifflin.

Tu, Wei-Ming. 1994. *The Living Tree: The Changing Meaning of Being Chinese Today*. Palo Alto: Stanford University Press.

Tuo Tuo (脱脱). 1985. 宋史 (*The History of Song, Song Shi*). Beijing: Zhonghua shuju.

Tuohy, Sue. 1991. Cultural metaphors and reasoning: Folklore scholarship and ideology in contemporary China. *Asian Folklore Studies*. 50: 189–221.

———. 2001. The sonic dimensions of nationalism in modern China: Musical Representation and Transformation. *Ethnomusicology*. 45 (1): 107–131.

Turner, Jessica. 2011. 壮族歌仙的定位刘三姐与音乐表演中的空间和性别问题 (Locating Goddess of Zhuang Song: Third Sister Liu and Issues of Place and Gender in Musical Performance). *Journal of Wenzhou University*. 24 (1): 30–43.

Uther, Hans-Jörg. 2004. *The Types of International Folktales: A Classification and Bibliography Based on the System of Antti Aarne and Stith Thompson*. 3 Vol. FF Communications Nos. 284–286. Helsinki: Academia Scientiarum Fennica.

Utley, Francis. 1974. The Migration of Folktales: Four Channels to the Americas. *Current Anthropology*. 15(1): 5–27.

Van Gennep, Arnold. 1909. *Les Rites de Passage*. Paris: Emile Nourry.

Van Oost, Joseph. 1918. *Dictons et Proverbes des Chinois Habitant la Mongolie Sud-Ouest (Varietes Sinologiques No. 50)*. Shanghai. American Presbyterian Mission Press.

Vaz da Silva, F. 2010. The Invention of Fairy Tales. *Journal of American Folklore*. 123 (490): 398–425.

Vibeke, Børdahl. ed. 1999. *The Eternal Storyteller: Oral Literature in Modern China*. London and New York: RoutledgeCurzon.

Waley, Arthur, trans. [1937] 1960. *The Book of Songs*. New York: Grove Press.

Waley, Arthur. 1947. The Chinese Cinderella Story. *Folklore*. 58: 226–238.

———. 1963. *The Secret History of the Mongols and Other Pieces*. London: George Allen.

Wan Jianzhong (万建中). 2007. 歌谣学运动的代表性成果: 评钟敬文先生的客家山歌研究 (The Representative Results of Ballads Movement: About the Comments on Mr. Zhong Jingwen's Study on Hakka Folk Songs). *Journal of Gannan Normal University*. 5: 7–11.

———. 2010. *Introduction to Chinese Folk Culture*. Beijing: Beijing Normal University.

———. 2011. *New Introduction to Folk Literature (Minjian wenxue xinbian)*. Shanghai: Shanghai Wenyi Chubanshe.

———. 2016. 民间文学引论 (*An Outline of Folk Literature*). Beijing: Beijing University Press.

Wang, Chi-chen. 1944. Predestined Marriage. In *Traditional Chinese Tales*. New York: Columbia University Press. Pp. 104–107.

Wang Houchen (王厚臣). 2002. *A Collection of the Xun Songs* (埙曲集). Beijing: Shijie tushu chubanshe.

Wang Jiangying (王江英) 2012. 对外汉语教学及教材的俗语研究 (A Study of the Proverbs in Teaching Chinese as a Foreign Language and in the Textbooks). Diss., Ocean University of China.

Wang Jianli (王建莉). 2018. 古谣谚二十四节气谚语研究 (Studies of Weather Proverbs in the Ancient Proverbs). *Chinese Classics and Culture*. 3: 127–133.

Wang Jushan and Yu Haiguang (王巨山, 于海广). 2008. 中国文化遗产保护概论 (*An Introduction to Intangible Cultural Heritage in China*). Jinan: Shandong daxue chubanshe.

Wang Lei (王蕾). 2009. 孙毓修与中国现代儿童文学的开拓 (Sun Yuxiu and the Beginning of Modern Chinese Children's Literature). *Tianfu xinlun* (*New Stories of Tianfu*). 4: 148–150.

Wang Li (王利). 2006. 谚语中的中国古代女性文化透视 (The Female Culture in Ancient Chinese Proverbs). *Lanzhou Studies*. 12: 180–183.

Wang Shifu. 1991. *The Moon and the Zither: The Story of the Western Wing*, ed. and trans. with an introduction by S. H. West and W. L. Idema. Berkeley: University of California Press.

Wang Suzhen and Gong Jue (王素珍、贡觉). 2014. 俗说、谣谚与叙事 (Sayings, Proverbs and Narratives). *Folk Culture Forum.* 1: 65–73.

Wang Tiechui (王铁锤). 2010. *A Grand Introduction to the Xun* (埙基础大教本). Changchu: Jilin dianzi chubanshe.

Wang Weihua (王卫华). 2012. *The Spring Festival Customs and the Female Identity Awareness (Chunjie xisu yu nuxing shenfenyishi)*. Beijing: Shangwu Yinshuguan Guoji Youxian Gongsi.

Wang Wenbao (王文宝). 1987. 中国民俗学发展史 (*The Developmental History of Chinese Folkloristics*). Shenyang: Liaoning Daxue Chubanshe.

———. 1995. 中国民俗学史 (*A History of Chinese Folkloristics*). Chengdu: Bashu Chubanshe.

———. 2003. 中国民俗研究史 (*A History of Chinese Folklore Studies*). Harbin: Heilongjiang Chubanshe.

Wang Wenzhang (王文章). 2013a. 非物质文化遗产概论 (*An Survey of Intangible Cultural Heritage*). Rev. ed. Beijing: Jiaoyu kexue chubanshe.

———. 2013b. 非物质文化遗产保护研究 (*The Protection and Study of ICH*). Beijing: Wenhua yishu chubanshe.

Wang Xin (汪欣). 2015. 中国非物质文化遗产保护十年 (2003~2013 年) (*The Ten Years of ICH Protection in China, 2003–2013*). Beijing: Zhishi chanquan chubanshe.

Wang Yi (王轶). 2015. 两汉谣谚兴盛探源 (The Reasons for the Popularity of Proverbs in the Han Dynasties). *Studies of Classics.* 2: 10–19.

Wang Yunxia (王云霞). ed. 2012. 文化遗产法教程 (*A Textbook for Cultural Heritage Law*). Beijing: Shangwu yinshuguan.

Wang Zhiqing (王志清), 2016. 民族志 (Folkloregraphy). In *A New Introduction to Folkloristics*, ed. Li Xing. Beijing: Beijing Shifan Daxue Chubanshe. Pp. 338–370.

Wang, Juan. 1996. "Fatalism Seen Through Chinese Proverbial Expressions and Folk Beliefs." *Folk Narrative and World View.* 10: 823–834.

Waterman, Patricia P. 1987. *A Tale-Type Index of Australian Aboriginal Oral Narratives.* Bloomington: Indiana University Press.

Watson, James, and Evelyn Rawski. 1988. *Death Ritual in Late Imperial and Modern China.* Berkeley: University of California Press.

Weber, Max. 1968 [1915]. *The Religion of China.* New York: Free Press.

Wen Ruizheng (温端政). 1989. 古今俗语集成 (*Complete Collections of Chinese Vernacular Sayings*). 6 Vols. Taiyuan: Shanxi jiaoyu chubanshe.

———. 2000. 二十世纪的汉语俗语研究 (*Studies of Chinese Proverbs of the 20th Century*). Taiyuan: Shanxi renmin chubanshe.

———. 2002. 中国歇后语大词典 (*A Grand Dictionary of Chinese Two-Part Proverbs*). Shanghai: Shanghai cishu chubanshe.

———. 中国谚语大全 (*A Complete Collection of Chinese Proverbs*). 2 Vols. Shanghai: Shanghai cishu chubanshe.

———. 2011. 中国谚语大辞典 (*A Grand Dictionary of Chinese Proverbs*). Shanghai: Shanghai cishu chubanshe.

Weng, Jianhua. 1992. Körperteilbezeichnungen in deutschen und chinesischen Phraseologismen. *Proverbium.* 9: 249–266.

Werner, E. T. C. 1922a. *Chinese Ditties*. Tientsin: The Tientsin Press.

———. 1922b. *Myths and Legends of China*. Revised ed. 1994. Dover Publications.

Wilhelm, Richard. 1921. *The Chinese Fairy Book*. New York: Frederick A. Stokes.

Wilkinson, James. 1761. *Hau Kiou Choaan or the Pleasing History*. 4 vols. London: R. and J. Dodsley.

Wilson, William A. 1988. The Deeper Necessity: Folklore and the Humanities. *Journal of American Folklore*. 101 (400): 156–167.

Wu Qinan (吴其南). 1992. 中国童话史 (*History of Chinese Fairy Tales*). Shijiazhuang: Hebei shaonian ertong chubanshe.

———. 2007. *Developmental History of Chinese Fairy Tales*. Beijing: Shaonian ertong chubanshe.

Wu Xiaoqun. 2015. *Folkloristics: Disciplinarity and Paradigm (Minsuxue: xueke shuxing yu xueshu fanshi)*. Zhengzhou: Henan Daxue Chubanshe.

Wu Zhao (吴钊). 1981. 篪笛辩 (Differentiating the Chi and Di). *Yinyue yanjiu* (音乐研究) 1: 10–15.

———. 1988. 陕西半坡、姜寨仰韶文化埙类乐器的音高测定及相关问题 (Problems about the Pitch of the *Xun* in Banbo, Jiangzai and Yangshao Relics). In *The Report of the Jiangzai Excavation* (姜寨—新石器时代遗址发掘报告). Vol. 1. Beijing: wenwu chubanshe. Pp. 549–554.

Wu, Ka-Ming. 2015. *Reinventing Chinese Tradition: The Cultural Politics of Late Socialism*. University of Illinois Press.

Wugou Daoren (无垢道人). 1937. 八仙全传 (*Complete Stories of the Eight Immortals*). In *Xu Gu Yi Cong Shu* (续古逸丛书). Beijing: Dazhong Shuju.

Xiao Yuanping (肖远平) and Chai Li (柴立). eds. 2015. 中国少数民族非物质文化遗产发展报告(2015) (*The Development Report on China's Intangible Cultural Heritage of Ethnic Minorities, 2015*). Beijing: Shehui kexue wenxian chubanshe.

Xiao, Fang. 2017. The Predicament, Revitalization, and Future of Traditional Chinese Festivals. *Western Folklore*. 76: 181–196.

Xie Yujie. 2010. 孙毓修与童话出版 (Sun Yuxiu and the Publication of *Fairy Tales*). *China Publishing Journal*. 3: 49–52.

Xing Li. (邢莉), ed. 2016. 民俗学概论新编 (*New Introduction to Folkloristics*). Beijing: Beijing Normal University Press.

———. 1995. 中国女性民俗文化 (*Chinese Female Folk Culture*). Beijing: Zhongguo Dangan Chubanshe.

Xing Lu (邢璐). 2005. "和光同尘": 浅论司马迁的道家思想 (Mingle with the Light and Dust: A Brief Discussion on Sima Qian's Daoist Ideas). *Journal of Taiyuan Institute of Education*. 23 (1): 40–43.

Xu Ganli (徐赣丽). 2010. 民间信仰文化遗产化之可能: 以布洛陀文化遗址为例 (The Possibility of Heritagization of Folk Beliefs: A Case Study of the Buluotuo Culture Relics). *Journal of Southwest University of Nationalities*. 4: 30–36.

Xu Jin and Li Shuxin (许晋, 李树新). 2016. 20 世纪中国谚语搜集整理与出版 (The Collection and Publication of the 20th Century Chinese Proverbs). *China Publication*. 18: 64–66.

Xu Kuisheng (徐奎生). 1989. 徐奎生采录故事集 (*Stories Collected by Xu Kui Sheng*). Beijing: Zhongguo minjian wenyi chubanshe.

Xu Shen (许慎). 1963. *Shuo Wen Jie Zi* (说文解字). Beijing: Zhonghua Shuju.

Xu Yimin (许逸民). 1984. 唐以前歌诗谣谚的总集 (Anthologies of Proverbs before the Tang Dynasty). *Knowledge of Literature and History*. 10: 10–15.

Xu Zhongyuan (徐中原). 2009. 水经注研究 (Studies of the Annotated Water Classic). Tianjin: Tianjin guji chubanshe.

Xue Chengzhi (薛诚之). 1936. 谚语研究 (Proverb Studies). Master thesis. Yenching University.

Xue Lei (薛雷). 2007. 夏商陶埙研究综述 (A Survey of the Studies of the *Xun* from the Xia and Shang Dynasties). *Yishu baijia*. 23 (5): 111–115.

Yan Zhi Tui (颜之推). 2011. 颜氏家训 (*Family Book of The Yans*). Beijing: Zhonghua shuju.

Yan, Haiming. 2016. World Heritage and National Hegemony: The Discursive Formation of Chinese Political Authority. In *A Companion to Heritage Studies*, eds. By William Logan et al. Wiley-Blackwell. Pp. 229–242.

Yan, Hairong. 1995. The Concept of 'Face' in Chinese Proverbs and Phrases. *Proverbium*. 12: 357–373.

Yang Lihui, trans. 1992. 怀念东方学者W.艾伯哈德 (In Memoriam: Wolfram Eberhard, 1909–1989). *Journal of Beijing Normal University*. 5: 31–4. (Original by Alvin Cohen, *Asian Folklore Studies*. 49: 125–133, 1990.)

Yang Li Hui and Zhang Chengfu. 2013. 中国神话母题索引 (*Chinese Mythology Motif Index*). Xi'an: Shaanxi Normal University Press.

Yang Lihui. 2016. My Re-interpretation of "Mythologism": Cause and Effect. *Journal of Yangtze University*. 5: 1–7.

Yang Shuda (杨树达). 1933. *The Weddings and Funerals of the Han Dynasty* (*Handai hunsang lisu kao*). Beiping: Shangwu Yingshuguan.

Yassif, Eli. 1999. *The Hebrew Folktale: History, Genre, Meaning*, trans. Jacqueline S. Teitelbaum. Bloomington: Indiana University Press.

Ye Shengtao (叶圣陶). 1922. 稻草人 (Strawman). *Ertong shijie* (*Children's World*). 5 (1): 3–28.

Yen, Alsace C. 1964. Red China's Use of Folklore. *Literature East and West*. 8: 72–87.

Ying Shao (应邵). 1980. *General Accounts of Customs* (风俗通义). Annotated version by Wu Shuping (吴树平). Tianjin: Tianjin Renmin Chubanshe.

Yuan Li (苑利). 2009. 非物质文化遗产学 (*The Studies of Intangible Cultural Heritage*). Beijing: Higher Education Press.

Yuan Qin (袁勤). 2013. 国内哈萨克谚语研究综述 (Studies of the Kasack Proverbs in China). *Journal of Changchun Normal University*. 1: 70–72.

Yuan Xingpei (袁行霈). 2005. 中国文学史 (*The History Chinese Literature*). 4 vols. Beijing: Gaodeng jiaoyu chubanshe.

Yuan Xuejun and Liu Han (袁学骏、刘寒), eds. 2006. 耿村一千零一夜 (*One Thousand and One Night in Geng Village*). 6 Vols. Shijiazhuang: Huashan wenyi chubanshe.

Yuan Zhen (元稹). 1982. Hui Zhen Ji (会真记). In *Yuan Zhen Ji* (元稹集). Beijing: Zhonghua Shuju.

Yue Yangfeng (岳洋峰). 2015. 魏晋南北朝谣谚研究 (A Study of Proverbs from the Weijin and South-North Dynasty). Diss., Northwest Normal University.

Yue Yongyi (岳永逸). 2019. 谚语研究的形态学及生态学: 兼评薛诚之的谚语研究 (The Morphology and Ecology of Proverb Studies: Review on Xue Chenzhi's Proverb Studies). *Studies of Ethnic Literature.* 2: 55–73.

Zhang Datong (张大同). 1992. 司马迁与道家思想的关系 (The Relationship between Sima Qian and the Daoist Ideas). *Journal of Literature, History and Philosophy.* 5: 35–41.

Zhang Jianqing. 2013. 孙毓修与童话丛书的编译 (Sun Yuxiu in Relation to the Editing and Translating of the *Fairy Tale Series*). *Dongfang Fanyi* (*Eastern Translation*). 5: 78–81.

Zhang Jiefu (张捷夫). 1985. 中国丧葬史 (*A History of the Chinese Funerals*). Taibei: Wenjin Chubanshe.

Zhang Jingrong (张静容). 2012. 现代化进程中的闽南俗语研究 (Research on Folk Sayings in the Southern Min Language in the Modernization Process). *Journal of Nanyang Normal College.* 8: 45–49.

Zhang Juwen (张举文). 2009. 传统传承中的有效性与生命力 (Validity and Vitality in the Transmission of Tradition). *Journal of Wenzhou University.* 5: 12–17.

———. 2013. Intangible Cultural Heritage and the National Identity in Rural Movie: About the Application of Guqin and Guxun (非物质文化遗产与乡土影视的民族认同情结: 浅谈古琴和古埙的运用). *Cultural Heritage.* 1: 57–62.

Zhang Liangcai. 2013. 中国风俗史 (*Chinese Custom History*). Beijing: Zhongguo Renmin Chubanshe. First published 1912.

Zhang Qizhuo and Dong Ming (张其卓, 董明). 1984. 满族三老人故事集 (*Stories Told by Three Manchu Elders*). Shenyang: Chunfeng wenyi chubanshe.

Zhang Yu and Fan Jinrong (张余、范金荣). 2019. 山西民间故事情节类型索引 (*Shanxi Folk Tale Type Index*). Beijing: Shangwu yinshuguan.

Zhang Zichen. 1985. 中国民俗与民俗学 (*Chinese Folklore and Folkloristics*). Hangzhou: Zhejiang Renmin Chubanshe.

Zhang, Lijun and Ziying You. Eds. 2019. *Chinese Folklore Studies Today: Discourse and Practice.* Bloomington: Indiana University Press.

Zhang, Hong. 1992. Spare Women a Beating for Three Days, They Will Stand on the Roof and Tear the House Apart: Image of Women in Chinese Proverbs. In *Locating Power*, ed. Kira Hall, et al. Vol. 2. Berkeley, CA: Berkeley Women and Language Groups. Pp. 601–609.

Zhang, Juwen and Jiang Fan. 2021. Fairy Tales from Tan Zhenshan in Contemporary China: An Introduction to "The Paper Maid Turned to a Real Bride" Translation. *Marvels & Tales.* 35 (1): 182–186.

Zhang, Juwen and Junhua Song. 2017. *Metafolklore: Stories of Sino-US Folkloristic Communication (Yaminsu: Zhongmei minsu xuezhe jiaoliu de gushi) (Chinese-English).* Guangzhou: Sun Yat-sen University Press.

Zhang, Juwen and Xing Zhou. 2017. Introduction: The Essentials of Intangible Cultural Heritage Practices in China: The Inherent Logic and Transmission Mechanism of Chinese Tradition. *Western Folklore.* 76: 133–150.

Zhang, Juwen. 2006. China Abroad. In *The Greenwood Encyclopedia of World Folklore and Folklife*. 4 vols., ed. William M. Clements. Westport: Greenwood Press. Vol. 2, Pp. 233–245.

———. 2012. Recovering Meanings Lost in Interpretations of *Les Rites de Passage*. *Western Folklore*. 71 (2): 119–147.

———. 2014. Cultural Grounding for the Transmission of the "Moon Man" Figure in the Tale of the "Predestined Wife" (ATU 930A). *Journal of American Folklore*. 127 (503): 27–49.

———. 2015a. Introduction: New Perspectives on the Studies of Asian American Folklores. *Journal of American Folklore*. 128 (510): 373–394.

———. 2015b. Chinese American Culture in the Making: Perspectives and Reflections on Diasporic Folklore and Identity. *Journal of American Folklore*. 128 (510): 449–475.

———. 2017a. Intangible Cultural Heritage and Self-Healing Mechanism in Chinese Culture. *Western Folklore*. 76: 197–226.

———. 2017b. *The Records of Mongolian Folklore by Xiao Daheng (1532–1612) and Two Rhapsodies on the Xun-Flute from Tang China (618–907)*. Lewiston: Edwin Mellen Press.

———. 2018. Folklore in China: Past, Present, and Challenges. *Humanities*. 7 (35): 1–20.

———. 2019a. Fairy Tales in China: An Ongoing Evolution. In *The Fairy Tale World*, ed. Andrew Teverson. London: Routledge. Pp. 335–346.

———. 2019b. Motif as Symbol in Context. In *Contexts of Folklore: Festschrift for Dan Ben-Amos*, eds. Simon Bronner and Wolfgang Mieder. New York: Peter Lang. Pp. 355–365.

———. 2020a. The Concept of Ethnic Genre as a Paradigm Shift. Special Issue in Honor of Dan Ben-Amos. *Western Folklore*. 79 (1): 13–44.

———. 2020b. Folkloric Identity Is the Thing. Archer Taylor Lecture at the 2019 Western States Folklore Society annual meeting. *Western Folklore*. 79 (2/3): 215–250.

———. 2020c. Rediscovering the Brothers Grimm of China: Lin Lan. *Journal of American Folklore*. 133 (529): 285–306.

———. 2022. *The Dragon Daughter and Other Lin Lan Fairy Tales*. Princeton: Princeton University Press. Forthcoming.

Zhang Wei (张伟). 2012. 殷墟埙的基本类型及其乐学特征 (The Basic Types and Music Characteristics of Ancient Porcelain wind-instrument *Xun* of the Yin Ruins). *Musicology in China* (中国音乐学). 3: 80–83.

Zhang Xiang (张翔). 1998. 周代乐器组合之观察 (An Observation of the Ensemble Instruments of the Zhou Dynasty). *The Yellow Bell*. 3: 48–54.

Zhao Binghuan (赵炳焕). 1993. 河南新郑发现七音孔陶埙 (The Seven-Hole *Xun* from Xinzheng Henan). *Wenwu*. 4: 28.

Zhao Jingshen. 2003 [1930]. 民间故事丛话 (*A Series Folktale Studies*). In 典藏民俗学丛书, Vol. 3. Ed, Ye Chunsheng. Harbin: Heilongjiang renmin chubanshe. Pp. 2531–2571.

Zhao Liangshan (赵良山). 1991. 埙演奏技巧探索 (An Exploration of the *Xun* Techniques). *Chinese Music* (中国音乐). 3: 54–56.

Zhao Yaodan (赵瑶丹). 2009. 中国古代谣谚研究三十年 (1978–2008) (Thirty Years of the Studies of Ancient Chinese Proverbs). *Review of Social Sciences.* 1: 108–123.

Zhaxihuadan (扎西华旦). 2011. 藏族谚语研究 (A Study of Tibetan Proverbs). Diss., Minzu University of China.

Zheng Hongfeng and Jiang Ruiliang (郑宏峰、姜瑞良). 2008. 中华谚语 (*Chinese Proverbs*). 4 vols. Beijing: Xianzhuang shuju.

Zheng Tuyou (郑土有). 2006. 研究者、编辑家、出版商共同构建的学术空间 (The Intellectual Space Commonly Built by the Researcher, Editor, and Publisher). *Folklore Studies.* 1: 94–117.

Zheng Zhenduo (郑振铎). 1938. 中国俗文学史 (*A History of Chinese Folk Literature*). Beijing: Shangwu yinshu guan.

Zhong Jingwen and Fang Xiao. 2008. 中国民俗史 (*History of Chinese Folklore*). 6 vols. Beijing: Remin Chubanshe.

Zhong Jingwen and Lin Yongfu, eds. 1991. *Fairy Tales of Chinese Nationalities.* Beijing: New Bud Publishing House.

Zhong Jingwen (钟敬文), ed. 1980. 民间文学概论 (*An Introduction to Folk Literature*). Shanghai: Shanghai wenyi chubanshe.

———, ed. 2009. 民俗学概论 (*Introduction to Folkloristics*). 2nd ed. Shanghai: Shanghai wenyi chubanshe. First published 1998.

———. 1927. 客音情歌集 (*Love Songs of the Hakka Tones*). Shanghai: Beixin shuju.

———. 2001. 谣俗蠡测: 钟敬文民俗随笔 (*Glimpses at Ballads and Customs*). Shanghai: Shanghai wenyi chubanshe.

Zhongguo minjian gushi jicheng: Liaoning Juan (The Grand Collection of Folktales in China: Liaoning 中国民间故事集成·辽宁卷). 1994. ed. Editorial Committee of the Grand Collection of Folktales in China, Liaoning Volume.

Zhongguo Yinyue Wenwu Daxi (A Grand Collection of Chinese Music Antiquities: Henan Volume (中国音乐文物大系: 河南卷). 2001. Beijing: Daxiang chubanshe.

Zhou Xing (周星). 2006. "民俗宗教" 与国家的宗教政策 (Folklore Religion and the National Policies on Religion). *Open Times* (开放时代). 4: 124–136.

Zhou Keqi (周可奇). 2011. 埙初级教程 (*Basics of the Xun*). Changsha: Hunan wenyi chubanshe.

Zhou, Xing. 2017. Folk Belief and Its Legitimization in China. *Western Folklore.* 76: 151–166.

Zhou Yang, ed. 1984–2009. 中国民间文学集成 (*The Grand Collections of Folk Literature in China*). 298 vols. Beijing: Zhongguo ISBN Zhongxin. Including, *The Grand Collection of Folktales in China; Grand Collection of Folk Songs in China;* and *Grand Collection of Proverbs in China.*

Zhou Yanliang (周延良). 2009. 河姆渡遗址土玦、埙与原始宗教礼法 (The Jue and *Xun* from Hemudu and the Ancient Religious Ritual System). *Zhongguo lishi wenwu* (中国历史文物). 6: 58–62.

Zhou, Yanxian. 2016. *Two Thousand Zhuang Proverbs from China with Annotations and Chinese and English Translation.* New York: Peter Lang.

Zhu Jiefan (朱介凡). 1989. 中华谚语志 (*Paremiography of Chinese Proverbs*). 11 vols. Taibei: Shangwu yinshuguan.

Zhu Zaiyu (朱载堉). 1997. 乐律全书 (*Yue Lu Quan Shu*). Beijing: Beijing Tushuguan Chubanshe.

Zhu Zuyan (朱祖延). 1985. 汉语成语大词典 (*A Grand Dictionary of Chinese Idioms*). Zhengzhou: Henan renmin chubanshe.

Zipes, Jack, Pauline Greenhill, and Kendra Magnus-Johnston, eds. 2016. *Fairy-Tale Films beyond Disney: International Perspectives*. New York: Routledge.

Zipes, Jack. 1987. *The Complete Fairy Tales of the Brothers Grimm*. New York: Bantam.

———. 2008. What Makes a Repulsive Frog so Appealing: Memetics and Fairy Tales. *Journal of Folklore Research*. 45 (2): 109–143.

———. 2011. The Meaning of Fairy Tale within the Evolution of Culture. *Marvels & Tales*. 25 (2): 221–243.

———. 2012. *The Irresistible Fairy Tale: The Cultural and Social Evolution of a Genre*. Princeton, NJ: Princeton University Press.

———. 2013. *Golden Age of Folk and Fairy Tales*. Indianapolis: Hackett.

———. 2014. *The Original Folk and Fairy Tales of the Brothers Grimm: The Complete First Edition*. Princeton, NJ: Princeton University Press.

———. 2015. *The Oxford Companion to Fairy Tales*. 2nd edition, Oxford University Press.

Index

About the Author

Juwen Zhang is professor of Chinese and folklore at Willamette University, Salem, Oregon, United States, with his PhD in Folklore and Folklife from the University of Pennsylvania. He is a Fellow of American Folklore Society, Archer Taylor Lecturer (2019), and current president of Western States Folklore Society. His research interests range from folklore theories, folkloric identity, *rites de passage*, folk narratives, folk music, filmic folklore, to Chinese/Asian American folklore. In leisure, he makes and plays traditional Chinese bamboo and clay flutes.

Some of his recent publications in both English and Chinese include, "Folkloric Identity Is the Thing" (Archer Taylor Lecture, *Western Folklore,* 2020); "Rediscovering the Brothers Grimm of China: Lin Lan" (*Journal of American Folklore,* 2020); *Epidemics in Folk Memory: Tales and Poems from Chinese History* (Old Johnson Place, 2021); *The Dragon Daughter and Other Lin Lan Fairy Tales* (Princeton University Press, 2022); *The Magic Love: Fairy Tales from Twenty-First Century China* (Peter Lang, 2022); *Ten Lectures on Folklore Studies* (In Chinese, 2021).

His Chinese translations of classical works include: Arnold van Gennep's *Les Rites de Passage* (2010) and Audrey Richards's *Chisungu: A Bemba Girl's Initiation Ceremony in Zambia* (2017), and English translations include, *A Translation of the Ancient Chinese The Book of Burial by Guo Pu (276–324),* Preface by Patricia Ebrey (2004), and *The Records of Mongolian Folklore by Xiao Daheng (1532–1612) and Two Rhapsodies on the Xun-Flute from Tang China (618–907): Two Primary Sources of Chinese and Mongolian Folklore and Music,* Preface by Pamela Kyle Crossley (2017).